The Company I Kept

The Connecticut Academy of Arts and Sciences

2001–2002 Officers

President	Franklin Robinson
Secretary	Margot Kohorn
Vice Presidents	Harvey M. Feinberg Jeffry Rider Howard R. Lamar Bruce M. Stave Borden Painter
Treasurer	Leonard V. Wesolowski
Librarian	Scott Bennett
Legal Counsel	Ralph G. Elliot
Members–at–Large	Thomas N. Byrne Carl W. Rettenmayer Stanley E. Flink H. Catherine Skinner Nicholas M. Greene Richard V. Szary Peter C. Hereld Robert G. Wheeler Claude Rawson Dorsey Whitestone

The Company I Kept

THE AUTOBIOGRAPHY OF A GEOLOGIST

BY

JOHN RODGERS

VOLUME 58
224 PAGES
OF THE TRANSACTIONS OF
The Connecticut Academy of Arts and Sciences
POST OFFICE BOX 208211
NEW HAVEN   CONNECTICUT 06520–8211   USA
CAAS@YALE.EDU
HTTP://WWW.YALE.EDU/CAAS

Copyright © 2001 by
The Connecticut Academy of Arts and Sciences
All rights reserved

First published in 2001 by the Academy
New Haven, Connecticut

Printed and bound in the United States of America

This book was typeset in Adobe Caslon, based upon type first released by English printer William Caslon in the 1720s. The digital version was designed for Adobe by Carol Twombly and is based on samples from Caslon's press from the middle to late 18th century.

Composed by Charlotte Hitchcock
Maps drawn by Carol Ann Phelps
Printed and bound by Thomson-Shore, Inc., Dexter, Michigan

The paper used in this publication meets the minimum requirements of American National Standard for Information Sciences — Permanence of Paper for Printed Library Materials, ANSI Z39.48–1984

ISBN 1-878508-23-7

Publications of the Connecticut Academy of Arts and Sciences can be obtained directly from the Academy, P.O. Box 208211, New Haven, Connecticut 06520-8211.
CAAS@YALE.EDU

Table of Contents

List of Figures & Maps 7

Prologue 11

Family and Education
Chapter 1 — In Albany 15
Chapter 2 — At Cornell 28
Chapter 3 — Yale & Its Continuing Influence 40

The Second World War
Chapter 4 — Before the War 56
Chapter 5 — The Military Geology Branch of the USGS 70

The Post-War Decade
Chapter 6 — In the United States 82
Chapter 7 — Abroad 98

The Later Fifties
Chapter 8 — In North America 116
Chapter 9 — In Norway 126
Chapter 10 — The Alpine year 131

The Sixties
Chapter 11 — In the United States 142
Chapter 12 — Abroad: Greece & the Soviet Union 151

The 1970s & After
Chapter 13 — In the United States 173
Chapter 14 — Later Trips to the Soviet Union 179
Chapter 15 — In Australia and New Zealand 191
Chapter 16 — In Africa and China 203

Epilogue 216
Publications 217
Index 221

List of Figures & Maps

Page	Chapter
14	Map 1–1 The Northeastern United States
15	Fig. 1–1 John Rodgers
17	Fig. 1–2 The Allen Gate, Pittsfield, Massachusetts
19	Fig. 1–3 a & b The infant John Rodgers
19	Fig. 1–4 John Rodgers with Louise
20	Fig. 1–5 Eagle Lake in the Adirondack Mountains
21	Fig. 1–6 The Rodgers family
29	Fig. 2–7 John Rodgers at Cornell
29	Fig. 2–8 Caricature of John Rodgers
40	Fig. 3–9 Carl O. Dunbar and John Rodgers
42	Map 3–2 The Western United States
44	Map 3–3 The Southeastern United States
59	Fig. 4–10 Preston Cloud with John Rodgers
69	Map 5–4 Western Pacific Region
71	Fig. 5–11 In uniform
88	Fig. 6–12 Professor G. Lincoln Hendrickson
91	Fig. 6–13 Keith and Rachel Wilson
95	Fig. 6–14 Jane Rodgers, John Rodgers, and Anne Conklin
101	Map 7–5 Western Europe
103	Fig. 7–15 Field excursion in Wales, 1948
108	Map 7–6 The Alps and Surrounding Regions
118	Fig. 8-16 John Rodgers and Sidney Quarrier, 1985
125	Fig. 8–17 Arthur Snoke, John Rodgers, & B. Clark Burchfiel
127	Fig. 9–18 John Rodgers by Alison Krill
146	Fig. 11–19 Harold Williams and John Rodgers, 1994
152	Map 12–7 Greece and Adjoining Countries
161	Map 12–8,9 Parts of the Former Soviet Union
165	Map 12–10 Tian-Shan in the Former Soviet Union
170	Map 12–11 Lake Baykal in the Former Soviet Union
172	Fig. 13–20 Willie Ruff's Branford seminar, 1972
175	Fig. 13–21 Willie Ruff, John Rodgers, and Dwike Mitchell
176	Fig. 13–22 John Rodgers and Jonathan H. Rodgers, 1994
187	Fig. 14–23 Lake Imandra, USSR, 1989
190	Map 15–9 Australia & New Zealand
202	Map 16–10 Togo & Bénin
207	Fig. 16-25 "Pan-Xi rift" in Sichuan, China, 1985
208	Fig. 16–26 Turkey, 1987
209	Fig. 16–27 Hills north of Beijing, China, 1986
212	Map 16–11 China
213	Fig. 16–28 Lecture at Anhui, China, 1986

The Company I Kept

Prologue

WHILE I WAS STILL A HIGH-SCHOOL STUDENT in Albany, New York, I learned what geology is about; the subject simply fascinated me, and I made up my mind to become a geologist. Then I could not have anticipated all the glorious outdoor experiences that decision would lead to, all the different parts of the world I would get to see, all the mountain ranges I would go climbing in, all the wonderful people I would meet and get to know in the many countries I would visit. Now I can look back over my geological life after two-thirds of a century, and I decided to write it up as a series of sketches of the many people who have helped me to make it so rich and so joyful. To them and to the many others who helped me to grow up and to live that life, I dedicate this book.

Always having been fond of climbing around in mountains, I chose the natural history of mountain ranges, their "comparative anatomy," as the center of my geological research. Mountain ranges are among the most prominent features of the Earth's surface, and their origin has long been debated. At first they were just supposed to have been "blown out" as they now appear when the Earth was originally created, but gradually those who studied them realized that mountain ranges too have a history, and many theories were proposed to explain that history. When as a graduate student at Yale I studied structural geology with Professor Longwell, he had each student in his class take one of those theories and present it to the class. But a couple of decades later a new theory appeared, the theory of plate tectonics, and for most of us it explained the facts so well — the details of individual ranges, the history of their growth and decay, and the patterns they make across the face of the Earth — that it simply pushed all the other theories aside as obsolete.

According to plate tectonics, the Earth's crust and outer mantle, its outer few hundred kilometers where the rocks are colder and hence stiffer and less plastic than farther down, consist of a fairly small number of relatively rigid plates separated by narrower zones where the plates can move relative to each other. Where two plates pull apart, new oceanic crust and upper mantle form by the up-welling and gradual cooling of hot viscous to molten rock from below, as is happening today in the "mid-ocean ridges" on the floors of the Atlantic, Indian, and southwest Pacific Oceans. Where two plates move laterally past each other, the zone between is a major line of faulting along which there are many big earthquakes; the great San Andreas fault, extending from the coast of northern California southeastward to the head of the Gulf of California, is such a zone. Where two plates push together, one must be pushed down under the other, thus balancing the new crust created where two plates pull apart.

If the crust that is being pushed down is oceanic it becomes part of the underlying mantle, but if it is continental its lower density prevents that and the whole crust is thickened, projecting both upward as a mountain range and downward as a mountain root. This process is in full operation today in mountains like the Himalayas, which are still growing as India pushes under the rest of Asia; it is just beginning in Indonesia as Australia approaches Asia, and it is quite over in older mountain ranges like the Appalachians of eastern North America and the mountains of northern Europe. In these ranges stream erosion is now gradually wearing the mountains down, but very slowly because a volume of rock equal to the mountain root must also be disposed of.

I don't pretend that all the memories I've here recorded are entirely accurate, but I have leaned quite heavily on the diary that I've kept faithfully since 1930, the year I discovered geology. If I have emphasized my travels around the world more than my years of sitting still, teaching, reading about geology everywhere, and writing up the results of my scientific investigations, it is because the travels provided most of the materials for the investigations.

Family and Education

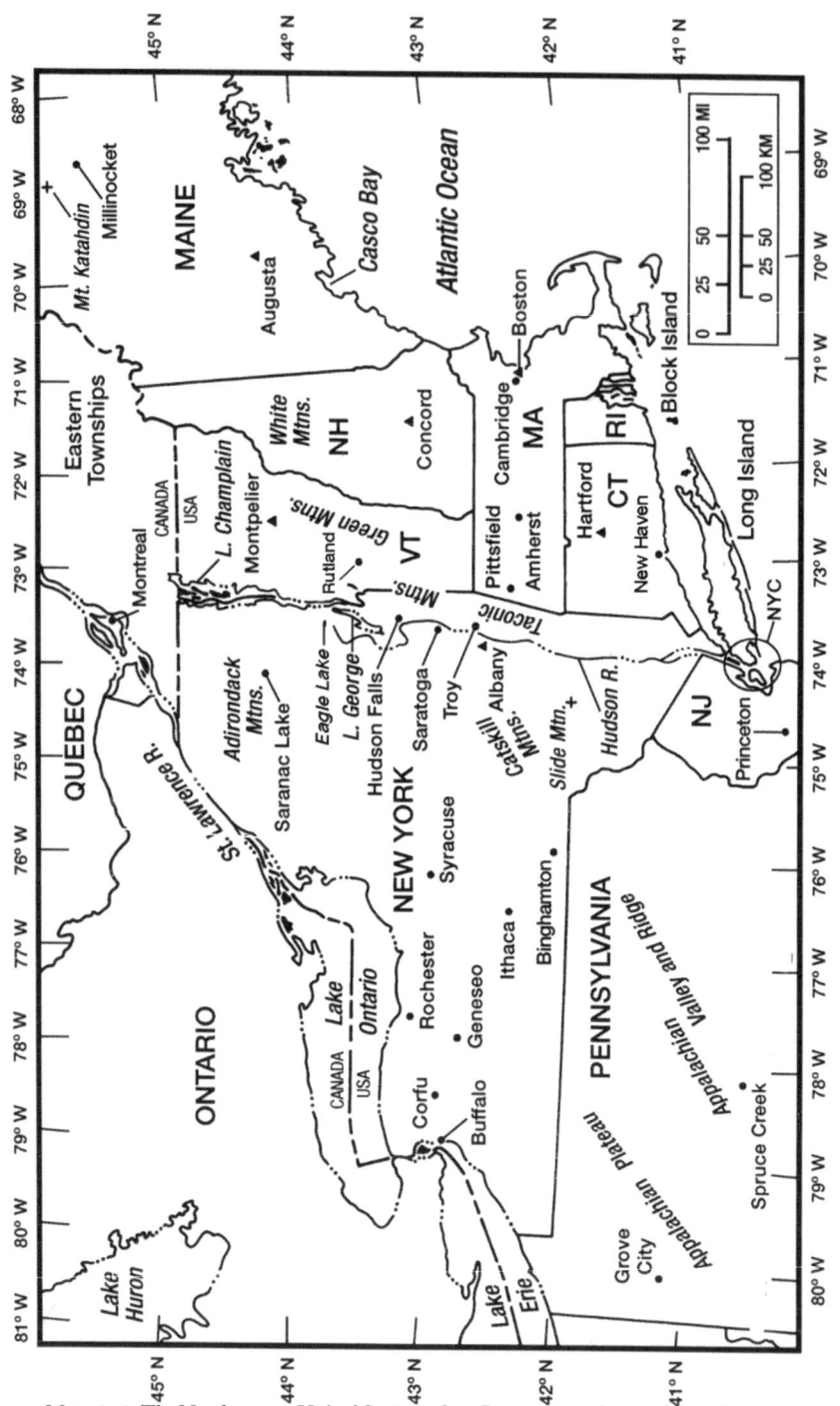

MAP. 1–1. *The Northeastern United States, where I grew up and was educated.*

1 — In Albany

My Parents:
Henry Darling Rodgers (1879-1957)
Louise Woodward (Allen) Rodgers (1880-1966)

ACCORDING TO THE FAMILY BIBLE, James Rodgers (1769-1834) emigrated to the United States in 1805 from Girvan in Ayrshire in Scotland, probably staying some time on the way in Glasgow and perhaps in Belfast. When I was in my teens, my parents visited Girvan looking for Rodgers relatives; they found them only in the graveyard. I visited Girvan myself in 1984 on a geological excursion, but I made no genealogical inquiries. The family Bible was in our home when we were growing up; it is now in the possession of my oldest nephew, Judge Frederic Barker Rodgers.

There is a significance to the date 1805. The Treaty of Amiens in 1802 seemed to have brought to an end the wars in which the other European powers had tried to destroy the French Revolution; they had to recognize Napoleon, by then the First Consul, as the ruler of France. But the treaty was only a truce, as all the powers understood; in 1804 Napoleon named himself Emperor of the French, and the British stepped up their preparations for the inevitable renewal of the war, sending out press-gangs to "recruit" soldiers for the Army. I can readily believe that my ancestor decided to leave home and come to the United States at just that time in order to escape Army service; thus he was a "draft-dodger" as the term has been used in recent years in this country. But we Americans should never forget that the United States was largely peopled and indeed created by draft-dodgers and similar folk unwilling to accept oppression, military or religious; the term should certainly not carry a stigma.

James Rodgers established himself in Albany, New York, and started a business building carriages and the like. His son, John Rodgers (1809-1866), carried it on, and their firm was well known in the northeastern states for, among other things, its fire engines (horse-drawn, of course). I was named for my great-grandfather, though probably indirectly

FIG. 1–1 *John Rodgers, my great-grandfather*

through an uncle John who died as a boy. John's son James wanted to be a (Presbyterian) minister, but his father decreed that he enter the family business. He did serve in the Union Army during the Civil War and was an officer, I think a Captain; his sword was around the house when I was young. His wish to be a minister was reflected however in his children, of whom seven lived to marry and raise families; my father was the sixth. James, the oldest, and two daughters, Anna and Mary, went into the ministry and became missionaries — James and Anna in the Philippines and Mary in China. Anna married another missionary, Will Wright, and Mary married August Larson, a Swede who was a leading merchant and factor in north China and Mongolia (see his autobiography written in collaboration with Nora Waln, *Larson, Duke of Mongolia*; Little, Brown, and Co., 1930). The second son, Albert, earned an M.D. In 1930 all seven and their spouses had a reunion in Rochester at the home of their youngest sister, Margaret; my sister Louise and I were there too.

Evidently there was money enough in the family to provide for the education of the older children but, by the time my father, Henry Darling Rodgers, was growing up, his father had died and the money seems to have run out. He had to leave high school before finishing, and he went to work as an office boy in the Albany Savings Bank. There he worked his way steadily upward; when I was growing up, he was Treasurer and had a very good salary. Later he was appointed President, the first President of that bank not to belong to one of the old Albany families. Lacking a college education himself, he saw to it that his children went to good private schools in Albany and on to college, and all four of us did, each going to a different college. In my own case, he paid my full tuition for four years at Cornell, although in fact I had won a good scholarship there; moreover I graduated in the middle of my senior year and hence had only the lower tuition in the Graduate School to pay for the second term. The justification for his paying the full amount was that I could put the extra money aside to see me through graduate school; I never had to ask him for any further support, though in fact he did make me several further gifts and I received my share of his estate.

One of my father's aunts was involved in a rather romantic episode that ended when her suitor jilted her; the story was told in a series of letters that were around the house, and I may not have it quite right. On the rebound she married a Scotsman named Alexander Kennedy, who settled in Pittsfield, Massachusetts. They had four children. As they grew up, two of the daughters, Mary and Ethel, became the closest friends of a Miss Louise Allen, the daughter of a reasonably well-to-do family there. My father, growing up, used to visit his cousins in Pittsfield, and he met and became more and more attracted to Miss Allen. In due course he proposed to her, but she refused him, for she was planning to become an (Episcopalian) deaconess and go out as a missionary. But after a little while, Miss Allen decided she had made a mistake, and the story of how she cajoled her bashful suitor into repeating his proposal, so that she could accept it, was one of the favorite stories around our home during my childhood. When the engagement was announced, the Pittsfield newspaper printed it under the headline: "The heathen will rage; Miss Allen will wed," publicity that my father and mother never forgot and never forgave. If any of us children had chosen to go into newspaper or other journalistic work, I really think we would have been disinherited.

Louise Allen's family traced its ancestry back to the *Mayflower* in 1620. At the time of the American Revolution, they were established in Pittsfield. My ancestor in that generation, Thomas Allen, became known as "The Fighting Parson" because he preached a fiery sermon and then led many of the men in his congregation to the support of General Stark at the Battle of Bennington (or Battle of the Walloomsac) in 1777. The battle was fought to prevent a contingent sent out by the British General Burgoyne from capturing munitions stored by the rebels at Bennington shortly before the battle of Saratoga, after which Burgoyne had to surrender his entire army. Actually it was not fought at Bennington, where it is commemorated by the Bennington Monument, but along the Walloomsac River in what is still New York State (though Bennington and indeed all Vermont were legally, if not willingly, part of the New York colony and then of the state until after the Revolution).

The Allens had a large farm just east of Pittsfield. The great arch at the entrance to the farm, made of Missouri granite (the family had strong connections to St. Louis and the St. Louis, Iron Mountain, and Southern Railway), still stands on the north side of Dalton Avenue, giving its name to Allengate Avenue, which enters at that point. Before my mother's time, the Allen farm had become famous for its trotting horses, who won many trotting races in the Northeast; my mother had many

FIG. 1–2. *The Allen Gate, gate to the original Allen farm, Pittsfield, Massachusetts*

stories to tell about them. I think however that her father, like my father's father, was less successful in business than his forebears; the farm ceased to be a profitable venture and ultimately was sold off. All his four children received a college education, however; my mother, the youngest, graduated from Wellesley in 1903. The only grandparent whom I remember was my Grandma Allen, my mother's mother; she lived comfortably in the Hotel Wendell in Pittsfield, and we often went to Pittsfield to visit her, and usually Cousins Mary and Ethel Kennedy as well.

My parents were married on 4 September 1907. Their first child, a son named Henry Allen Rodgers though he was always called Harry to distinguish him from his father, was born on 10 June 1908. The second son, Prentice Johnson Rodgers, was born on 22 November 1909. At about that time, however, my mother discovered that she had tuberculosis, and she went to the Trudeau Sanitorium in Saranac Lake, New York, then the standard treatment for the disease. I was told later that her disease was "glandular TB," and she had a long scar on her neck, with marks of many stitches, from an operation to remove diseased tissue. There was a story in the family that, when she returned to Albany, my father took his two young sons down to the station with him to meet her, and that only Harry, the older son, recognized his mother — after some hesitation. I think her return was in October 1913; I was born on 11 July 1914 and my sister, Louise Allen (Rodgers) Ackerman, on 15 July 1915.

When my parents were married, my father arranged with his former schoolteacher, Miss Utter, to rent her cottage on Eagle Lake (then Chilson Lake) in the Adirondacks for the honeymoon. Many years later, in 1921, he bought the cottage from Miss Utter, and thereafter our family spent most of each summer there, though my father was ordinarily able to come up only for a few weeks plus occasional weekends. When my father died in November 1957, my mother sold the cottage, as she did our home in Albany and, although she later went back to the Lake during several summers, she stayed in a rented cottage on the other side and never revisited the cottage that had been theirs.

After she grew up, my mother reacted against the Allen family's assumption that they had socially superior status, in good part I think because she was always very solicitous that my father never feel his lack of a college education as social inferiority. One might say that she "leaned over backwards" to prevent any such implication. Indeed my father once told me he regretted that his wife had deliberately refused to take the position in Albany "society" to which her family background entitled her.

What matters is that they were deeply in love for the whole of the fifty years they lived together, and that each was continually thinking of the other, of how any action or even interpretation of an action would affect the other. My mother once told me that an in-living maid said to her, in amazement: "Mrs. Rodgers, I have never heard you or Mr. Rodgers speak a harsh word to each other." The doctor who attended my father on his deathbed, speaking to me just afterwards (I had had a small upset), told me he thought my not having married might be because, having witnessed the happiness of their marriage, I was unwilling to try, for fear that mine would never be as happy and perfect.

My mother lived on in Albany for nearly nine years after my father's death, and she lived an active life, in good part centered around the Episcopal Church. But, from what she said to me once or twice, I believe that every night, when she went to bed, she prayed to the Lord to let her die that night. Both my parents were fortunate in their deaths, each having a short illness of only five days before the end. "There is no good way to go, but there are better ways and worse."

There can be no doubt that my mother has influenced me much more than my father. Physically I was rather slow to grow up; I was not strong, though not sickly. As a boy I played all the usual sports, but I was never much good at them, and I didn't come to enjoy them, except for tennis. My father would have liked to share sports with me, as he was inclined that way, but we never did much of that. Mentally on the other hand I grew up fast, perhaps too fast, and I read precociously and indis-

FIG. 1–3 a & b. *The infant John Rodgers with his mother and with his father in May 1915*

FIG. 1–4. *John Rodgers with his sister Louise at 150 South Pine Avenue, Albany in 1923*

criminately. Somewhere around the age of nine I discovered that playing the piano well could serve as a substitute for failure in schoolboy sports, and somewhere around twelve I discovered the same thing about my studies. From then on I studied and practiced avidly and effectively, and I graduated from the Albany Academy, one of the best private schools in the country, at the head of my class.

Conversely, I was never much interested, and still am not, in practical matters, like earning money in the summer to have pin money during the rest of the year, as my older brothers did, and I suspect my father may have worried about whether he might not have to support me for the rest of my natural life. And throughout my life I have always avoided responsiblity as much as possible, though of course it has very often not been possible.

Then, in what would correspond to the tenth grade, I discovered geology and made up my mind to be a geologist. My father wasn't at all sure I could make a living at that and asked practical questions, but he never said "No," and he evidently consulted his business friends and decided I might make it. In the end he saw me established; I rather doubt however that he had ever expected a son of his to become a professor at Yale.

On the other hand, I certainly absorbed a large part of my major intellectual interests from my mother — languages and literature, history, comparative religion, philosophy, and perhaps even geology, for she had taken a small course in that at her finishing school and there was a copy of *Dana's Manual of Geology* around the house, though I cannot remember that I ever read it; I did study *White's First Greek Book* quite thoroughly. During those years, there was a brief but popular fad for a book called *I've Got Your Number*; one answered five sets of questions about one's likes and dislikes, one's habits and aversions, and the numbers of the sets for which the answers were mainly positive led to a paragraph giving

FIG. 1–5. *Eagle Lake in the Adirondack Mountains, New York, from the family cottage*

an analysis of one's character. I remember vividly that my paragraph began: "Were you tied to somebody's apron-strings too long?" That is quite unfair to my mother but perhaps not to me; I probably tagged right along without needing to be tied to any strings.

My Siblings:
Henry Allen Rodgers (1908-1999),
Prentice Johnson Rodgers (1909-1980),
Louise Allen (Rodgers) Ackerman (1915-

MY TWO BROTHERS, Harry and Prent (baptismal names Henry and Prentice) were six and four years old when I was born, so I don't think they felt me as a competitor within the family. As I grew up, I looked up to them, especially, I think, to Harry as the older. Because he played the piano (Prent played the violin), I wanted to play it too, and he taught me the rudiments, including how to read simple music and to play it. Miss Olive Schreiner, the piano teacher for all us children, told me years later that, when I came to my first piano lesson, I was playing simple Chopin mazurkas with the most awful fingering she'd ever seen in her life. After about a year of lessons, I got somewhat bored with them, presumably with the discipline of practicing for them, and I wanted to quit. My parents sensibly let me do so, and within a few months I was clamoring to have them back again. I kept them up until I went to college, practicing hard and regularly. After that I never took any more formal lessons, but for the rest of my life I have never stopped practicing — and playing. During my years doing geology in East Tennessee and vicinity, I would always seek out a piano wherever I was, generally in the Baptist church.

FIG. 1–6. *The Rodgers family*
Front: Mrs. Rodgers, Louise, Mr. Rodgers
Back: John, Prent, Harry

Curiously, Harry did not keep up his piano-playing in his later school years. Indeed he and Prent got well into jazz, took up the clarinet, the saxophone, the trumpet, and the trombone, and played in local jazz bands, but I stuck with the piano and classical music.

I wanted to imitate Harry in other ways too. He had been quite a good student at the Albany Academy, being almost always in the top five or so of his class, and so was I, at my six-year interval; at the end I did even better. Prentice on the other hand, following a year after Harry and expected to be like him, wasn't gaited that way; he found that expectation unfair, and eventually he shifted to the Albany High School, which he found more congenial.

Both my brothers went on to college, Harry to Hamilton, a small college in central New York State, Prent to Amherst. I visited them both during their college years, and if I had gone to a small college it would certainly have been Hamilton. But after I got into geology it became clear that I should go to a larger school (as mentioned below, the choice was Yale or Cornell, and I chose Cornell). On one of my visits to Harry at Hamilton, however, I met and was taken on a short field trip by Nelson C. Dale, Professor of Geology there. Harry was always good in languages, which he made his major in college; indeed he took his junior year abroad in France. My great interest in languages may also stem in part from my wanting to imitate him.

My brothers graduated from college in 1930 and 1932, in the pit of the Great Depression. Neither had any clear vocation like the one I already had for geology. Harry had had the idea of going into railroading, but jobs were disappearing faster than they were opening in that field. My father, being a banker, found them both jobs in other banks in Albany. Prentice stayed with his bank and ultimately rose to be its CEO; Harry on the other hand threw up his job after six years and went west, to Albany, Oregon, "to seek his fortune." After a few discouraging months, he felt a call to the ministry, and he went to the San Anselmo Theological Seminary in California, where he was ordained in the Presbyterian church and where he met Elizabeth — "Betty" — Nielsen. They were married in 1937, and I visited them that year on my first trip west. They lived very happily together for over sixty years, though there could be no children, which I think was a great disappointment for them both. At first Harry had parishes here and there in towns around middle California; I visited them in one of these on my return from the Pacific in 1946. Then he decided he wanted to teach, and he held positions in several small Presbyterian colleges across the country teaching Bible and Greek, especially New Testament Greek. His longest spell of teaching was in Grove City College in western Pennsylvania, where I visited them several times. When he retired, they moved into a home for retired Presbyterian ministers in Pasadena, California, and I visited them there too.

For one of my visits to Grove City, Betty, who was fond of surprises, engineered one. Harry's and my parents were visiting them over one Thanksgiving Day, and Betty found some pretext or other to get the parents to drive to the Youngstown, Ohio, airport, and then to watch the arrival of a particular plane. Suddenly my mother spoke up: "Why, that man getting off the plane looks like John; why, it is John!" Fun for all.

As I've mentioned above, in my earlier years I wanted to imitate Harry, but later I came closer to Prentice, whom I saw more often because he continued to live in Albany. Among other times I saw him nearly every Christmas until 1966, the year my mother died. Even from our college years, we shared many musical and other intellectual interests. He and his wife Jane raised a family of five children, all of whom went their separate ways — the three boys went into, respectively, the law, Arabic languages, and computers; the two girls married happily, one a lawyer, one a leader in a commune she had joined. I already have about a dozen great-nephews and nieces in that family and about half a dozen in my sister's.

In my sketch of the Conklin family, I mention the second home that Prent and Jane established at Ajijic in western Mexico.

My sister Louise and I, only a year apart, were inseparable companions as we grew up, though we squabbled much of the time. I don't think I ever felt "threatened" by her and her abilities, for I went my own way, but I'm pretty sure she felt seriously overshadowed by me — a boy, older, good at school, and sure of myself. She went to Vassar College, where she became more and more interested in religion, in which she majored. After her college years, she decided to go to a theological seminary (she chose Hartford) and become an ordained minister. As neither the Episcopalian nor the Presbyterian Church accepted women as ministers at that time, she joined one of the Congregational denominations, and for about seven years she was a pastor in Congregational churches in western Vermont. One of her fellow students at the seminary, William Ackerman, had asked her to marry him about when they graduated, but she had refused him. Seven years later he came back and asked again, and that time he was accepted.

He was also an ordained minister, but he found more congenial employment as a sociologist of religion for various county and city planning agencies, all across the country from New York (near Albany) to Texas, where they lived for a considerable time, notably in El Paso and Fort Worth. Naturally their three children moved around with them; indeed the children came to think of themselves as Texans. During my frequent travels, I was able to visit them in nearly every place they lived. At their daughter Nancy's wedding to Kenneth Schofield, when the two young people graduated from Grinnell College in Iowa, her two parents, both ministers, officiated. I remember particularly that at one point, as part of the ceremony, Nancy asked her father and mother to accept her new husband into their family, and Ken asked his parents to do the same for his new wife. I never saw that done at any other wedding, but I was deeply impressed by its beauty and rightness.

Only at the end of his life did Bill Ackerman take a parish, that too in Texas. Since her husband's death, my sister has lived with Nancy and Ken Schofield in Wisconsin, and I have visited that happy family several times.

Chris Andrew Hartnagel (1874-1962)

WHEN DURING MY TENTH GRADE YEAR I decided I wanted to be a geologist, it turned out that my Latin teacher at the Albany Academy, Mr. Stetson, lived next door to the Assistant State Geologist of New York, Chris A. Hartnagel, and Stetson asked him to talk to this high-school student about what a geologist's life is like. Dr. Hartnagel found that I was quite serious about the matter, and he suggested that I come to his office in the New York State Museum one afternoon a week for a little lesson in geology. That was easy for me, for the State Museum was in the upper floors of the State Education Building, opposite the State Capitol and only a block or so uphill from the Albany Academy building, a fine, if old, brownstone building in downtown Albany opposite the City Hall. In that building in the 1820s, Joseph Henry, then teaching there, did the experiments that demonstrated the useful magnetic properties of electric currents, leading directly to telegraphy and electric motors. The Academy didn't moved uptown to its present site on Academy Road until 1931, and my class there, '32, was the first to graduate from the new building, as I made sure to mention in my valedictory speech at that commencement.

I was already quite familiar with the public exhibits of the New York State Museum, having been taken there many many times by my parents, I suppose when they found my sister and me difficult to handle on rainy Saturdays or holidays. The exhibits, prepared by the successive State Geologists, Paleontologists, Zoologists, Botanists, and Anthropologists, were excellent and very instructive; the "Indian groups," four dioramas that illustrated Iroquois life, were in fact quite famous. I knew all these exhibits well and was particularly taken with the relief maps. There was a careful relief model, with trees, houses, etc., of the Hill Cumorah, a large drumlin in western New York State where Joseph Smith found the Book of Mormon, and a very large-scale relief map of the whole state colored to show the geological formations, around which I had walked many times, gradually learning to understand it.

Maps have always fascinated me. When I was a little boy and my parents wanted to keep me out of mischief, they would sit me on the floor with a big heavy atlas in my lap, and I would turn the pages for hours, memorizing the names and shapes of states, countries, and continents. They also bought me cut-out "picture puzzles" of the states of the Union, of the counties of New York and of Pennsylvania, and of the European countries as they were both before and after the First World War; to this day I can draw from memory reasonably accurate maps of any part of the world. By the time I was ten, I was adept at reading contour maps, and indeed I subscribed to the monthly lists of such maps published by the U. S. Geological Survey, not guessing I would one day join the Survey.

Dr. Hartnagel began his lessons by sending me out into the Museum to make drawings of the fossils, the good old Agassiz technique. Soon he found that I already had some idea of the stratigraphy of New York State, for I had been buying secondhand geology books at a bookstore downtown, and indeed I acquired quite a number of books from the library of John M. Clarke, State Geologist and Paleontologist of New York, who had died in 1925. Dr. Hartnagel therefore set me the task of working out the formations penetrated by a well at Corfu in western New York from the rotary-drill cuttings, helping me to recognize the different rock types from the cuttings. I well remember how at one point I was much puzzled by cuttings that should have been the "Niagara limestone" (the rock that forms the lip of Niagara Falls) but that failed to fizz in dilute hydrochloric acid, as ordinary limestone should do, and that looked granular, more like sand grains. He showed me that the "sand grains" wouldn't scratch glass, as quartz sand grains would have done, and then he told me to powder them and try the acid again; this time they fizzed. That was my introduction to the mineral and rock dolomite, which has since been one of the leitmotifs in my geological life.

When I had worked out the stratigraphy of the well and knew the depth at which it reached the top of the different formations, especially the Medina sandstone (it was drilled to look for natural gas in the Medina), he gave me similar information from other wells in the region, and from them I constructed a structure-contour map of the top of the Medina in western New York State. Then he had me make a north-south cross-section, based on the surface geology and the wells and extending into

Pennsylvania, where I used an atlas of geological maps of the Pennsylvania counties. There my cross-section encountered the gentle folds in the strata of the Appalachian Plateau and then the great folds in central Pennsylvania — my first introduction to the Appalachian Valley and Ridge province, which has been one of my central interests throughout my career. He also helped me to understand the geological jargon I had been reading in the books I had bought, and he taught me to recognize many minerals and rocks. Thus in the two and a half years I worked with him he gave me a thorough basis in geology, especially in the geology of New York State. When I got to college I already had the equivalent of the introductory course in geology and a good start on several of the advanced courses.

 Dr. Hartnagel was not the only person at the State Museum who took an interest in me and my geological education. The State Geologist in those years was Dr. David Newland, who was known to my family, especially the family of my brother Prentice's wife, Jane Weed. I remember that he took me on a field trip to Lake George in the southeastern Adirondacks and helped me to understand the complicated geology. The Assistant State Paleontologist then was Dr. Winifred Goldring, a highly regarded specialist in fossil crinoids; again the Goldring family was well known to my parents. Finally there was the State Paleontologist, Dr. Rudolf Ruedemann (1864-1956), who was for many years the leading expert in North America for graptolites, a long-extinct animal group (hence known only from the fossils) whose relations to living animal groups are still obscure.

 Dr. Ruedemann was brought up and educated in Germany in the last part of the nineteenth century, earning not one but two PhD degrees (in petrology and paleontology), but he became quite discouraged by the lack of opportunity there. In 1892, urged on by his wife, he came to the United States, finding employment first as a school teacher in towns in central New York State. Studying the rocks in their vicinity, he came upon an extraordinary deposit of fossil graptolites, and he published a short description of his find, first in German in Germany. It came to the notice of Dr. John M. Clarke (mentioned above), who had it published in English and then encouraged Ruedemann to take a Civil Service examination for Assistant State Paleontologist. He was appointed in 1899, and he became State Paleontologist in 1925 when Clarke died. Dr. Ruedemann was particularly kind to me, and he delighted in telling me stories about geology and geologists, some of which were hardly appropriate for a youngster just starting in the profession. Long after I left Albany to go to college, I would visit all my old mentors at the Museum or in their homes whenever I came back to see my parents. Dr. Ruedemann, even after his retirement, kept telling me his stories in a strong German accent that seemed to thicken with the years. Nearly twenty years after his death, I was privileged to write his Biographical Memoir for the National Academy of Sciences, of which he had long been a member.

My friends at the State Museum also encouraged me to join them in field meetings of geologists of the state (held at least once a year, though not always near enough to Albany for me to attend). They helped me to understand the geology being demonstrated, and they introduced me to many other geologists, especially the geology professors in the various colleges in the state. On one of these field trips, in a limestone quarry near Schoharie, Dr. Ruedemann found a curious piece of rock, a cone with rough striae diverging from the apex, though the apex was broken off and replaced by a shallow depression containing low-relief markings with a fourfold symmetry. He explained to me that it was a percussion cone formed by the explosion of dynamite in a drill-hole, the fourfold markings having been made by the drill bit. Then, with me tagging along, he took it around to the other paleontologists on the trip and asked each of them what kind of fossil it was. Each gave his opinion, all different, but none recognized what it really was. In this way Ruedemann taught me always to be ready to doubt the opinions of professed experts, especially self-professed experts; the lesson was premature no doubt for a high-school kid, but I've not forgotten it.

In December 1934 in Rochester, New York, as I particularly remember, Dr. Hartnagel took me to the first meeting of the Geological Society of America (GSA) that I attended; by then I was a junior at Cornell. Moreover he took me to the Society's Annual Banquet as his guest; at that banquet the then relatively new Penrose Medal of the Society, the highest honor in North American geology, was awarded to Professor Charles Schuchert of Yale (see below). Professor Schuchert had been called to Yale from his position in Albany with Dr. Clarke, and hence Dr. Hartnagel had known him there. After the medal presentations, Dr. Hartnagel took me up and introduced me to Professor Schuchert; then he asked him to let this young undergraduate student hold the medal! Both Professor Schuchert and I were completely unprepared for this request; nevertheless Schuchert graciously put the big gold medal in my hands for a minute — then I gave it back to him. Nearly fifty years later, when I in my turn was awarded the Penrose Medal, I recalled that incident in my acceptance speech.

2 — At Cornell

Charles Merrick Nevin (1892-1975)

I MAY HAVE MET PROFESSOR NEVIN of Cornell University on one of the geology field trips that I took with my New York State Museum mentors during my senior year at the Albany Academy. In any case my diary records that I had thought of going to his geological field camp in central Pennsylvania in the summer of 1932, *before* going to college, but that Dr. Hartnagel advised against it, judging me not yet mature enough to profit from it. He did talk to Professor Nevin about me, however, and Professor Nevin suggested I make him my adviser if I came to Cornell.

All during that year I was trying to decide whether to go to Cornell or Yale for my undergraduate work, vacillating as my geological advisers suggested one or the other. For some reason, when I had to list my college choices, I listed Cornell first, and in August I got a rather glum (one might even say peevish) letter from Yale, hoping that I had been accepted by the college of my first choice; they knew that as first in my class at the Albany Academy I would have been accepted by any college in the country.

That letter may even have been what decided me in favor of Cornell; later, when I could compare the two universities, I realized that I never made a better decision in my life. Undergraduate Yale, *at that time*, as I learned when I came there as a graduate student, was monolithic. There was one accepted pattern for a Yale man, in large part set by the big Senior Societies, of which Skull and Bones is the most famous, and boys who didn't fit that pattern (as I would certainly not have fit) found themselves somewhat out of place and had to expend much of their energy maintaining their right to be "different." Cornell on the other hand was a pluralistic society; fraternities and sororities were important, but for only about half the student body. There were "senior societies" imitated from those at Yale, but they had little influence outside some of the most "fashionable" fraternities; no one else paid them much attention.

Thus I was able to find my niche without difficulty; I did join one of the lesser fraternities, and living there was very useful for me in teaching me how to get along with many different kinds of people. I was rather a prig in those years and got over it only after I left Cornell. When I was fourteen my father said several times that I was a curious mixture of four and forty; by the time I reached forty I suspect I was a curious mixture of fourteen and eighty-four.

But my central interest all through my undergraduate years was not in the sports, dates, and dances that were the core of life for many of my fraternity brothers but in my studies, not only in geology and the other sciences but also in the "humanities," especially languages and literatures, English and foreign. The Albany Academy had given me a thoroughly "classical" education — French from the fifth grade, Latin from the eighth; then in the tenth one had to take either German or ancient Greek, and I got some of both while there. On the other hand, science was perhaps the weakest part of the Academy curriculum. At Cornell I also got deep into music; I not only kept on practicing the piano, but I audited several music courses, thus becoming acquainted with several members of the Music faculty. Right away I joined the Cornell Instrumental Club or "Mandolin Club," and already in my freshman year I was chosen to play the solo piano part of Gershwin's *Rhapsody in Blue* with the Club in several concerts, at Ithaca and on tour. Later I got into the Cornell Glee Club, though at first only as pianist. In my senior year I was the pianist for several performances of the Gilbert and Sullivan operetta *H.M.S. Pinafore*; indeed I memorized the whole piano score, and I played it all the way through

FIG. 2–7.
John Rodgers at Cornell; taken by Eleanor Murphy Moorhouse during the 1930s.

FIG. 2–8.
Caricature of John Rodgers, drawn by an itinerant artist named Ward during the 1930s.

from memory at one of the later rehearsals. The music professor who was conducting (and who had chosen me to play the piano) realized what I was doing but didn't interfere; afterwards however he made me promise under no circumstances to try any such stunt during the performances.

To get back to geology, I conferred with Professor Nevin about my courses as soon as I got to Ithaca in September 1932, and he was my adviser from then on. I took the elementary course in Geology of which he was one of the instructors, and after that I took all his courses and seminars and indeed virtually every course offered in the department. During the summer after my freshman year I did go to his geological field camp at Spruce Creek, Pennsylvania, in the heart of the Appalachian Valley and Ridge province,. There Professor Nevin converted my fairly extensive book-knowledge of geology into a thoroughly practical basis in geological field work and mapping. I loved it; such field work has ever since been for me the most enjoyable side of geology, much as I also enjoy the theoretical side — assembling evidence for, working out, and testing hypotheses and theories to explain the larger geological phenomena. Right from the first I was fascinated both by stratigraphy, the study of strata as a key to the depositional history of such regions as the Appalachian Mountains, and by structural geology, the study of the deformation that affected those strata after their deposition, in the process of building them into the mountain ranges.

Professor Nevin was perhaps best known for his textbook *Structural Geology*, which went through four editions from 1931 to 1949 and was highly respected. Indeed, when I came to Yale for graduate work, I found that Professor Longwell was using it in his courses.

But Nevin's own publications and research were at least as much in sedimentation, in the detailed study of the processes by which strata are laid down; thus by studying with him I was able to deepen both the interests mentioned above.

After my sophomore year I went again to the summer camp in Pennsylvania, but at that point Professor Nevin suddenly developed appendicitis, and the camp was run by Professor Burfoot. Again I learned a lot, and the following summer I began to use my newly acquired field techniques to make a geological map of part of the southern Champlain Valley in Vermont and New York, near enough to our summer camp on Eagle Lake in the Adirondacks for me to live at the camp and do field work day by day, using one of my father's automobiles. For my first spell of field work, however, I lived in Shoreham, Vermont, and went out in the field on a bicycle. This work gradually added up to a solid piece of geological mapping, and it became the basis for my Master of Sciences thesis. Naturally Professor Nevin was the adviser for my Master's thesis; it ultimately became my second published article.

Nevin was a very good teacher — in his own way. After he had given us the basics, he would almost never tell us his opinion on any doubtful question but would force us to argue it out with him and with the other students in the class. For example, in those days Continental Drift, the idea that the Americas were once right up against Europe and Africa but then drifted thousands of miles away over the long geological eras, was considered very unlikely, if not impossible, by most North American and European geologists. Bailey Willis, a well known structural geologist, published an abstract entitled *Continental Drift, ein Märchen*. But Nevin never revealed his own opinion; he would point out the great mechanical difficulties in the way of accepting the idea of whole continents moving on the surface of the solid Earth, but he would also point out how neatly it could explain the known distribution of the very widely scattered late Paleozoic Southern Hemisphere glaciations (an Ice Age nearly 300 million years old, quite other than the "recent" Ice Age of the last million years or so), bringing them all into an area no larger than that covered by the "recent" ice sheets of the Northern Hemisphere. That is why Southern Hemisphere geologists always tended to favor the idea, whatever the Northern Hemisphere geologists might think of it. In one of Nevin's seminars we argued our way right through the book *Our Wandering Continents* by the South African geologist Alexander du Toit, studying the good arguments and the bad arguments but reaching no firm conclusion. That was Nevin's way of teaching, and I found it very valuable. When he died, I was asked to write a Memorial for him for the Geological Society of America, and I worked quite hard on it. But my principal conclusion was that, as a geologist, Nevin was a superb poker player (he was anyway; he loved games of all kinds but even more he hated to lose), and the Society decided it wasn't very complimentary and didn't publish it.

The Feud in the Department of Geology

BY TAKING ALL THEIR COURSES, I CAME TO KNOW all the members of the Cornell Geology Department, and gradually I learned that the Department was riven by a great feud, which had apparently been going on for decades; I never did learn how it began. The main leaders of the two opposing parties, which I will call Party A and Party B, disliked each other intensely — the word hatred is not too strong — but, as they were all full professors with tenure, there was little they could do to hurt each other. But they could and did take out their dislikes on the younger men of the other party, the assistant professors and graduate students. I came to know of egregious examples of unconscionable actions on both sides of the feud. As I was only an undergraduate till my last year, I could be as it were "just a little mouse in the woodwork," observing these actions but being careful not to identify myself with either party and to keep on good terms with everyone. I got into the habit of making little evening calls on all the full professors and many of the younger men and their wives, and indeed they were all very cordial and helpful to me throughout my five years there. Naturally I never mentioned to members of the one party that I was visiting those of the other. After I left Cornell, I often came back to Ithaca to visit, and on such occasions I made a point of trying to see them all. But these experiences sensitized me to the presence of such feuds, where they exist, and made me vow never to allow myself to become part of such a feud — never "to choose up sides and smell armpits," as the vulgar saying goes. These matters and many others are treated in William R. Brice's book: *Cornell Geology Through the Years: Cornell Engineering Histories*, vol. 2, 230 p., 1989.

One of the senior members of Party A was Professor Gilbert D. Harris, Professor of Paleontology. He retired at the end of my sophomore year at Cornell, and I never took a course from him, though his protégé, Dr. Kenneth Caster, had him give a few lectures in his courses. As Party B had the upper hand all during my years at Cornell, Professor Harris felt unwelcome in the Geology building and, rather than continue to work there, he built his own laboratory on his property some distance from the campus, the Paleontological Research Institute, from which he published a well known series of *Bulletins of American Paleontology* that he had started in 1895. Thanks to Caster I did get to know him, and I would visit him too, when I returned to Ithaca.

Another leader of Party A was Professor O. D. von Engeln, Professor of Geomorphology; he was reputed to be difficult to deal with but, although I didn't take his course till well along in my college career, I got along quite well with him. Indeed, a small project I did while taking his course interested him enough that he urged me to write it up and publish it; with his help I did so, sending it off to the *American Journal of Science* at Yale where it was accepted. That was my first published article; I never guessed that later I would edit that journal for half a century.

The leader of Party B was Professor Heinrich Ries, Professor of Economic Geology; during my years he was Head of the Department — not Chairman but Head, which seemed to mean that he could, if he chose, make major decisions such as those about hiring or firing younger faculty members without consulting the full Department. I came to know him rather quickly, and he too was very friendly and helpful. I took all his courses, notably his famous seminar on clays, for he was recognized as the outstanding expert in North America on the geology of clay. He and Professor von Engeln particularly disliked each other, and neither made any effort to conceal it. When, after leaving Cornell, I began to work on a doctoral dissertation in East Tennessee, I wrote letters about it to all my former professors at Cornell. In his reply, Professor von Engeln urged me to keep working for the Ph. D. "The PhD is only a label," he wrote, "but one can get to be President of the Geological Society of America on labels alone." I knew, and he knew that I knew, that he was referring to Professor Ries, who had been President of the GSA in 1929. When, forty years later, I was named President of the GSA, I wanted very much to write him and say: "Look, Dr. Von, I made it, on labels alone!" He would have loved it, but unfortunately he had died a few years earlier.

On one occasion when I returned to Ithaca to see my friends there, at a time when Party A had regained the upper hand and Professor von Engeln was Chairman (or Head; I'm not sure which), I visited Professor Ries, who had recently retired, and he complained bitterly to me that he had been forced to vacate his office in the Geology building, though in fact friends of his in Chemical Engineering had found him an office in their building. I knew, but of course I didn't say so, that Dr. Von had done it deliberately because, when Professor Ries was Head, he had forced Professor Gill of Mineralogy, a member of Party A, to vacate his office when he retired; ironically friends in the Chemistry Department had found Professor Gill an office there. So now the wheel had come full circle.

Professor Nevin had been brought into the Department by Professor Ries and hence belonged to Party B, though he was never belligerent about it. He and Professor von Engeln were none too fond of each other, but their feelings were much less intense, and they never visited them on me.

My years at Cornell were of course during the "Great Depression." It happened that, when the Depression struck, the Geology Department had just hired a new group of young instructors or assistant professors; in view of the dismal job situation, they were permitted to stay on in the Department beyond the usual time limit when they would ordinarily have been either promoted to tenure or let go. I knew all these men well, for they were the instructors in my elementary geology laboratories and in certain advanced courses; in the long run all but one moved on. I want particularly to mention two of them.

The first is Dr. Kenneth E. Caster, who was Professor Harris' choice as successor in invertebrate paleontology. I got along splendidly with Ken Caster and, more than with any other member of the department, I used to go on field trips with him around New York State, both to the regular annual or semiannual meetings of geologists and on more informal trips here and there. About my Junior year, Professor Ries (Party B) ended the, always temporary, appointment of Dr. Caster (Party A), and, when Caster then applied for a good position in the U. S. National Museum in Washington, Ries was asked for his opinion and Caster didn't get the job. Instead he had to make do with a temporary position at the State Normal School in Geneseo, New York. But a couple of years later he moved to the University of Cincinnati (always a mecca for paleontologists), where he had an illustrious career and, when he left Geneseo, he arranged for one of the other instructors at Cornell, one who "belonged" to Party B but by then had also to move on, to take his position there, where the latter made his career. The enmity between the leaders of the two parties did not extend down among the younger men.

The other younger man whom I wish to mention is Professor J. Dabney Burfoot, a mineralogist; he alone among the younger men who were at Cornell at that time achieved tenure. He came from Virginia (we dubbed him The Colonel) and had a strong southern accent; at first I had a good deal of difficulty understanding him. He knew his mineralogy well, but unfortunately he was not good at explaining it; only if one already understood what he was explaining did one find out how thorough his knowledge was. I got to know him first when I took his elementary course in the spring term of 1934, then at Nevin's camp that summer; after that I took several more courses from him, and he evidently found me an apt student. Then at the beginning of my senior year he found himself faced with an overload of students in his elementary mineralogy course, and he persuaded the Department to make me a laboratory assistant for that year; I served not only in that course but in the elementary geology courses as well. We got along famously, and I evidently did well enough the work he wanted done, for the next year I was appointed Instructor, again for the laboratories in elementary mineralogy and geology. The resulting work was extremely valuable experience for me; I learned how to prepare and give labs and how to make my explanations accurate and at the same time intelligible and interesting to the students, who were not always anxious to learn.

Professor Burfoot also helped me greatly as I was learning how to deal with the feud in the Department. He had been brought in by Professor Ries for Party B, but from the first he worked hard to be on good terms with all parties, and he showed me how to follow suit. His wife, Marian Burfoot, was Secretary of the Department during my time there, and she too was very helpful to me in finding my way, both materially and personally, within the Department.

An amusing incident: the Geology Department had its own quite good library, which was shelved all around the walls of the Department office and in an upper level of stacks there. From the first, building on my training in Albany, I made use of the library and became very familiar with what was there and how to use it. It happened that the library shelves were behind a railing on which hung a sign: Undergraduates not allowed behind this railing. As a Geology major, I paid no attention to this sign, and nobody ever questioned my right to go behind it, but I resented it nonetheless. So one lunchtime, when I was alone in the office, I simply stole the sign and hid it away, soon transferring it to my own room. Several weeks later, at another lunchtime, someone noticed its absence, and everyone commented; they were quite sure it had been there that morning and had only just disappeared. Knowing that it had been gone for weeks, I just kept quiet, but I learned something about the value of eye-witness accounts.

A major debt I owe to Professor Burfoot was his urging and encouraging me to follow in detail the George Fisher Baker Lectures in Chemistry during the second term of my sophomore year (the same term that I took his own elementary course). The Baker Lectures were given by Sir William Lawrence Bragg, the younger of the two Braggs who just at that time were introducing the use of x-ray diffraction in determining the atomic structure of crystalline materials, thus creating the new field of structural inorganic chemistry. The new methods were especially useful in studying minerals, as the Braggs well knew, and Bragg's lectures were an extraordinary revelation; aspects of mineralogy that had been very difficult to understand because they seemed to have no sense or meaning, notably the chemical formulas and classification of the silicate minerals, suddenly became crystal clear and the foundation for many other parts of geology. As a result of that lecture series, Bragg published his seminal book *The Atomic Structure of Minerals*, and in it he pays a handsome tribute to Professor Burfoot for his help in dealing with mineralogical conventions. Bragg's lectures were a major step forward in my intellectual history; not only had a field of knowledge that had seemed impossibly obscure suddenly become clear and beautiful, but I learned that as science advances it becomes not more complex but simpler and that such simplification, clarification, and "beautification" is in the long run the real test of major scientific hypotheses.

Mrs. H. H. Heller (née Lillian Purvis) (1882-1957)

IN 1905, MISS LILLIAN PURVIS from Dryden, New York, a member of the Class of 1904 at Cornell, married Mr. H. Howard Heller, a member of the class of 1903; they had met there a few years earlier (there were no children). Mr. Heller was a brilliant engineer; they lived on Long Island, where he became Works Manager for the Ford Instrument Co., a major instrument company, until his death in 1927. In 1930, Mrs. Heller returned to Ithaca, where she first rented and then bought an unique house at 122 Eddy Street. The house had been built in 1876 by William H. Miller, Cornell's first graduate in Architecture and, almost immediately thereafter, the official University architect. He lived in that house until his death in 1922. According to the story we were told: "Mr. Miller was a hartchitect, and whenever he had a new idea he tried it out in his own house." Thus the house became a sort of split-level rabbit-warren of rooms and passages, including such ideas as a built-in organ and even a windmill off to the side.

Mr. and Mrs. Heller had always wanted to "do something" for Cornell students and, when Mrs. Heller moved into 122 Eddy Street, she decided to offer rooms in the house at very nominal rent to seven or eight women students; in all some 25 lived there. But in 1934, after four years of girls, she decided, not without some trepidation, to try boys, and accordingly eight men were selected to fill the house; they included architects, engineers, and a chemist-organist chosen specifically to play the organ and piano. The men took over with a will, not only relieving Mrs. Heller of many household chores but concocting large schemes for the improvement of the house.

The first major project, undertaken that first year, was a complete redecoration of the "garden room." The artistic taste, ingenuity, and sheer work that went into that project are still apparent, for the room stayed as the boys finished it in one all-day-all-night session. From then on project followed project under Mrs. Heller's gentle but firm guidance and, sparked by a succession of architecture students, room after room was redecorated or recreated, the old windmill house was transformed into a garage (the boys' original plans called for a combined garage and dovecote), and many other improvements were made. Materials for these projects came out of the mysterious depths of the innumerable closets or were found on expeditions into the country, to auctions, or to brook-beds in the search for "hollowed-out stones", much prized for the garden or for Mrs. Heller's famous flower arrangements; one of her flower arrangements won first prize in the New York Flower Show of 1948. Thus her enthusiastic helpers gradually transformed an already remarkable house into one in which every nook and corner, almost every article of furniture and bric-a-brac, had its own story. Yet with all the changes, the house, like the continually changing "family" within it, always reflected her perfect taste, her gracious charm, and her generous personality.

With this kind of stimulating activity going on, and even more because of Mrs. Heller's unfailing interest in each person and her wise and good-humored tolerance of their collective brainstorms, the succeeding groups from the first women students of 1930 on became a close-knit family: Mrs. Heller's family of 122 Eddy Street. Among many amusing incidents, let me tell one: the boys and Mrs. Heller were holding a council on some project or other, and one of the boys, noticing that some were absent, asked if a quorum were present. Another replied that, with Mrs. Heller there, a quorum was certainly present. She was called "The Quorum" by us all from that day on.

Except for a short interruption during the Second World War, Mrs. Heller continued to fill her house with young men until 1952, when she became seriously ill; although later she tried to carry on, it soon became impossible. She died in 1957, bequeathing the house to Cornell's School of Architecture to be used as a residence for visiting professors, instructors, and graduate students in the School. But the nearly 200 Cornellians who as students knew the joys of life in 122 Eddy Street under Mrs. Heller's serene direction "rise up and call her blessed."

As it happened, the chemist-musician of 1934, Donald Flower, was a good friend of mine, and I visited him there several times that year, my Junior year; thus I became acquainted with Mrs. Heller, and she with me. Don Flower graduated in 1935, but by then I also knew a fine tenor who lived there, Edwin Miller, so I kept visiting, often to accompany his singing. After the middle of my senior year, when I had become a graduate student and was concentrating more and more on geology, life in the fraternity house became distasteful to me, and Miller, knowing this, suggested to Mrs. Heller that I take Don Flower's place as resident pianist-organist; she agreed, and I happily moved in during April 1936. I lived there for the rest of that school year and all the next, a wonderful time for me. After I left Cornell, I kept up my connection with 122 Eddy Street for many years, as long as Mrs. Heller lived there, and I was always welcome whenever I came back to Ithaca to visit Cornell and its geologists.

I'd like to tell an amusing story about Don Flower. When he graduated, he took a job as a chemist in industry, but after several years of that he decided that he'd rather be a failure as an organist than a success as a chemist; he quit his job and enrolled in the Eastman School of Music in Rochester, where he'd been working. After graduating, he took a job as organist and choir director in a church there, but before long he realized that he was doing exactly as he'd planned; he was a failure as an organist. So he went back to chemistry for a living, this time in Syracuse. But Don had other interests and talents; he was fond of working with automobiles, especially old ones, and he and a friend started a little garage for foreign cars. Right after the Second World War, they obtained the franchise for Syracuse for an unknown German car called the Volkswagen. Needless to say, the franchise was brilliantly successful, and lucrative, and before long Don could quit chemistry again; he constructed a home on the outskirts of Syracuse and built a good-sized organ into it. When I was preparing to go to Europe and study the Alps for my first sabbatical year, 1959-1960, I arranged to buy a Volkswagen camper from Don (campers were quite new then), to be delivered on the dock at Le Havre; I could deal with him instead of with the local VW agent because the car was to be delivered overseas.

Ethel Newcomb

ONE NOVEMBER EVENING IN MY SENIOR YEAR at Cornell, two undergraduate friends of mine, John Longyear and Paul Mattice, took me down to the village of Whitney Point, 30 miles east of Ithaca, to hear the retired pianist Ethel Newcomb. She had gone to Europe in the earliest 1900s to study with the famous piano teacher Theodor Leschetizky in Vienna and then had become one of his principal assistants. After his death in 1915, she had a long career as a piano teacher and concert pianist, mainly in Europe; finally she returned to the United States and retired to her native village where, on Saturday evenings, she would play the piano for whoever came to listen. Moreover, one of her pupils had been Olive Schreiner, who was my piano teacher in Albany before I went off to college.

The next April I and my friend Don Flower went down to hear her play; that time she discovered that I could play and that I had actually studied the Schumann Piano Concerto, so she sat me down at the second piano to play the orchestral part as she played the solo part on her first piano. As I knew the music, I did reasonably well, and she was pleased enough to suggest that we play together again when I came down; my diary says I went home that night "reeling in ecstasy."

Several times later that school year and a dozen times the next I went down to Whitney Point to hear her, and often we played piano concerti in the same way — oftenest the Schumann *Concerto* but also the Chopin

E minor, Beethoven's *Fourth and Fifth*, and the Saint-Saens and Grieg *Concerti*. Some of these I had never seen or heard before, but I was able to read them adequately; it isn't required for the accompanist to play all the notes exactly, only to keep the rhythm and the line of the music going. One time indeed, I was able to take my own teacher, Miss Schreiner, down to hear her — and the two of us playing together. And sometimes she would have other people play too; she even had me play pieces I knew, especially Bach. On one such occasion she paid me a supreme compliment: "John, you don't play well but you do play beautifully."

After I left Ithaca, I had fewer opportunities to get to Whitney Point and hear Miss Newcomb play, but I managed to get there once every year or two, except during the War, until the middle 50s, and she usually put me to work at the second piano. But after that she had to go to a nursing home (with no piano), and she died a few years later, in her late eighties.

3 — Yale & Its Continuing Influence

Carl Owen Dunbar (1891-1979)

HAVING IN EFFECT MAJORED IN STRUCTURAL GEOLOGY with Nevin at Cornell, I decided to concentrate more in stratigraphy during the rest of my graduate studies, as I worked toward a PhD degree. For that degree I decided to go to either Harvard or Yale, and early in my last year at Cornell I wrote letters to the professors of paleontology and stratigraphy at the two universities, Professor Percy Raymond at Harvard and Professor Carl Dunbar at Yale. I had in fact met Professor Dunbar in June 1936 on a field trip out of Rochester (he was a passenger in my car for that trip), and quite possibly he had checked with my professors at Cornell, perhaps also with the geologists at Albany, to find out whether I was acceptable material. Apparently he decided that I was, for he wrote me a friendly letter arranging for a visit in December.

When I arrived in New Haven Professor Dunbar met the train, and he installed me in a guest suite in the tower of the Hall of Graduate Studies at Yale. The next day he showed me around the university. Then he took me to the Peabody Museum of Natural History, where all the paleontologists had their offices and laboratories, and we conferred about what I had already done and what I might do if I came to Yale. As soon as I showed him what I was doing for my Master's thesis, he took me down to the other geology building to confer with Professor Chester Longwell, Professor of Structural Geology, Professor Adolph Knopf, Professor of Petrology, and Mrs. Eleanora Knopf, a fine geologist in her own right although Yale never gave her an appointment or allowed her to teach a formal course. They all showed much interest in what I wanted to do, and

FIG. 3–9: *Carl O. Dunbar and John Rodgers on Prospect Hill near Clinton, NY during a field excursion of the New York State Geological Association in 1955 — courtesy of John H. Johnsen, Secretary of the NYSGA.*

before I left New Haven it was clear to me that I would get excellent guidance there as I carried my education forward.

My letter to Harvard was answered not by Professor Raymond but by Professor Kirk Bryan, Professor of Geomorphology there, a fine scientist whose work I have always greatly admired. He explained that Professor Raymond was not well and had turned my letter over to him, and he set up an appointment at his own office. It happened that a good friend of mine from Cornell was then a graduate student at MIT, and he arranged a room for me in Cambridge for my night there. After talking to Professor Bryan about what I might study at Harvard, I particularly asked about going to see Professor Raymond, who would after all be my major adviser if I came; Professor Bryan tried to discourage me, but I insisted and, after calling Professor Raymond, I made the trip out to his home in Lexington. He was cordial and friendly, but it became quite clear that he would not be able to give me much help or guidance; in fact his health continued to deteriorate, and he retired a couple of years later. Thus the matter was decided; I applied to the Graduate School at Yale and was accepted.

At Yale I took both of Professor Dunbar's major courses, Stratigraphy of North America and Invertebrate Paleontology, and they were both superb, very well organized and full of material carefully checked for accuracy. The only hitch was that the stratigraphy course was so full of material about the Paleozoic Era ("Ancient Times", geologically speaking), which was Professor Dunbar's main interest and also mine, that we never got to the later parts of geologic time, the Mesozoic and Cenozoic Eras ("Medieval" and "Modern" Times). Several of us in the course therefore asked Professor Dunbar if he would be willing to offer a course in that stratigraphy the next year, with us doing a lot of the work, and he graciously agreed.

His course in Invertebrate Paleontology was a splendid introduction to the animal kingdom, so thorough that many graduate students in Zoology also took it to complete their zoological training. As I worked along on various projects he assigned me, such as a suite of well preserved Permian brachiopods from East Greenland, it became clear to me, and to Professor Dunbar, that I do not have the ability nor the temperament for the attention to detail required for work in taxonomic paleontology. What attracted me in paleontology was rather the grand sweep of organic evolution, building from "simple" unicellular animals, and indeed originally from the bacteria, up to such complex animals as insects and vertebrates.

For vertebrate paleontology I was lucky to take the course offered at Yale by Dr. G. Edward Lewis, a brilliant if somewhat dogmatic scientist who did not remain long at Yale. I well remember that, when we came to the evolution of humans and the various finds of fossil hominids that

MAP 3–2 *The Western United States*

illustrate it, he stated flatly that Piltdown Man cannot be accepted as evidence, being no more than a combination of a human skull and a chimpanzee jaw. Nearly twenty years later he was proved right, though he may not have realized that the combination had in fact been fraudulent. For paleobotany, on the other hand, I had been able to take a good course from Dr. Charles Merriam at Cornell, though he was not himself a paleobotanist; he had been appointed by Professor Ries to the position in invertebrate paleontology there after Dr. Caster was let go.

During my last year at Cornell, I took the U. S. Civil Service Exam for Junior Geologist, the first that had been offered since the beginning of the Great Depression, and apparently I did quite well in it. Comparing notes with others afterwards, I found that my "book-larnin'" had enabled me to answer more questions more quickly (we weren't expected to finish) than men with much more practical experience in geology than I had. In the spring of 1937 I was offered a summer job with the United States Geological Survey (USGS) in the West, and I jumped at the chance; both my professors at Cornell and Professor Dunbar, with whom I was to work the next fall, urged me to take the job for the experience it would give me. Being told that I would go to work in eastern Montana, I bought a car and drove out to California to visit my newly married oldest brother in Oakland. That was my first trip west of Ohio. Preparing for the trip, I arranged with another student at Cornell, who wanted a ride to California, to drive out with me, and he then persuaded me to drive day and night in order to get there sooner. We got all the way to Laramie, Wyoming, before we were both too sleepy to drive on; then after five hours' sleep we drove the rest of the way, making it from Ithaca to Palo Alto in three days — there were no superhighways in 1937.

While I was waiting in Oakland for definitive instructions from the Survey, I improved the time touring in middle California. But 1937 was the year that President Roosevelt, after his landslide victory in 1936, tried to get Congress to increase the number of Justices in the Supreme Court from nine to fifteen, so that he could overcome the conservative majority on the Court that was standing in the way of several "New Deal" projects. Congress bogged down on this issue and for the first time (I think) failed to pass the major appropriation bills before 1 July, the beginning of the new fiscal year. As this hadn't happened before, no one knew how the government was to be kept going. Later, however, that became almost routine, and Congress would just pass enabling legislation to keep the government going till they got around to the appropriation bills. Hence my summer job was first postponed and then cancelled, and instead I was offered a year's job in Florida, in a branch of geology in which I had neither competence nor much interest. Taking it would have prevented my going to graduate school at Yale in the fall, so I drove right back across the country to Washington (alone, in six days), to confer with my presumed bosses on the Survey. I finally declined the job, though I was warned I would never again have a chance to join the Survey. That was quite untrue; each of the next three summers I was offered a job, and I took it, and for several years I was a full-time member of the Survey. But I had virtually wasted the summer of 1937, except for seeing so much of the country.

Because of my summer jobs with the Survey, I was unable to start work on a project for my dissertation at Yale. Finally in the winter of 1940 I started work on one in East Tennessee (see below). But by then the Second World War had begun in Europe, and young men like myself were subject to the draft. Hence, after my two years of graduate work at Yale, I joined the Survey full time in mid-1940 and was put to work on "strategic minerals," materials in short supply — first manganese, then zinc. I kept Professor Dunbar informed of what I was doing. Then, by the time my draft number came up (by the luck of the draw it came up very late), the Survey felt justified in asking for my deferment, and it was granted.

Later, the Survey assigned me a project of my own, a small but well delimited mineral district in East Tennessee with significant deposits of iron, manganese, zinc, and lead, and I prepared a full report. Then I wrote to the Yale Department, asking if that report could serve as the basis for a doctoral dissertation, and they agreed to consider it; during the War they tended to be more flexible in such matters. After revising it in the light of their criticisms, I submitted and defended it. It was accepted, and thus I received my PhD degree in June 1944, at a time when few others whose

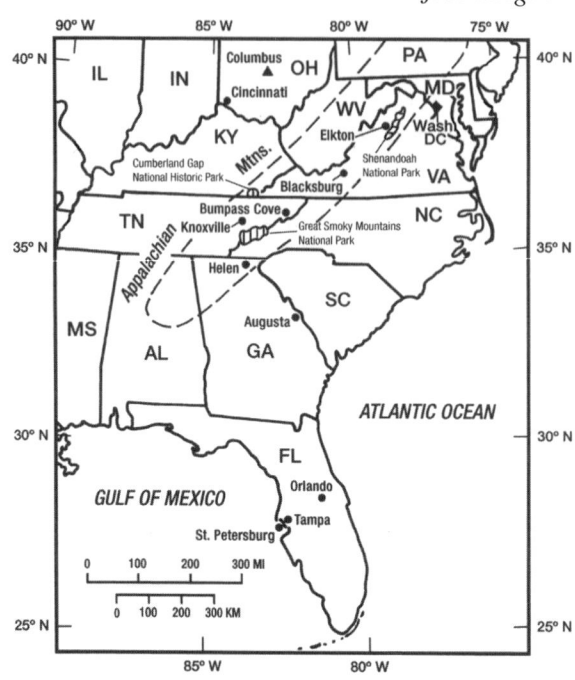

MAP 3–3 *The Southeastern United States*

graduate education had been interrupted by the War were so fortunate. For what it's worth, the title of my dissertation was *The Geology and Mineral Resources of Bumpass Cove*.

About that time I was transferred to the Survey's Branch on Military Geology; I worked for that branch for two years (1944-1946). In February 1946, during a trip that I made for them around the western Pacific, I received a cable from Professor Longwell, who was Chairman of the Yale Geology Department during and right after the War, asking if I would be interested in joining the Department to teach sedimentary geology; indeed I was, and I cabled right back. In May 1946 I came back to the States, and that summer I worked for the USGS in East Tennessee (as indeed for five summers running). Then in the fall I began to teach at Yale.

At this point in my career I had three very attractive offers for future work. I had already made up my mind that my geologic research would be in the Appalachian Mountains, beginning in East Tennessee and vicinity but by no means to be confined to that region. The Federal Survey made it clear that, if I wished, I would be kept permanently in the Appalachians (retaining my "overseas" Pacific salary, about $4,500 a year; remember that the dollar bought a good deal more in 1946 than it did a couple of decades later, let alone now). The Shell Oil Company was just then planning and setting up the Shell Development Corporation as its research arm, and they offered me a quite high salary (about $7,000 a year) and a free hand in choosing research projects. Later, when I visited their offices in Houston, I found the atmosphere very much that of a good science department in a major research university, but only a science department. As an Instructor at Yale I was on the "tenure track" leading in due time, if I made the grade, to a Professorship. The starting salary was $3,500 a year, and indeed I was asked not to mention the figure to the other young men then being added to the Department, who were getting only $3,000. But I was single and had no outside financial responsibilities; hence I could afford to take the lower salary. I told myself I would try it for a year or so, but within a very short time I knew that I had made the right choice; the university atmosphere suited exactly my interests, my abilities, and my temperament. Here I could pursue not only my geological research and my other scientific concerns but also all my other intellectual interests — music, literature, history, philosophy — and exchange ideas with outstanding scholars in all these fields. I had arrived where I belong.

As soon as I got back to Yale, Professor Dunbar asked me to join him in teaching a course on the Principles of Stratigraphy; he had always devoted to principles a first part of his course on the Stratigraphy of North America, but now he wished to make it a full course. Thus began a fruitful collaboration that continued until his retirement; I found working with him both personally and intellectually rewarding. The first year we divided up between us the subjects we wished to teach in the course; the second year we switched subjects, so that each of us would be familiar with the material in every part of the course; the third year and after we returned to our original subjects.

As it turned out, we didn't always agree; on those subjects each would present his own point of view, leaving it to the class to argue the matter out with us, and with one another. I found it amusing that some years the students would agree with him and beat on me, other years the opposite. A little later Dunbar invited me to join him in writing a book on the subject, to be based on the course, and I was delighted to accept. It took us nearly ten years, but it was a great experience. We divided the subjects as we had for the course; as we finished first drafts of our various chapters, each had the other look them over and criticize them. At the end, when we were about to turn in the final manuscript, we sat down in his office (he was by then Director of the Peabody Museum), and each would read his own chapters aloud, the other being free to make any comments or criticisms, which we would then discuss and decide about. Thus the book was the result of close collaboration, and each of us felt responsible for it all. The result speaks for itself; the book, called like the course, *Principles of Stratigraphy*, was published in 1957. It did very well for decades, and was translated into Russian, Spanish, Arabic, and Chinese, though I never obtained a copy of the Chinese translation. During my visits to the Soviet Union, I was often asked to autograph copies.

In 1959, when Professor Dunbar retired from teaching and from his position as Director of the Museum, he deliberately left his office and moved away from New Haven for good; he moved to Florida to be near his son in Dunedin, near St. Petersburg. He chose to do so because, as Director, he had had a difficult time with a former Director who insisted on retaining a large office long after he had ceased to do scientific work. For several years Dunbar came back to New Haven in the summer to work on his scientific specialty, late Paleozoic fusuline foraminifera, but later he gave that up too. He offered that part of his scientific library not wanted by the Museum and Department libraries at Yale to the newly established Geology Department at the University of South Florida in Tampa, and they gratefully made space available to him there for his continuing work. Thus he had an easy and gradual transition from full activity to full retirement. He died in Florida in 1979; I wrote his Biographical Memoir for the National Academy of Sciences.

Charles Schuchert (1858-1942)

JUST AS I WAS FIRST A GRADUATE STUDENT of Professor Dunbar at Yale and then became his colleague, both in teaching and in writing our book, so Dunbar was first a graduate student of Professor Schuchert there and then became his colleague and coauthor, indeed his successor as Professor of Invertebrate Paleontology and Stratigraphy. Charles Schuchert grew up in Cincinnati, Ohio, in a region famous for its abundant, well preserved, and easily collected fossil shells; at the end of the nineteenth century it produced quite a few outstanding paleontologists.

Another of these was E. O. Ulrich. Only a year older than Schuchert, Ulrich helped to steer him into scientific paleontology even though Schuchert's means had been inadequate for him to go to high school, let alone to go to college or to take any formal course in paleontology. In spite of that, the young Schuchert made a large collection of the local fossil brachiopods or "lamp-shells," now only a minor variety of "shellfish" but in Paleozoic or "Ancient" times the dominant variety. This collection became known, and in 1888 Dr. John M. Clarke, State Geologist and State Paleontologist of New York, called Schuchert to Albany, where they collaborated on a major monograph on brachiopods.

When Yale's Professor of Invertebrate Paleontology, Charles E. Beecher, died suddenly in 1904, Yale offered the position to Dr. Clarke, who refused it but strongly recommended Schuchert, and Yale appointed him. He used to mention that the first time he ever entered a college classroom was when he went in to teach his first class at Yale. He had a long and illustrious career at Yale and was well known and highly respected not only in the United States and Canada but in Europe. I have mentioned above that I was present when he was awarded the Penrose Medal of the Geological Society of America in 1934.

By the time I came to Yale as a graduate student, Professor Schuchert had retired; he used to spend a large part of each year in Florida, but he also spent some time in New Haven, where I had the chance to meet him a few times. Then, when I began to work on a doctoral dissertation project in East Tennessee in 1940, it turned out to be of much interest to Schuchert; I wrote him several letters about it before his death in 1942. He was interested because his first graduate student, Percy Raymond, had begun work on the same strata in the 1920s after he went to Harvard, where I met him in 1936. But Raymond's results turned out to challenge certain of Ulrich's fixed ideas on stratigraphic relations; Ulrich, already highly placed and influential, became quite annoyed, and Raymond had to drop the subject. Evidence in some of Schuchert's unpublished correspondence at Yale shows that, although Ulrich and Schuchert had been very good friends and had indeed written one very important joint article, Ulrich was also annoyed with Schuchert for supporting Raymond; he even launched a campaign to prevent Schuchert's election as President of the Geological Society of America, but it was unsuccessful. It is not irrelevant, I think, that when Schuchert was awarded the Penrose Medal in 1934, he chose Raymond, his first student, to present him (Ulrich had been awarded the Medal two years earlier).

The question raised by Raymond then lay dormant until I started to work on those strata early in 1940, not then knowing of Raymond's work. The evidence soon convinced me too that Ulrich was wrong, and I corresponded with Schuchert about it. Ulrich was still quite active in those days; I used to see him at geological meetings, setting forth his ideas with pontifical assurance. But by then those ideas were being seriously questioned in several other parts of the country; Raymond had been alone in disagreeing with him, but I was not. In any case, I soon became engaged in war work and had to drop the matter; by the time I got back to it after the War, Schuchert and Ulrich had both died. But I have always greatly admired Schuchert for being willing to pursue the evidence wherever it led, whether it supported his own previous ideas or not. When Professor Dunbar and I published our joint textbook in 1957, he suggested and I happily agreed that we should dedicate the book to Professor Schuchert.

Chester Ray Longwell (1887-1975)

I FIRST MET PROFESSOR LONGWELL on my trip to Yale in 1936 when I was deciding where to go for further graduate work after Cornell. While a graduate student at Yale, I took his regular graduate course in structural geology the first year and his seminar the second. I particularly remember that in the course he had each student present one of the plethora of "theories" then being proposed to explain the deformation that produces mountain ranges. From that exercise I learned that, when there are many diverse theories to explain a phenomenon — about one per theorist — some major clue is lacking, either a significant group of facts or a clarifying idea, or both. It was characteristic of Longwell that, although he was always much interested in how the rocks of the mountains came to be deformed, he proposed no theory of his own and he encouraged us to approach all such theories with skepticism. Roughly two decades after I was a graduate student in his courses, the geologists, and even more the geophysicists, brought in new facts from the ocean floors to complement those already known on the continents, and the clarifying idea appeared — what was later called plate tectonics — that the Earth's crust consists of several large plates, with some smaller ones, that slowly but steadily move horizontally with respect to one another. Thus Continental Drift falls out as a corollary idea. Longwell's part in this change of ideas, which was a veritable revolution in geological thinking, was simply to help clear the ground for it by his intelligent skepticism.

When I came back to Yale as a member of the Geology faculty, I soon began to work fairly closely with Professor Longwell, though never as closely as with Professor Dunbar, with whom I shared a course and the resulting book. Even in my first years I helped several graduate students find dissertation projects in the southern Appalachians, in East Tennessee and vicinity. Actually they were more Professor Longwell's students than mine, but together we visited them in their field areas. I also spent time with students of his who worked in the West, and I visited them there.

My original appointment to the Yale Geology Department was to teach Sedimentary Geology, how and where strata are laid down, a subject in a way intermediate between Professor Dunbar's Stratigraphy and Professor Longwell's Structural Geology. Part of my job was to set up a laboratory to study sedimentary rocks and their formation, and I worked quite hard at that, but slowly I came to see, and so did others, that my forte is not for laboratories and lab work but for field work and for general ideas. So only a few years later I specifically asked Professor Longwell, then approaching retirement, if he would approve my shifting into structural geology and preparing myself to fill the position he was soon to leave. He agreed, and before long I took over the undergraduate course he'd been teaching. When he went on leave for the year 1948-1949 I taught his graduate course.

Another major concern that Professor Longwell and I shared was the *American Journal of Science*. The *AJS* is the oldest still extant scientific journal in the United States, probably in the Americas. It was founded in 1818 by Benjamin Silliman, the first professor of "natural philosophy" (i.e., science) at Yale and one of the first in North America, and it was carried on by his son-in-law James D. Dana, then by the latter's son, E. S. Dana. In 1926, when it became clear there were no more Danas to edit it, E. S. Dana gave it to Yale University, with a small endowment to keep it going. Through the 1930s and the earlier 1940s, the Editor was Professor Richard Swann Lull, a vertebrate paleontologist who taught a very popular undergraduate course in Organic Evolution, but in the late 1940s his advancing age and failing eyesight forced him to resign. Professor Longwell was asked to become the Editor; he agreed if some younger man were appointed Assistant Editor, and I was chosen. Actually my first year as Assistant Editor was the year of Longwell's leave, so for that year I worked with Professor Lull. Professor Longwell was Editor until 1954, when he resigned as he prepared to retire from Yale and move to California, and I took over.

As Editor, Longwell insisted on high standards, and I was happy to follow his lead. Our philosophy was always that we should constantly "turn the screws a little tighter;" papers that would have been good enough ten years ago aren't necessarily good enough today. It's of some interest that James D. Dana, the Editor through much of the nineteenth century when the *AJS* was almost the only scientific journal in the country, introduced "peer review" for scientific articles, which is essential in keeping the scientific endeavor sound and forward-looking.

After joining the Yale Geology faculty, I decided to learn all I could about Connecticut geology, so I compiled a complete list of books and articles on the subject from the excellent USGS bibliographies. I was mildly astonished to find how relatively few they were, and how little known they were to most of my Yale colleagues; I mention below the lure of Western geology for Yale faculty and graduate students alike. Indeed I remember that once, brash young man that I was, I said to Professor Knopf: "It has always struck me that Yale has the oldest geology department in the country" (you could see him swell a little with pride) "and Connecticut is the least known state in the Union." He snapped back at once: "Except Massachusetts," but it wasn't true then, though later it might have been.

Although Longwell's chief interests were in the West, he had made himself acquainted with the main outlines of Connecticut's geology, and he knew many of the significant rock outcrops in our part of the state. He published with E. S. Dana a little guide to those outcrops, called *Walks and Rides in Central Connecticut*, and he showed me many of them. Connecticut had its own State Survey, called the Connecticut Geological and Natural History Survey; the State Geologist was Professor Troxell of Trinity College in Hartford. The Survey was not then a part of any state department but an independent organization governed by Commissioners who represented the five colleges in the state. Longwell was Yale's representative, and in May 1948, he organized a meeting to discuss and, as it turned out, to launch a campaign to map Connecticut's geology in detail, using as a base new large-scale topographic maps of the state just then being published. A cooperative program was arranged with the USGS, and in the next thirty years or so detailed maps and reports were issued covering most of the state, both maps showing the bedrock geology and maps showing the glacial geology, the deposits laid down by the continental glacier that covered Connecticut during the Great Ice Age of the last million years.

After Professor and Mrs. Longwell moved to California in 1955, I still saw them quite often on my fairly frequent trips there, when I would always visit the Knopfs as well, also at professional meetings and on geological field excursions, and when they came back to New Haven. After his death in 1975, I wrote his Biographical Memoir for the National Academy of Sciences, of which he had been a member for forty years.

Adolph Knopf (1882-1966)

I MET PROFESSOR KNOPF AND HIS GEOLOGIST-WIFE, Mrs. E. B. Knopf (see below), when I visited New Haven in December 1936, and their interest in me and my work certainly helped me to decide to come to Yale to study for my PhD degree. During my two years of graduate work there, I took both of Professor Knopf's major courses: Advanced General Geology and Petrology. The first course was devoted to a whole series of subjects that interested him and that he felt would serve to teach us how to reason geologically. In particular he took up the use of radioactive elements to determine the geological ages of rocks, a subject that he was one of the first geologists to study because of his friendship with

Professor B. B. Boltwood, who had worked out the decay schemes of uranium and thorium to isotopes of lead. The Petrology course was thorough and covered all three main groups of rocks, although strongest in igneous rocks, Professor Knopf's central interest.

Professor Knopf was a demanding teacher; if he found you ill prepared, he could be quite caustic. He had a habit of turning suddenly on a student, whipping off his pince-nez and seeming to glare at him (he was in fact short-sighted and a bit shy), and asking a pointed question; some students would virtually freeze, unable to articulate answers they knew perfectly well. For such students Knopf could be quite terrifying; "Knopfitis" was a well recognized disease among us graduate students. As he was also Director of Graduate Studies for the Department during those years, we all had to deal with him face to face in setting up our schedules at the beginning of each term and in consulting on how we were doing during the term and at its end. Furthermore he gave the oral examinations to test our ability to read German, then required of all graduate students; that examination just terrified many students. James Gilluly, an outstanding geologist who had been a graduate student at Yale some fifteen years ahead of me, told me of his own experience; on perhaps his second or third try at the exam, he felt he was doing badly, and he simply handed back to Knopf the book from which he had been reading, saying he'd work some more, then come back and try again. When he did so, and passed, Knopf told him he would have passed the time before if he'd only stayed around.

For myself, being bright, brash, and self-confident (too much so, no doubt), I was less afraid of him than most, but he knew well enough how to cut such a student down to size. And, even if he was both demanding and terrifying, he taught very well. Above all, he taught us to recognize good and bad reasoning and not to accept an idea simply because it was plausible or popular but to analyze it, and the evidence adduced for it, thoroughly and consistently. Thus we learned a great deal more than the particular subject that he was teaching, or rather that he was using as his means for teaching.

Eleanora Bliss Knopf (1883-1974)

ELEANORA BLISS, LATER MRS. KNOPF, WAS ONE OF THREE WOMEN who together took their doctoral degrees at Bryn Mawr College in the early 1900s under the direction of Professor Florence Bascom, herself a highly respected scientist. After graduation, all three joined the U. S.

Geological Survey, for whom Professor Bascom had also worked. The other two, Julia Gardner and Anna Jonas, later Mrs. George W. Stose, remained with the Survey throughout their careers, but in 1920 Miss Bliss married Adolph Knopf and moved with him to New Haven, Connecticut, where he became Professor of Petrology at Yale University. At that time, however, Yale had strict rules forbidding the appointment of two members of the same family, and Mrs. Knopf, despite her eminence and ability, never received an academic appointment or was permitted to teach formal courses, a great loss to Yale. But she was always very helpful to any geology students who sought her advice, as I and many others can attest, giving them informal instruction in her specialties and much encouragement in their work.

Mrs. Knopf was more concerned with metamorphic than with the igneous rocks dear to her husband. Moreover, although Professor Knopf's field work was in the West or in Alaska, hers was in the East, first in the Piedmont province of southeastern Pennsylvania and adjacent Maryland, then (when I came to know her) in the Taconic region of easternmost New York on the borders of Connecticut and Massachusetts. Her field area there included a sequence of lower Paleozoic carbonate rocks much like those I had studied in the southern Champlain Valley for my Master's thesis. Hence we compared notes on our sequences, we went out to see her rocks in May 1938, and she took me on as a field assistant for a short spell that November and for two spells the next spring; as she was working for the USGS, it was easy to fit me into her project. I may have been of some help to her; certainly I learned a great deal from her. For example, she was then experimenting with the use of stereoscopically viewed airplane photographs in field mapping — one of the first to do so, I believe — and she taught me the technique. We also worked together in the office; as we were both dealing with rocks made of the two carbonate minerals, calcite and dolomite, we needed ways to distinguish them accurately, and I took on the project of looking for and testing chemical stains that would differentiate them on polished rock surfaces. That led to my third research article, for which she was my adviser; perhaps she should have been co-author, but she graciously chose not to be.

In her work on metamorphic rocks, Mrs. Knopf had come to know and use a new method of study called petrofabrics or structural petrology, begun mainly by Professor Bruno Sander of Innsbruck in Austria. Sander was famous for the difficulty of his German; once indeed a fellow Austrian geologist told me, in jest to be sure, that when Sander published a paper the other Austrians waited until it was translated into English to read it. But both Professor and Mrs. Knopf were accomplished linguists (Knopf's parents had emigrated from Germany to California), and Mrs.

Knopf would have had little difficulty. During one of Professor Knopf's sabbatical leaves, they visited Sander in Innsbruck, and she mastered both the method and the ideas behind it. In the 1930s, moreover, she introduced those ideas to the American geological profession (in English) in several articles and finally a whole GSA Memoir. For my part, I had already encountered Sander's main book at Cornell, and my German was adequate to take me well into it, but I was happy to have Mrs. Knopf's help in penetrating further. Some years later indeed, she told me that, while I was her field assistant, sometimes when she had come in tired from a long day of field work I would take up whole evenings asking her difficult questions about the Sander method when she wanted only to rest. I met Professor Sander when I was in Austria in 1959; my diary records that I "had a long and very pleasant chat with him, but I learned almost nothing except that he sees little farther than his own work."

When, after my years with the USGS during the War, I returned to Yale as a junior colleague of the Knopfs, they both continued to be helpful and inspiring teachers, if only informally. I can take some credit for getting Mrs. Knopf to publish the results of her work in eastern New York. In 1951, when Professor Knopf retired from teaching at Yale, they at once moved back to his beloved California, where he had been brought up in San Francisco and on a ranch not far to the south, situated over the San Andreas fault. I suspect he thought of all his years at Yale, 1920-1951, as a Babylonian captivity. Furthermore, the Geology Department at Stanford University welcomed them both, gave them an office, and got them to do some teaching there; thus Stanford was more sensible than Yale in making good use of Mrs. Knopf's great knowledge and ability. On my frequent visits to middle California in those years, I always stopped by to see them, Professor Knopf until his death in 1966 and Mrs. Knopf until hers in 1974. I wrote the Memorial for Mrs. Knopf for the Geological Society of America; later I was asked to write the entry for Professor Knopf for the American National Biography.

The Second World War

4 — Before the War

Marland Pratt Billings (1902-1996)

I FIRST MET PROFESSOR BILLINGS on my visit to Harvard in 1936 when I was deciding between Harvard and Yale for further graduate work. If I had known that structural geology would be a larger part of my life work than stratigraphy, I might well have become his student, but at that time stratigraphy was more important to me, and I was right to choose Yale and Professor Dunbar.

Professor Billings came from Boston — he never lost his flat Boston accent — and his main interest throughout his career was the geology of New England. As it happened, a geologist of the U. S. Geological Survey had in a funny way "staked a claim" on the geology of Massachusetts, and Billings chose therefore to concentrate on the geology of New Hampshire and to find dissertation projects for his students there and in Vermont and Maine. Beginning in the 1930s, when I was still a student, his work revolutionized New England geology, laying the basis for all later progress.

When I was learning about Connecticut geology, and finding out how little was known, I set about to remedy that situation, and I saw that the way to start was to apply the results achieved by Prof. Billings and his students to Connecticut. In 1948 we invited Prof. Billings to New Haven to give a lecture on his New Hampshire work, and Professor Longwell and I took him out to see the rocks east of town; as we had suspected he would, he recognized rock units like those in New Hampshire, giving us confidence in applying his results. It was only a couple of months later that Prof. Longwell organized the meeting to discuss mapping Connecticut's geology in detail. Again Prof. Billings was invited, and again he told us of the work in New Hampshire and Vermont, which was obviously going to be important for us in Connecticut; new work in Massachusetts hadn't yet begun, but soon it did.

In preparing to teach courses in structural geology, I took time to compare the two leading textbooks in the field: Nevin's, then in its later editions, and Billings's, first published in 1942. Despite my admiration for and my great debt to Professor Nevin, it became clear to me that Billings's text was the better, though even so Longwell, who was already using it, and I found things in it to disagree with. Then in 1953, when Professor Billings prepared a second edition, the publisher asked me to review it for them; I agreed to do so, and I prepared a fairly long and fairly critical, review. When Billings saw that review, he didn't guess who had written it but was apparently impressed that anyone had studied his book so thoroughly, and he was quite appreciative. His younger colleague, the brilliant petrologist James Thompson, did recognize whose work it was and told Billings; when I next saw Billings at a field meeting that fall, he thanked me warmly. When the new edition was published, I found he'd accepted about half my criticisms.

In 1952 the Geological Society of America (GSA) was to meet in November in Boston, and Billings, with Thompson, decided to run a field excursion across New England before the meeting, but across southern Vermont and New Hampshire, avoiding Massachusetts! Knowing that I was familiar with eastern New York and adjacent Vermont, they asked me to join them in preparing and running the trip, which was to start in Albany, New York, and I was happy to accept. For most of the year preceding the meeting, we three were busy choosing outcrops to visit, writing text for the guidebook, and drafting its maps. I think that guidebook helped to crystallize thinking about the many problems in the relevant geology. Moreover the trip was taken by perhaps fifty persons, including some of the outstanding leaders of the profession — more than expected indeed, so that people had to double up in beds (I doubled up with Professor Longwell). At the start of the dry run in May, my parents kindly invited Billings and Thompson to stay in our home in Albany, and I think that may have been when my father became quite sure his son had "made it," when he saw a Full Professor at Harvard treating me almost like an equal.

After that I met Billings frequently at professional meetings and even more on geological field trips in various parts of the United States. He also knew that his student E-an Zen (see below) and I were seeing a lot of each other in the field, as our field areas were adjacent, and I think he approved, for he considered that my scientific work was sound. Indeed I suspect he wrote a favorable letter in my behalf when I was up for promotion to tenure, though of course I never saw it. One time when he was visiting in Zen's dissertation area, I came along.

In 1957, when I was Chairman of the Nominating Committee for the Geological Society of America, we proposed Billings as the next President of the Society, and the Council endorsed the nomination. In the next decade, E-an Zen and other students of his put together a "Billings Volume" of articles about the northern Appalachians (down past New York City), and I contributed an article — one of my best, I believe. The volume was to be a surprise for him, and the conspirators chose to present it at the banquet of the 1968 meeting, in New Haven, of the New England Intercollegiate Geological Conference (NEIGC). The NEIGC meets every fall to take field trips somewhere in or near New England, and I've been going to its meetings ever since I was a graduate student at Yale; to the comparable New York State Geological Association I've been going since I was in school in Albany. Mrs. Billings was brought into the conspiracy to insure that Professor Billings would be there, for he never much cared for banquets and the like; it came off beautifully.

When in 1981 I was awarded the Penrose Medal of the Geological Society of America, I think Zen and others of Billings's students were a little unhappy that he hadn't yet been so recognized, for his seminal work in New Hampshire was already being published when I was only a college student. But in 1987 that lack was remedied, and Zen kindly invited me to join a dinner party in Billings's honor after the award ceremony.

Preston Cloud (1912-1991)

Preston Cloud and I arrived at Yale as graduate students in Geology in the same week, and we met as we were waiting to appear before the faculty of the Department to discuss our courses of study. We came from quite different backgrounds — I from a standard four-year college course plus a Master's degree at Cornell, with adequate funds and a supportive family behind me, Preston from four years of night school at George Washington University while he held down a full-time job during the day at the U. S. National Museum, with almost no other financial backing. Fortunately Dr. G. Arthur Cooper, an outstanding paleontologist for whom Cloud worked at the Museum and who had himself taken his degree at Yale under Professor Charles Schuchert, called him to the attention of Professor Schuchert, who helped make it possible for him to go to graduate school full time.

Fairly soon Pres and I became close friends, but he told me later that, when he first met me that day, he was quite turned off, partly I suppose by my arrogantly displayed, though I hope unconscious, sense of intellectual and financial security. In a short while, however, our mutual love of ideas brought us together. He credited the change to a set of lectures I offered to my fellow graduate students that first year on the structural mineralogy that I'd learned at Cornell from Sir William Bragg. Curiously, none of the Yale faculty in Geology were then familiar with the Bragg's work; when I spoke about it to Professor William E. Ford, the Professor of Mineralogy, he said he knew it was important but felt he was too old to learn it. He died less than two years later.

As Cloud knew from the first that he wanted to become a paleontologist, and as my "major" was then in stratigraphy with a sort of "minor" in paleontology, we saw a great deal of each other during our two graduate years together. As that first year went on, four of us — Preston Cloud, Warren Hobbs, Hugh Beach, and I — became great friends, and by spring we were arranging to room together the next year in a large second-floor flat over a plumber's shop near the campus, along with a friend of Warren's, Ralph Roberts, who was coming to graduate school the next fall. It was a stellar group, and we got along famously. Hugh Beach was a Canadian, and he worked then for the Geological Survey of Canada; indeed his dissertation project was based on work he did for them in the Canadian shield. Later he joined the Canadian arm of the Texas Company; in the Texas Company he rose to Chief Geologist and Geological Advisor to the President. Warren, Ralph, and I soon went to work for the USGS; Warren and Ralph remained with the Survey throughout their careers. Preston stayed at Yale for a third year and completed his doctor's degree by June 1940; moreover, his dissertation won the A. Cressey Morrison Natural History Prize of the New York Academy of Sciences that year. After a year of teaching at Missouri School of Mines and a year's "post-doc" at Yale, he too joined the Survey, doing a fine piece of work on carbonate rocks in central Texas — rocks that were important to study as reservoirs of oil.

In 1946, after the War, Cloud was called to Harvard to the position in invertebrate paleontology vacated when Professor Raymond retired, and I was appointed to the Yale faculty; we saw each other quite often during the next couple of years. But, whereas I knew almost at once that I was where I belonged, Preston fairly quickly became dissatisfied — that was the only period when I remember him as a chain-smoker — feeling that he was not well supported in his efforts to build up the equipment and collections for paleontology, and after two years he returned to the USGS.

FIG. 4–10: *Preston Cloud with John Rodgers at the presentation of the* **Cloud Volume of the American Journal of Science**, *13 October 1990.*

On the Survey he first became chief of a party studying the geology of Saipan in the Marianas along with the ecology of the surrounding seas; then he was called to Washington as Chief Paleontologist, a position he held for ten years while he quadrupled the research staff of the Survey's Paleontology and Stratigraphy Branch. But he didn't allow his administrative duties to stand in the way of his research or of excursions or even new field work, notably in marine geology; e.g., the carbonate deposits on the Great Bahama Bank.

After thirteen years with the Survey, Cloud returned to academia as Professor of Paleontology or, as he preferred it, Biogeology at, successively, the University of Minnesota, the University of California at Los Angeles, and the University of California at Santa Barbara; this part of his life also occupied thirteen years. He kept up his connection with the Survey, however, especially at Santa Barbara where he organized a Biogeology Clean Laboratory to look for evidence of life — first in the rocks brought back from the Moon but then in very ancient strata on Earth, in which such evidence had mostly escaped notice. In 1974 he decided to "retire" from the University and return to full-time work for the Survey, but he kept on working as hard as ever. He took years off to be a visiting professor and for other travels, but he continued to make Santa Barbara his base. In October 1990 he was the innocent victim of a surprise party there to present him with the *Preston Cloud Volume of the American Journal of Science*, of which he had been an Associate Editor for twenty-one years. He died a few months later, in January 1991. I wrote his Biographical Memoir for the American Philosophical Society, to which he was elected in 1973.

While we were still graduate students at Yale, we went to an annual meeting of the Geological Society of America in New York City where, with other students to a total of ten, we attended the Annual Banquet as the guests of Professor Schuchert, although he was in Florida, to see the award of the Penrose Medal and other honors. We told each other then that some day we too would be famous geologists and would meet at such an affair and waggle our beards at each other (we were both clean-shaven then). In 1976 when Cloud was awarded the Penrose Medal, he had grown a beard but I had not; he therefore procured a false beard and insisted that I wear it, and waggle it at him, during the award ceremony and the preceding President's cocktail hour and Annual Banquet, to the astonishment of our mutual friends. By the time I was awarded the Penrose Medal (1981), I too had grown a beard; Preston was spending that year in Australia, but he suborned Neil Williams, a young Australian who had also been a graduate student at Yale and was now returning to the States to receive a medal of his own, to wear the same false beard and waggle it at me.

Preston's style and mine were always quite different; we remained very good friends throughout, but possibly it wouldn't have been easy if we had been close colleagues. I found my niche at Yale and made it the base for a wide variety of trips in all directions, wherever I could see new geology, and I found my central interest in the Appalachian Mountains, from which I opened out into the "comparative anatomy of mountain ranges." Pres kept moving around, not only geographically but scientifically — from fossil brachiopods to ancient carbonate strata to modern carbonate sediments to coral reefs to marine geology generally, then on to studies of the evolution of very ancient life and the conditions under which it had evolved. Indeed he used to boast that he had looked for the evidence of such life on every continent except Antarctica. His capacity for work was enormous, right from the start — earning a bachelor's degree in four years of night school while holding down a full-time job at which he worked equally hard, then a doctor's degree in three. He drove himself intensely, and he drove others the same way, but fortunately he was equally intense at play; he loved a good party and a good joke, and his laughter was forthright, uproarious, and contagious. He left strict instructions on how his family and friends were to commemorate him after his death, with a celebration of his life, a champagne-and-balloons party of the kind he so much enjoyed, and there was.

I WANT TO ADD A WORD about *Hugh Beach*, our mutual roommate at Yale. Hugh was one of the most lively, amusing, and witty people I have ever known. He was very able and could be deeply serious, as his rise in the world shows, but he always leavened it with his lively humor and good nature, even in his last years when he was suffering from extremely high blood pressure. He had the same sense of the irony of things that I have but was much less solemn about it. One of the last times we met, he claimed that long ago he and he alone had converted me, during the year we roomed together, from a teetotal prig into a regular fellow able to enjoy a companionable drink but not be ruled by it. He said he had done it by presenting the classification of alcoholic beverages as an intellectual problem, appealing to my rational nature and quite bypassing my New England Puritan upbringing. It's not easy to accept the idea that someone else has changed one's whole life without one's knowing it was happening but, reflecting on the matter, I strongly suspect he did just that for me. I had a lot of growing up to do in those days, and he is one of those who got me to do it.

William Walden Rubey (1898-1974)

IN 1938, the first summer that I actually worked for the U. S. Geological Survey in the West, I was assigned as field assistant to David Andrews, who was working along the eastern margin of the Bighorn Basin in northwestern Wyoming up against the Bighorn Mountains. Like many Survey geologists in the 20s and 30s, Andrews had been a graduate student at Yale, though I don't think he ever completed his degree. It was commonly said in those days that Harvard men did best on the Civil Service exams for Geologist but didn't take jobs with the Survey, whereas Yale men did take them. Indeed in those years many of the higher positions in the Geological Division, one of five divisions in the Survey, were held by former Yale graduate students, with or without PhDs, right up to Gerald Loughlin, the Chief Geologist when I joined the Survey. Andrews was mapping the geology in his area by plane table, a technique in which I had gotten some training at Nevin's summer camp, and he helped me to convert my fairly good but theoretical knowledge into practical know-how. That season I stayed in the field through October and hence got back to Yale a month late; the Yale faculty was a bit unhappy about that but let it pass, for the preceding spring I had passed with honors the oral qualifying examination for candidacy for the PhD degree, the chief hurdle in our way as graduate students, and the faculty knew how valuable the extra field experience would be for me.

The next summer, 1939, I was sent out to the "phosphate country" in the mountains along the Wyoming-Idaho border, in a kind of geology quite different from that in the Bighorn country and more like that in the Appalachian Valley and Ridge province, as around Nevin's camp. Whereas the summer before Andrews and I had worked on foot out from trucks in open sage-brush country, that summer we worked mainly on horseback, using trucks mostly to move from one field camp to another; some of the field camps were well isolated in forested mountains, commonly by rushing streams full of trout! I had in fact learned to ride horses in Albany, for my father had enlisted in the cavalry during the First World War, though he never went overseas; he kept up his cavalry connections after that War, and he made sure that his children learned to ride, though our riding was mostly indoors and, even when outdoors, was around in a ring, so that I never saw the point of it. But in the West we rode over beautiful mountain country, the horses doing most of the climbing, and I loved it. I remember how astonished the horses were when I would post on them, an Eastern trick never used in the West.

For the first two months of that summer, in westernmost Wyoming, my party chief was William W. Rubey, and I have often said that I learned more in those two months than in any other year of my life. Rubey was both a superb field geologist and a deep thinker about geological principles, indeed about all principles, and I owe him a great debt for what he taught me in both directions. After my years of being very successful academically (first in the class at my school, for instance), I was pretty cocky about my intellectual abilities, sure of my conclusions and good at arguing for them, but Rubey taught me to be far more cautious in my reasoning and to explore alternative hypotheses much more thoroughly than I was used to doing. Since that summer I have always maintained that Bill Rubey was the best geologist I ever knew, and one of the finest people.

Apparently David Andrews had been asked, after that first summer, to turn in a report on me and my abilities, on whether I should be offered permanent employment on the Survey; his report had been mixed, by no means wholly favorable, whereas the Yale professors well known to the Survey bosses, many of whom had been their students, had written quite favorably. Rubey was therefore asked to observe me carefully and to write an estimate of my potential, and he wrote a fairly long letter about me to our mutual Branch Chief, George Rogers Mansfield, one of the pioneer geologists in the very phosphate region where Rubey and I were working. Mansfield then decided to send the letter, or at least a large extract from it, on to me; Rubey told me many years later that he hadn't expected that to happen and was quite upset, thinking I suppose that this brash kid would take umbrage, raise a row, and ruin our ability to work together. Receiving that letter was, I can certainly say, one of the most difficult pills I ever had to swallow but, because of my already deep admiration for Bill Rubey, instead of taking umbrage I resolved to accept its criticisms and try to use them to make myself a better geologist and a better person. Rubey told me at that later time that he never knew on what day I received the letter; he only knew that I had received it because I began to alter my "style." The receipt of that letter was a major turning point for the better in my life.

For the rest of that summer and into the fall I was in southeastern Idaho as assistant to Louis Gardner; his name had been Bumgardner, but he had it changed legally, he told me, to save his children the rough joking he had to endure while growing up. I had met him a couple of times at Yale, where he had been a graduate student of Longwell's just before I arrived. Then in the fall he took me down to St. George in southwestern Utah, to assist him in work he was doing there for the Survey; I believe he was hoping to use it as the basis for a doctoral dissertation, but the War came along and I don't think he ever completed it. From him too I learned much, and I got to see still another kind of Western geology, along the western margin of the Colorado Plateau. The next summer I was again Gardner's assistant in southeastern Idaho.

I never worked with Bill Rubey again, but I kept in touch with him and always stopped by to see him when I was in Washington or wherever he was, and he was always cordial and helpful. In 1950 he was President of the Geological Society of America, and his Presidential Address was on the Geological History of Sea Water, a subject that no one before had ever dug into so deeply and thoroughly. Later I became involved in the affairs of the Society and, during my term as Councillor, I was named Chairman of the Committee on the Penrose Medal. That year, 1963, Rubey's name was among the candidates, and I was very happy to see, and to help, it be chosen. At that time, moreover, the Chairman of the Committee presented the Medalist to the President at the awards ceremony during the Annual Meeting — before and after that, the Medalist was allowed to decide who should present him — and I was happier still to have that privilege. In my presentation I came as close as I dared to expressing my deep conviction that he was the finest geologist in North America. That year's President, Harry Hess, another great geologist and a few years later the Penrose Medalist, did say it, as he handed Bill the Medal: "There isn't anyone I'd rather give it to."

Philip Burke King (1903-1987)

WHEN I WAS STUDYING GEOLOGY, a majority of United States geology students wanted to do field work in the West because of the dry climate, the relatively scanty vegetation, and the excellent rock outcrops. That was especially true of students at Yale who worked with Professors Longwell and Knopf, as their work had been entirely in the West; indeed at one point Professor Longwell was arranging for me to work in the Virgin Mountains in southwestern Utah. But, having already made a good start in the East at Nevin's summer camp in Pennsylvania and for my Master's thesis in the Champlain Valley, I told my Survey bosses that I would be willing and happy to work in the East and, after my three "apprentice" summers in the West, they decided to use me there. In part my reasoning was that, as few young geologists were working there, "in the land of the blind the one-eyed are king." What's more, I made it; later on I was actually referred to a few times as "the king of the Appalachians."

Somewhat before that, however, at the beginning of 1940 after my summer and fall working with Louis Gardner, I found myself at a loose end; it was Josiah Bridge, whom I met when visiting the paleontologists at the U. S. National Museum, who suggested I pick a dissertation project in East Tennessee, the advantages being not only the presence of fewer competitors but the existence of superb new and detailed topographic maps, just then being published for the Tennessee Valley Authority, and also the possibility of working there all year long. I worked there all that winter and spring.

In October 1940 then, after my second summer with Gardner in Idaho, the Survey took me on full time and assigned me as field assistant to Philip B. King for a manganese project at Elkton, Virginia, just southwest of the Shenandoah National Park; manganese was at that time a "strategic mineral," one in short supply in the United States as the Second World War began. King too was being switched to the East; up to that point he had worked mostly in Texas, especially in West Texas where he was a highly respected expert. The manganese deposits we were studying were in the immediate foothills of the Blue Ridge, and the project was fruitful and exciting geologically — less so, I'm sorry to say, for the manganese deposits — and we much enjoyed our field work there. Because of King's considerable field experience, I learned a great deal working with him.

At Elkton also, I came to know Mrs. Helen Carter King, whom King had met and married in Washington where she was a well recognized poet. Knowing the Kings was not only geologically but "humanistically" rewarding. At that time I was already reading widely in the works of the great philosophers from Aristotle through Kant to the pragmatists, and I was beginning to piece together my own philosophical position — Thorough Pragmatism, pragmatism in the light of Kant's first Critique. Phil and especially Helen generously gave me their time and attention and helped me much in working out my ideas and learning how best to express them.

When the Elkton project was finished, King and I were sent down to northeast Tennessee to work on similar manganese deposits in the mountains there. It was at that point that we met Herman W. Ferguson, who worked for the Tennessee Division of Geology — in effect the state's Geological Survey — and who was assigned by the State Geologist, Walter F. Pond, to work with us. Up to that time Ferguson had worked only in the flat-lying strata of central Tennessee, more indeed in the office than in the field, studying the cuttings from oil wells, so we had the fun of inducting him into the challenging geology of the East Tennessee mountains, underlain by the strongly deformed strata of the Appalachian Mountain chain. He took to it like a duck to water, and soon he was a coequal colleague; our collaboration was cordial, complete, and very fruitful.

The geology in that part of East Tennessee turned out to be even more exciting than that in Virginia, and soon we were working out new hypotheses to explain it; each manganese district that we studied seemed to provide new evidence and new ideas for testing our hypotheses. After we got started, we divided up the various districts; ultimately we three, with Lawrence C. Craig, who like me was assigned by the Federal Survey as an assistant to King, put together a major report, setting forth not only the information about the manganese deposits but also the striking new geology we had worked out.

There were other manganese deposits in East Tennessee than those we were studying, and two small ones happened to be in precisely the strata I had begun to study for my doctoral dissertation; I was therefore assigned to work on them, and that work added much evidence for the dissertation project, even if there wasn't much manganese. Then, back in northeast Tennessee, I was given a particular, well marked-off district to study, one that had produced not only manganese but iron, zinc, and lead; it was the report I wrote on that district that I finally used for my doctoral dissertation, for the other project had far less relevance for "strategic minerals," and there was no likelihood that I could pursue it further while the War was on.

As the manganese work wound down, the presence of zinc and lead in my "own" district resulted in my transfer to a project to look at zinc deposits elsewhere in East Tennessee and in southwest Virginia. Zinc deposits, though considerably more abundant than manganese deposits in the United States, were also in danger of exhaustion because of greatly increased demand during the War, and my job was to study prospective deposits in some detail (there were already two big zinc mines in East Tennessee). As there were many such deposits, in several different geological settings, studying them gave me an excellent grasp of the general geology of a quite large region in the Appalachian chain. On this project I worked independently or even as chief of a small party. My overall boss for this work was Charles H. Behre, Jr., Professor of Economic Geology at Columbia University but on loan to the Survey during the War. Professor Behre was not only a fine geologist from whom I learned a great deal but also a charming and cultivated person, as was Mrs. Behre, who often came with him on his visits to our party; they too provided a part of my continuing education, geological and humanistic. The zinc work went on for two years, 1942-1944. All this work in Virginia and Tennessee was part of my training as a geologist; from then on I concentrated on Appalachian geology.

While I was involved in this zinc work, King and Ferguson with Craig's help were engaged in writing the major report on the northeast

Tennessee manganese deposits mentioned above; as I was also a coauthor, I made quite a few trips back to northeast Tennessee to work with them. We were all working very hard at that time, not only on that report but on our other projects, and I confess that, having become quite tired, I "lost my cool" more than once in our writing sessions and blew up at Phil King. Phil, also working at full pitch, took considerable umbrage at these outbursts, and for a while would hardly speak to me. I am forever grateful to Helen King for making it possible for me to present proper apologies to Phil and for getting him to accept them; the storm blew over, and we became good friends again.

In 1944 I was brought into Washington to join the Branch of Military Geology. When that work was over, the Survey brought me back to East Tennessee, and I worked there for five consecutive summers (in the fall of 1946 I began my teaching career at Yale). For two summers I did detailed mapping, but then, at Ferguson's instigation, the State and Federal Surveys together assigned me the task of compiling a geological map of the whole of East Tennessee, with which I was by then quite familiar. That was one of the most satisfactory projects I ever undertook; I spent three summers on it, and the third summer I wrote a report to accompany the map — one of my best efforts. The map and report were published by the State of Tennessee in 1953; I was quite proud afterwards when I learned that they came to be used almost as a textbook for geology courses at the University of Tennessee in Knoxville.

King too returned to East Tennessee after the War; he continued as a member of the Federal Survey for the rest of his career, and for his first post-War project he chose the geology of the Great Smoky Mountains National Park in Tennessee and North Carolina. For that project he was the chief of a good-sized party, and they turned out a group of fine reports, including one for non-geologists visiting the Park. During my five summers in East Tennessee I often visited the Kings and his field party; indeed I made use of their results in compiling the map of East Tennessee.

In my opinion Philip King was one of the outstanding geologists in North America during his lifetime; wherever he worked, he made major, seminal contributions. Throughout his career he not only provided sound and thorough detailed studies of the regions where he worked, but he thought about the "big picture." Early in his career, in connection with the International Geological Congress of 1933, held in the United States, he prepared a small-scale tectonic map of the country, with explanatory text, which was published as a guidebook for the Congress. When the Committee on Tectonics of the Natural Research Council decided to sponsor a large-scale tectonic map of the United States, Professor Longwell, as Chairman of the committee for the project, asked King to assemble the materials and prepare the map; Longwell had known King when King was a graduate student at Yale, and he knew of his great skills as a draftsman. King did so; indeed he was working on it much of the time he was also working on the Appalachian manganese deposits. That map, one of the first major tectonic maps of a large country, led later to his being asked to prepare a tectonic map for the whole of North America, which in its turn served as a model for tectonic maps of other continents. Thus King became well known internationally.

It has seemed to me however that King was never fully appreciated by the geological community in his own country. Partly because of his own strong and sometimes difficult personality, he was not always easy to know and to work with; he had strong admirations and dislikes, which he never hesitated to express bluntly, and he tended to arouse the same in others.

As graduate students at Yale, he and his brother Robert, who became an outstanding oil geologist with the Texas Company, had been the leaders of one faction in a serious feud among the graduate students there (happily there was no corresponding feud among the faculty), and some members of the other faction, who also became outstanding geologists and rose to influential positions, were unable ever to forget the feud or to accept and appreciate Phil's good qualities and great ability. Some very influential older geologists also shared that inability, as I found when I tried to urge his election to the National Academy of Sciences, for which in my opinion he was fully qualified.

Intellectual qualifications are, however, not always enough. At the very first meeting of the Academy in 1863, William B. Rogers told the assembled members never to forget that there were at least as many qualified scientists outside the Academy as within it. That is still true. Rogers, one of the founders of the Massachusetts Institute of Technology, its first President, and later a President of the Academy, was no relative of mine; his father left Ireland in 1798, the year of a major Irish rebellion, obviously one jump ahead of the police, whereas my ancestor left Scotland in 1805, one jump ahead of the press gang. On the other hand, in an organization like the Academy, election to which is decided by those already elected, persons with difficult and prickly characters can be detrimental to the aims of the organization; often they are precisely the ones who stand in the way of electing other fully qualified scientists. Phil King also was never a Councillor or officer of the Geological Society of America, although his brother Robert had a very successful term as Treasurer, but Phil did serve as Chairman of the Publications Committee, and as such he handled a difficult problem very well. Finally, in 1965 he was awarded

awarded the Penrose Medal of the Society, in just recognition of his great ability and his major contributions to North American geology. After his death in 1987, I wrote his Memorial for the Geological Society.

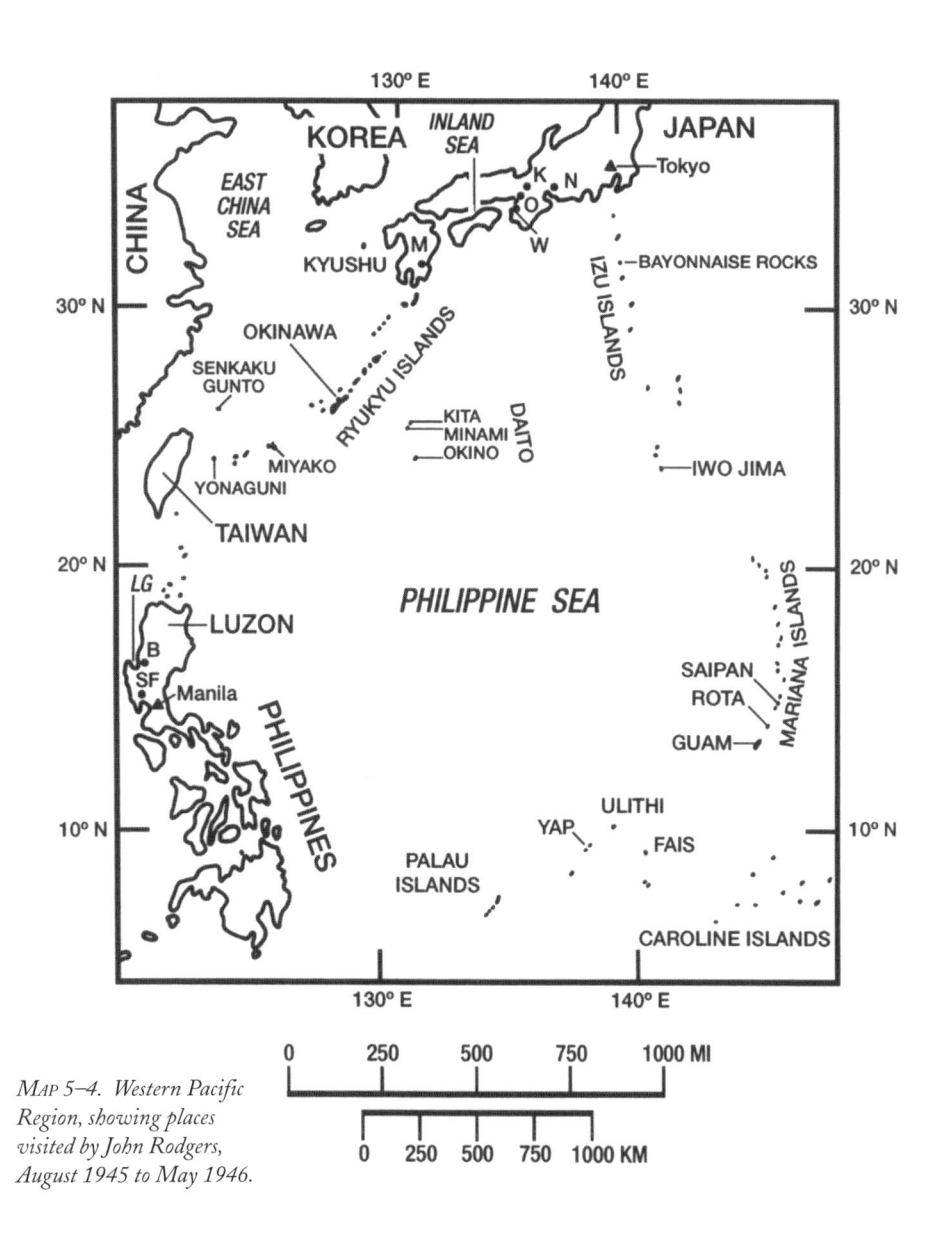

MAP 5–4. *Western Pacific Region, showing places visited by John Rodgers, August 1945 to May 1946.*

5 — The Military Geology Branch of the United States Geological Survey

During the War

As the Second World War began in Europe and then engulfed the United States, the USGS organized a Military Geology Branch to work with the Army Engineers and assemble information useful to them in the various war theatres: information on topography, trafficability, materials for building roads and airfields, and water supply. Indeed, such a unit had been organized during the First World War.

In May 1944 the Survey transferred me from field work on the zinc project in East Tennessee to office work with the Military Geology Branch in Washington. For the first three months I worked on road problems; my chief in this project was Dr. G. Edward Lewis, with whom I had studied vertebrate paleontology during my second year of graduate work at Yale. Then two of us in the unit were assigned to work on beaches and sent out to the Beach Erosion Board of the Army Engineers, located in a pleasant parklike reservation at the edge of the District of Columbia. My partner was Robert M. Garrels, a brilliant geologist of about my age whom I found delightful to work with. This move we made in midsummer; back in downtown Washington we'd been working in air-conditioned offices, but at the Board there was no air-conditioning, only open windows to the hot and humid outside air, and I well remember that, for the first two weeks, Bob and I went to sleep over our desks regularly every afternoon. Here we worked first with William Krumbein, an outstanding student of sedimentary geology on loan from Northwestern University where he had built up a fine department — indeed, after the War he got Garrels to join that department — then with Eleanor Tatge. We studied beaches and coastlines all along the western Pacific rim from Kamchatka to China, to help the planners decide in which areas an invasion would be feasible and in which not.

About the time I joined the Military Geology Branch, a team of geologists from the Branch had been sent out from Washington to MacArthur's headquarters in the Southwest Pacific to work closely with the Army Engineers there, providing detailed terrain information for the invasions in that theatre. Then about the beginning of October it was decided to send a similar team to Central Pacific headquarters on Oahu, and I was chosen as the "beach expert" for that team; we finally got there

Fig. 5–11: In uniform as "scientific consultant" to the U.S. Army Engineers in the Central Pacific theatre between November 1944 and May 1946.

in mid-November. We called ourselves the Engineering Terrain Intelligence Team.

Like the earlier team, we were in fact still civilian employees of the USGS, but we were called "scientific consultants," given an "assimilated rank" (my "rank" was Captain), and put in the uniform of Army officers but with the regular insignia of rank replaced by little brass US's — greatly confusing the enlisted men, who never knew whether to salute us or not. In view of our ambiguous status, our ability to be useful depended very largely on the personal relations we could establish with the Army officers with whom we were dealing. Our chief was Philip Shenon, a fine Survey geologist but also a shrewd "Blarney Irishman" who was very successful in establishing cordial relations with the individual officers and obtaining their confidence and respect, also in dealing with the Army regulations and red-tape, so that our team could fulfill its potential. I learned a tremendous amount just watching him "operate;" moreover he helped me a great deal in a certain amount of growing up I still had to do.

In Washington we had assembled terrain information from all available published sources, for we had access to the full collections at the Library of Congress, and we had become expert at putting such information together. But on Oahu we had access to much unpublished, classified and even "secret," information, especially to the airplane photographs of our invasion targets. There we were assigned offices and living quarters with, successively, two Engineering Topographic Battalions, who were making most of the maps for the Central Pacific theatre. Thus we were working with the latest available maps and, even more important, with the airplane photographs from which those maps were made. The second battalion (the 30th) worked in an underground facility, so we worked there too; when we were working on rush jobs, there would be times when we didn't see the sun for several days running. After a few months, another group was sent out from the Branch in Washington to work with us; one of them was Bob Garrels, who joined me in the work on beaches.

At first we did a little work for the invasion of Iwo Jima, which was imminent when we arrived, but then our big job was on the Ryukyu Islands, especially on their largest island, Okinawa. For that invasion, my job was to provide information not only on the beaches across which our troops would fight and on the terrain behind — on how it would favor defense or attack — but also on the coral reefs that lay offshore, which posed serious problems for the invading troops. The invasion of Tarawa earlier that year had shown how vital it was to know all about the coral reefs and to take them into account. Moreover, my rapidly growing knowledge of these coastal matters led to my working closely with Navy units concerned with harbors and with planning for the transfer of munitions and other supplies from ship to shore, once a foothold had been secured.

Okinawa consists of a larger, mountainous northern part, of almost no military interest, and a much lower, well inhabited southern part, on which we were planning to establish airfields from which to carry the war to Japan; the two parts are joined by a fairly narrow isthmus. The initial invasion was rapid and successful because we had led the Japanese to think that we would invade the south coast, but actually we invaded the west coast of the low southern part, a little south of the isthmus, and our troops crossed the island on the first day; they then turned south to complete the conquest. But nearly all the earlier invasions of Pacific islands, mostly much smaller ones, had been decided on the beaches; hence the airplane-photograph and map coverage for Okinawa was excellent for the coastline but rather mediocre inland, where the invasion was more difficult. When, for our next job, we took up the invasion of Japan itself, the airplane-photograph coverage we had was complete and superb.

My part of the job on Japan was of course to learn everything I could about the beaches. There were several large and beautiful beaches on which we could invade but, generally speaking, the terrain around them strongly favored the defense. The beaches lay at the heads of broad but quite shallow bays whose offshore gradients were so nearly flat that our LSTs would ground stern-first, forcing troops and tanks to plow through considerable water before reaching the beaches. Behind and parallel to each beach was a line of sand dunes; behind that a line of little swamps; behind that another line of older sand dunes; behind that another line of swamps; behind that — etc. Behind the last sand dunes were the rice paddies, which could of course be flooded in short order; behind or beside the rice paddies were flat-topped terraces, a few tens of meters above the paddies, made of volcanic ash layers. These terraces had to be the first main objective of the invasion, for only there could we build our airfields; without land-based air cover the invasion would remain precarious. But the volcanic ash lent itself readily to the construction of subterranean defenses, and air photographs taken in May 1945 showed that such underground fortifications were already being built; the invasion itself was scheduled for November.

The Japanese knew perfectly well that we were planning to invade their home islands; they were saving for it everything they still had, considerably less than before to be sure but by no means negligible, and they would be fighting for their homes. I am convinced that, if we had invaded Japan — and we would have succeeded, after a while — the invasion would have taken many, many more *Japanese* lives, not to speak of American lives, than the atomic bombs took — which was about 50,000. To put it baldly, the invasion of Japan would have made the invasion of Okinawa, bloody as it was, look like a Sunday-School picnic. Afterwards indeed the Japanese told us that the atomic bombs were the second worst disaster of the War; the first was the fire-bombing of Tokyo, which took 70,000 lives. And the atomic bombs finally and completely discredited the War party, which had been in control of Japanese foreign policy since before the invasion of China, of Manchuria, in 1930; the Peace party finally took over, and before the second bomb messages were coming through the Swedish embassy to ascertain our terms for surrender.

That the Second World War began in 1930 must never be forgotten. A friend of mine from graduate school, Charles R. Warren, had been brought up, the son of missionaries, in Miyazaki in southern Kyushu; after the war he went back there to visit. I met him in Tokyo, where he was acting as an interpreter, and he told me that, for the people he knew there, the whole period from 1930 to 1945 had been one steady crescendo of economic difficulties. Each year, as things got worse, they were told to tighten their belts, soon things would get better — but they never did. The American part of the War, with at the end the bombing of their cities, was merely the final fortissimo. Hence I have always maintained that the dropping of the atomic bombs was fully justified. War is a brutal business but, if we fight at all, we fight to win. I can understand a fully pacifist position, for my two brothers and my sister were pacifists in that War, but I happen to believe that there is no absolute right and wrong in human affairs, only various gradations between, and that our fighting, and winning, that War produced a considerably better gradation in the world than the alternative.

After the War, in Japan

IN ANY CASE, JAPAN WAS NEVER INVADED. Instead our troops occupied the country. When the War ended in August, most people wanted to go home to their families and take up a "normal" life again, but I was single and thus free to accept the invitation to accompany the occupying forces, still in my capacity as a geologist and "scientific consultant" to the Army Engineers. I had indeed already been picked to join an Engineer Construction Brigade attached to the headquarters of the Sixth

Army as a part of the invasion of southern Japan — not in the first wave, of course, but when the Army headquarters went in — so I was assigned to them. I was flown to Manila, and in early September the Sixth Army assembled near Lingayen Gulf on the west coast of Luzon. I even had the opportunity to drive up into the mountains to Baguio, though it had been almost entirely destroyed; my Uncle James and his wife had died there during the Japanese occupation. In late September a quite large convoy sailed from Lingayen Gulf to the port of Wakayama at the eastern entrance to the Inland Sea, and I was chosen to drive a jeep from Wakayama through the bombed-out city of Osaka (which has long been one of the five largest cities in the world) to Kyoto, the old capital of Japan before the Shogun made Yedo into Tokyo, the Eastern Capital. Like the shrine cities of Nara and Nikko, Kyoto had never been bombed; we were trying to tell the Japanese people that we weren't fighting the old Japan but the new Japan of the War party, and I think they understood.

In Kyoto our outfit took over the comfortable quarters of the German-Japanese Friendship Club, where we found not merely records of speeches by Hitler and Goebbels (in German) but many fine records of the best German music, which we much enjoyed — plus excellent German literature.

My job in Kyoto was to drive around the countryside looking for gravel and "subgrade," for the Army Engineers felt they needed to rebuild the roads and especially the airfields to accommodate our trucks and planes. Two of us, Charles Johnson and I, were assigned a jeep, and we had a delightful time exploring the Kyoto region, which includes Japan's largest lake, Biwa-ko; a couple of times we were sent over to Nagoya on the same mission. There was absolutely no danger from the Japanese; the Emperor had spoken, and we were honored guests. We got into several towns and areas before any other Americans; at one prefecture boundary we were met by the Prefect himself and a large staff, including a charming lady interpreter, and we had to explain that the real occupying troops would be along in another hour or so. When we got to the city of Okazaki, there was a big banner across the main street saying: "Welcome, Allied troops. After your long and strenuous campaign from the Philippines, we welcome you to Okazaki." The only trouble I ever heard of was from one or two young Japanese men who bitterly resented American soldiers going out with their girls. Early in the occupation, a soldier from the 1st Cavalry Division, General MacArthur's favorite unit, raped a Japanese girl, and MacArthur, after a proper trial, had him shot, with full publicity; after that there were no more rapes, but American soldiers, with food, had no difficulty getting what they wanted.

After a month or so in Kyoto, I was called into the main headquarters in Tokyo to join the Natural Resources Section of MacArthur's Far Eastern Command. The chief of the section was Lieutenant-Colonel Hugh Schenck, a Professor of Paleontology on leave from Stanford University, another very shrewd person from whom I learned a great deal. Although only a Lieutenant Colonel, he held his own against Brigadier and Major Generals in the infighting within headquarters. From him I learned especially how to get along with Army officers, a lesson that stood me in very good stead later on. The principal job of the Natural Resources Section was gathering statistics on the mineral resources of Japan to determine what might be available as reparations for the countries she had overrun and then exploited during the War. I was assigned coal and ferro-alloys but also phosphate, because of my field work in the phosphate country of the western United States in 1939 and 1940.

I remember nothing about the coal and ferro-alloys, but phosphate turned out to be important. Phosphate is used principally as a basis for fertilizer, and Japan, which has no reserves whatever in the home islands, has always imported a great deal. During the last years of the War, however, our Navy had been sinking every Japanese ship they could find, right down to small fishing boats close to the home islands, so that no phosphate, or anything else, had been coming in. As a result the production of rice had fallen precipitously, and there was real danger of famine that first winter after the War. Now one ton of phosphate rock when treated with sulphuric acid — and sulphur is one thing in which the volcanic Japanese islands are rich — makes nearly two tons of superphosphate fertilizer, which under the circumstances might produce three extra tons of rice. Looking at the statistics on phosphate imports into Japan over the preceding decades, I found that roughly a quarter had come from the United States, for we have very large reserves and can afford to ship it out, a quarter from then French North Africa, a quarter from islands in the south Pacific and Indian Oceans — Nauru, Ocean, and Christmas — and a quarter from the islands in the western Pacific that we had just taken away from Japan. The phosphate in the southern Pacific was needed for Indonesia and other countries nearby; that in French North Africa was needed for Europe and adjacent Africa; that in the United States was available, but shipping costs would be high. So I asked: "Why doesn't someone go to see if the phosphate deposits in the western Pacific could be used, as they're so much closer?" and the answer was: "Well, why don't you go?" So we wrote my orders for the trip — fantastic orders telling everyone who saw them to see that I got to such and such islands "and any others necessary for the accomplishment of his mission" by plane, ship, train, bus, automobile, "or any other means of transportation" — got them signed at a high level in MacArthur's headquarters, and early in the morning of 1 January 1946 I took off.

After the War, Around the Western Pacific

I SPENT THE MONTHS of January and February on that trip and visited 20 different Pacific islands; I took a couple of week-long cruises and was flown hither and yither. My first goal was three tiny islands well out in the Philippine Sea, the Daito Islands — Kita, Minami, and Okino: north, south, and far. I flew to Okinawa, presented my orders to the Military Government officers there, and they arranged for me to join a Military Government group that was then cruising the southern Ryukyu islands in an LST but would soon be heading out to the Daitos. Accordingly I was flown down to Miyako-Jima, a largeish island, to wait for them.

The surrender of 20,000 Japanese troops on Miyako had been taken by a colonel with perhaps 25 American soldiers, but the Emperor had spoken, and they surrendered and laid down their arms like little men; then they arranged and policed their own "prisoner-of-war" camp while they waited to be sent home. The colonel told me that, when he came ashore to take their surrender, he'd arranged with the captain of the destroyer that brought him that, if he had trouble, he would make a certain signal and the destroyer would shell a certain point on the shore, in the hope that the Japanese would back off, but in fact there was no trouble of any kind. I happened to know that there were some quite small phosphate deposits on Miyako, and I asked to go see them; they were too small to be of any interest, but on the way we drove right by the POW camp. That evening the Miyakans put on a three-hour show of dances, skits, plays, and almost an opera, accompanied by samisens, drums, and falsetto voices in unison — interesting, but three hours was a little much.

A couple of days later the LST came in, and I transferred. At first I think the Military Government group and the crew were rather suspicious of this ambiguous character in an Army uniform, but we quickly got acquainted, and it was a fun cruise. First we cruised around the southern Ryukyus, going out to the Sento-shosho or Senkaku-gunto in the East China Sea, a group of tiny volcanic islands — we landed on the largest, about a mile long — then to Yonaguni, the southwesternmost island in the Ryukyu chain. We had rough seas getting there, and I was seasick; when I landed on Yonaguni and climbed up the mountain behind the port, I was happy to be on land and in hills again, but I did notice that the island rolled perceptibly. Then we sailed east 600 kilometers into the

Philippine Sea and came to Okino-Daito, where I went ashore to see the phosphate deposits. They had been fairly large but clearly were almost entirely mined out; here however I became acquainted with "karrenfeld" topography, the extremely irregular surface that forms on limestone by solution beneath a soil cover in a humid climate. Then we sailed north to the two other Daitos, two raised atolls; on each a wall of limestone tens of meters high and one or two hundred meters wide surrounds a central flat at sea level containing a fresh-water lake that rises and falls with the tide. But by then the northwest monsoon, blowing out of winter Siberia, had taken over, and the captain decided it would be unsafe to land. We made a figure 8 around the two islands, and some native islanders rowed out to see us; they reported that there too the deposits had been mined out but that a considerable stock of phosphate rock, an unusual aluminum phosphate, was waiting on the dock for lack of shipping. When I got back to Okinawa, I cabled this information to Tokyo, and ships were sent down to get the phosphate rock before I returned from my trip.

The Military Government people on Okinawa had been so helpful that I also cabled Tokyo asking that an official commendation be prepared and sent from headquarters there; that was done. I spent a few days on Okinawa and then was flown to Manila and on to Guam. Thence, on the advice of Harry Ladd, a good friend from the Geological Survey whom I kept meeting here and there around the Pacific, I flew down to the Palau group. The main American headquarters was on Peleliu, but the chief phosphate deposits are on Angaur, the southernmost island. There at last I found a sizeable reserve, and I radioed the information to Tokyo; not long afterwards, a Japanese firm reopened that deposit. Angaur was at that time my farthest south, 7° north of the equator, and I remember sitting on its southern beach, with a cool drink in my hand, looking at the southern stars. The Military Government officer with whom I was sitting told me that, after he had gained the confidence of the local chief, the chief asked him: "Well, how long are you people going to be here?" It was a fair question; the Spaniards had arrived about 1880, the Germans had taken over in 1898, the Japanese had driven out the Germans in 1914, and now we Americans had driven out the Japanese — this one man had witnessed it all. In fact, after a few decades the Americans granted independence to Micronesia, if always as a sort of protectorate.

Before I left the Palaus, I had the fun of an airplane ride over the whole chain, including the big northern island of Babelthuap, arranged by a friendly colonel. Then I flew back to Guam and presented my orders to the Military Government group there; they too were very helpful. Phosphate deposits were reported on several of the Mariana Islands, and I visited those on Rota and Saipan, but again there was almost nothing left.

On my return from Saipan, I found a radio message from the Geological Survey, asking me if I would accept assignment to a party to study the atoll of Bikini, already selected as the site for the next atomic-bomb test. I thought about it for 24 hours — and decided against it. The same day that I sent off my reply, a cable arrived from Professor Longwell, asking me if I would care to be considered for an Instructorship in the Geology Department at Yale. About that offer I had no doubts and I accepted at once.

In the meantime the Military Government people had been arranging to get me to the tiny island of Fais in the westernmost Carolines. They decided to use a net-tender (a small vessel about half the size of the LSTs in which I had travelled before) that was lying idle in the harbor; moreover one of their officers, a Lieutenant Commander, decided to go along to visit MG groups on various islands, and then the chief medical officer for the region, a Navy Captain, decided to come along "to inspect medical conditions on the islands" — i.e., for the cruise. So we took off on a week's cruise, not just to Fais but to the other islands that the officers wanted to visit.

We went first to Fais, where I looked over the phosphate diggings and "refinery." Fais is a low limestone plateau, perhaps 20 meters above the sea; the plateau is open and flat, where not cut up by the phosphate diggings, and the native islanders (no Japanese here) had flattened most of them out and were raising crops on the rich phosphatic soil. Clearly not much phosphate rock was left, and I saw no reason to disturb them for the little that remained.

From Fais we went on to Ulithi, where I had the chance to see a "regulation" atoll, then to Yap. I was very happy to see Yap, whose rocks are decidedly continental, mostly green schist, quite out of place so far out in the Pacific. Yap is also the site of the stone money, great rings of calcite and coral rock like overgrown beads, evidently brought there from Palau, for there is no raised coral rock on Yap. The Military Government crew on Yap struck me, however, as quite inferior to the others I'd met; moreover Yap-town, the principal settlement, is inhabited mostly by Chamorros brought in from the Marianas by the Spaniards. In reaction against them, their Western clothes, and their Catholicism, the native Yap Islanders have retained their original grass breech-clouts and skirts and their animism, and they still inhabit little villages scattered over the four islands of the group. These villages are connected by beautiful stone pathways made of the local rock, also used for stone walls and pavements beneath the houses. The Navy Captain, the medical officer, wanted to visit the other islands too, so a boat trip was arranged and I went along, on the pretext of looking at some bauxite deposits (there was nothing worth mining). On each of the four islands, native islanders climbed up coconut trees and cut down coconuts for us, and we drank the fresh coconut milk.

Of all the Pacific islands and groups I visited I liked Yap the best. Later, back in Tokyo when we were arranging to make geological surveys of the various western Pacific groups, I sang Yap's praises to Charley Johnson, telling him however to get out of Yap-town as soon as he could. He went there and quickly made friendly contact with the real Yap people; moreover he was able to supply DDT to the wives of the native chiefs and, for the first time in their lives, they could get rid of the insect fauna in their grass skirts and be truly comfortable. There are curious advantages to being a geologist.

From Yap we sailed back to Guam, and early in March the Navy, not the Army, flew me to Tokyo; on that trip we stopped in Iwo Jima. There we had a half-hour trip around the island looking for breakfast, and I had just a chance to see it and its rocks. Iwo consists of two volcanoes, a broad flat one and a sharp little cone (we didn't get to that), connected by an isthmus of black volcanic sand. It was fascinating to see steam coming out of cracks in the volcanic bedrock; neither volcano has erupted in historic time, but that's not very long there, and clearly neither is extinct. Farther north, near the Bayonnaise Rocks, we flew over a new volcano just sticking its head above water — a great plume of steam streaming off to the southeast in the monsoon, a few masses of black rock projecting out of the sea, and a remarkable greenish stain in the blue water extending northeast with the Japanese Current.

As soon as I got back to Tokyo, in early March, I ran into a Survey friend, Tom Hendricks, whose job was to start geological surveys of the various Pacific islands, and he at once asked me to take on the Geological Survey of Okinawa. Because of the possible job at Yale, I couldn't do that, but I agreed to go for a month or so, until someone else could take over. Actually we didn't leave for over a month, by which time I had a party of three; moreover, when we got to Okinawa I looked up a geologist in the Army, Gilbert Corwin, whom I'd met in January, and started working to add him to the party. I got to do some geology, helping the party get started, but actually my main contribution was dealing with the Army and Military Government to smooth the way; it amazed me how good I had become at that kind of thing. But my previous experience, and above all my having asked headquarters in Tokyo in January to send down a commendation for the recipients' "201 file," made everyone very cooperative. My replacement turned up in less than three weeks, and I could return to Tokyo (early May by now), then a week later to the States.

Thus ended my two years with the Military Geology Branch of the Survey. In 1947, in recognition of my work in the Pacific theatre, the U. S. Army awarded me the Medal of Freedom, its highest honor for civilians.

The Post–War Decade

6 — In the United States

Byron Nelson Cooper (1917-1971)

IN 1940 I STARTED A DISSERTATION PROJECT in East Tennessee and worked at it off and on for a while, but I had to drop it for war work, a part of which I was then able to parlay into a dissertation and a PhD. But the original problem continued to intrigue me and, during my summers in East Tennessee right after the war, I pretty well carried through my research on the subject. Already during the war years I became aware that Byron Cooper was working on the same rocks in southwest Virginia and that his conclusions were very different from mine; moreover he became aware of my work. It would be hard to explain most of our differences in terms intelligible to a non-geologist; perhaps the easiest to explain, and one of the most important for both of us, had to do with how the great rock folds in the western Appalachians formed — whether by pushing the rock layers from the side over an unyielding floor or basement (my view) or by draping them over individual "floor-boards" that moved separately, alternately up and down (Cooper's view). After the war Cooper joined the Geology Department of the Virginia Polytechnic Institute in Blacksburg; he soon became its head and built it up into one of the finest geology departments in the Southeast, and in the nation.

One might have thought that our strongly differing geological hypotheses would have separated us, but in fact we became very good friends. Each of us greatly respected the other's geologic work in our respective regions, and we much enjoyed arguing about our differing hypotheses and scoring debater's points off each other, acknowledging the good ones, but neither of us changed our main opinions. Already in 1949 Cooper, who was arranging a geological session at a meeting of the Virginia Academy of Sciences in Richmond, had me invited to give a guest lecture on my ideas. They allotted me 40 minutes, quite long for such a meeting (I think he allotted himself time to reply, as was his perfect right). Later we met in the field many times to look at each other's evidence, to argue about it, and to show it to our students. Moreover, whenever I came to Blacksburg, as when I was driving through or attending various meetings there, Professor and Mrs. Cooper would greet me, and often they took me into their home as a guest; I hope I made some recompense by playing the piano for them, for they both seemed to enjoy the classical music I played. And we also invited Professor Cooper to come up to Yale to present his ideas to us.

As soon as we each had published articles presenting our hypotheses, I made a point of assigning them to my students, hoping to show them that scientific hypotheses can seldom be called "true" or "false" but only, and slowly, better and better, or worse and worse, approximations, and that a controversy like ours, if it can be kept free of personalities, is the best way to arrive at such approximations. I used to tell them, somewhat but by no means entirely in jest, that the persons involved in such controversies seldom if ever change their minds but that sooner or later they do die off, leaving the younger generation — you students — to decide finally which hypothesis is "right" (they liked that idea). Then you will start arguing about other controversial hypotheses and, when you die off, the next younger generation will make those decisions (they weren't so sure they liked that idea). One year (1961) Byron Cooper ran a field excursion right across the Appalachian mountains, from western North Carolina across southwest Virginia and into West Virginia. I went on that trip; my diary records that "there was a delightful running battle between him and me ... but all the exchanges were good-natured and full of light humor."

Then at a geological meeting in Blacksburg in 1963, Professor Cooper and his staff arranged a "symposium" of six papers on Appalachian structure, the last two being by me and him; as organizer he had the right to the last word. My diary states that afterwards I was "given many broad hints by oil geologists" (who had access to unpublished subsurface information from their oil wells) "that I'm right, but then Byron was probably given exactly the same treatment by others." At another meeting we had breakfast together and were "as cordial and as diametrically opposed as ever."

In November 1969, at the annual meeting of the Geological Society of America, intrigued by its title I went to listen to a paper by William A. Thomas, a student of Byron Cooper's whom I had come to admire as a geologist and to like as a person. As I came into the room I saw Byron, so I went to sit beside him. It turned out that the whole point of Thomas's talk was that Rodgers is right in one part of the orogenic belts, the embayments of the craton, and Cooper is right in another, the protuberances. Byron and I were so amused by the idea that anyone would try to reconcile us that we both burst into loud laughter; poor Bill Thomas, up on the podium, must have been quite disconcerted, for he knew perfectly well who we were. But as the years went on, I came to realize that Bill's idea was quite correct; more than once since then, I have apologized to him for my unseemly laughter on that occasion.

When volumes of articles were prepared in honor of Professor Marland Billings of Harvard and of Professor Ernst Cloos of Johns

Hopkins, I was asked to contribute to both; for the Cloos volume, I presented a sort of extension of my hypothesis. I specifically requested the organizers of that volume to invite Professor Cooper to write an article rebutting mine, of which I had sent him a draft copy; he chose to do so, and it certainly seemed that he had won that argument. But in the early 1980s, Fred Diegel, then a graduate student at Johns Hopkins, discovered outcrops on the shore of a TVA reservoir in East Tennessee that could well be taken as evidence of my extended hypothesis, so the question remains open.

In 1971 I was again invited to present a paper on my ideas, this time to a conference in West Virginia, and again I suggested that Professor Cooper be invited to present his views, but that time he didn't. Two months later came the shocking news of his sudden death by heart attack. I've lived a quarter century since then, and I think I can say that my main hypothesis has gradually prevailed, but probably I should hold off boasting about that until a quarter century after my own death.

Two months after Professor Cooper's death, a major geological meeting was held at Blacksburg, one that he had prepared and largely planned; indeed his shadow hung over the whole meeting. I was asked to prepare a paper on the subject he had assigned to himself; in it I tried to present his line of thinking, despite the unwanted advantage of having the last word. Later the staff there put together a Cooper Volume in his memory, and we at the *American Journal of Science* were proud to publish it as our vol. 273-A.

(George) Evelyn Hutchinson (1903-1991)

Evelyn Hutchinson (the first two syllables are sounded and accented as in evil) was an outstanding biologist and also limnologist, indeed a "Renaissance man." Born and educated in Cambridge, England, in 1928 he was called to the Yale Zoology Department where he spent the rest of his career. I was fortunate to meet him and get to know him already during my first year on the Yale faculty; in January 1947 he gave a lecture on the Pacific phosphate islands, and I could tell him that I'd recently visited some of them and could give him copies of two reports I'd written for the Army Engineers after my "phosphate" trips in early 1946. He was startled to find one of them marked classified, but I'm pretty sure it had already been declassified, and in any case it was written not during the War to help defeat Japan but afterwards to help avert famine there.

When I became Assistant Editor of the *American Journal of Science*, I found that Professor Hutchinson was the Associate Editor for Biology;

he advised us which biological books to have reviewed in the *Journal* and whom to ask to review them, likewise whom to ask to review articles with a biological component. For some years he was also chairman of the Yale Committee that oversaw the *Journal* . Thus I quickly became familiar with his extraordinary breadth and depth as a scientist, and indeed as an intellectual. I remember that once, when Mrs. Bernard Knox and I met him in the Yale Library, she mentioned that she had just come back from a vacation on Block Island, and he gave us a two-minute dissertation on the unusual characters of Block Island mice. For many years he wrote a column called "Marginalia" in the *Sigma Xi Quarterly* (later the *American Scientist*); it was famous for the breadth, understanding, and insight it displayed.

I've mentioned above that in 1948 Professor Longwell organized the conference that started a campaign of geological field mapping in Connecticut. A few years later, when Longwell was preparing to move west to live in California and work in Nevada, Professor Hutchinson took his place as Commissioner and I became informal "straw boss" for the Survey's geological mapping program. I was therefore invited to many meetings of that Commission, generally luncheon meetings in or near Middletown, so about twice a year Professor Hutchinson and I would drive up and back, talking all the way. Then in 1959 he resigned as Yale's Commissioner, and I was appointed to succeed him.

In 1837, more than a century and a half ago, a small group of New Haven men, including some Yale professors, organized a club that met every two weeks or so, except in the summer, for dinner in somebody's home; they discussed a subject, chosen by some member or by mutual consent — political issues, for example. As time went on, The Club, as it called itself, became more and more exclusively Yale faculty (only quite recently, about seven years after I became a member, have we elected women). In 1958 both Professor Hutchinson and I were elected, and we were both quite faithful members because of the great intellectual stimulus it provided. In our first year, because it was the centennial of Darwin's *The Origin of Species*, which had indeed been discussed in The Club when it was first published, we arranged to discuss it in two successive meetings, mine on the intellectual climate of the time, his on the book itself and its impact.

In 1969 I had the opportunity to visit Lake Baykal in Siberia and even to take a ten-day cruise on it. Lake Baykal is unique, for it is the deepest lake in the world and the largest in volume; it has existed as a lake for something like 30 million years since it was cut off from the (now distant) ocean, and it contains many, many unique forms of life, including fresh-water seals, which evolved out of the ordinary seals that got trapped in the lake when it was cut off. Of course Professor Hutchinson as the world's leading limnologist knew all about it, but he had never been there; now this younger colleague was about to go. He very kindly talked to me about it before I went; then when I got to the lake, I met Dr. Galazyy, the Director of the Limnological Institute of the Soviet Academy of Sciences there. Of course he knew Professor Hutchinson by reputation, and he gave me a copy of his handsome *Atlas Baykala* for Evelyn; I had already bought my own copy. And when I got back to Lake Baykal in June 1973, we wrote a joint postcard to Prof. Hutchinson.

My close friend Willie Ruff, when he was an undergraduate in the Yale School of Music, nevertheless took courses outside the School, including a course in biology that deeply impressed him; one of his instructors was Professor Hutchinson. When he came back to Yale in 1970, he was happy to come to know him better; in due course we nominated Willie for The Club and he was elected, increasing their contacts. When Willie started his seminar on rhythm in 1980, he had Evelyn and me present the rhythm in our respective subjects - I for crystals in space and Evelyn for seiches in lakes and predator-prey cycles in biology. Then in Prof. Hutchinson's last years, Willie went out of his way several times to go to see him and to help him get to meetings of The Club.

Early in 1991, Evelyn's second wife died, and his sister came over and took him back to England to look after him. A few months later we heard that he had died there but that he was to be buried in New Haven beside his first wife, with whom he had lived for more than 30 years.

The Fellowship of Branford College

The College system at Yale was instituted in 1933; in the next few years the already existing Memorial Quadrangle, the premier undergraduate dormitory, was divided into two colleges and eight new ones were constructed. That Yale was given the money for this construction at that time helped New Haven enormously during the Great Depression. Basically the colleges were big undergraduate dormitories with dining halls and other amenities, but in each lived a Master, who was always married, his wife being an important part of the "family atmosphere" he was expected to create, and to each was assigned a group of Fellows, senior and junior members of the faculty representing the various disciplines in Yale College and the Sheffield Scientific School and also in the professional schools — Music, Law, Divinity, Medicine, Architecture, Art, Drama. Fellows had the privilege of taking meals in the College dining halls; part of the time they were expected to eat with the undergraduates but part of the time with each other, generally at fixed times — e.g., lunch once a week, dinner once a month — and conversations between scholars from different disciplines were certainly among the most valuable results of the Fellowship system. Until much later, not all Yale faculty members who taught undergraduates were Fellows of Colleges; the choices were made by the Master with help, if he wished it, from the already appointed Fellows and depended on estimates of eminence, "clubbability," and other vague criteria.

In the spring of 1947, at the end of my first year on the Yale faculty (Fellows were never appointed before they had been on the faculty a year), Prof. Alan Bateman, back from his war work in Washington and by now Chairman of the Geology Department, began arranging for me to become not just a Fellow of one of the Colleges but a Resident Fellow, who would actually live in a suite in the college dormitory (Resident Fellows were always bachelors). I was appointed to Branford College, part of the Memorial Quadrangle, and in the fall I moved into a large and handsome second-floor suite looking out over the Branford Court, in many ways the central court of the University; it was there for instance that the Senior Societies conducted their ritual Tap Day, the selection of their members in the next senior class. I lived in the College for thirty-five years, I think a record.

The Master of Branford then and for many years afterwards was Professor Norman S. Buck of Economics, always called "Steve" or else "Dean Buck," as he was Dean of Freshmen; he lived with his wife and daughters in a fine house built right into the Memorial Quadrangle, and I came to know them quite well. It was Dean Buck who assigned me my "duties" as Resident Fellow, but they were really quite vague. When I ate in the dining hall, as I generally did, I was expected to join the young men at table and converse with them, if they wanted to converse with me; some did, some didn't. I was also to be available for conferences or counselling, academic or personal, again when they wished it; sometimes that was no more than lending a young man a few dollars over a weekend.

There were a few other duties. As soon as I moved into the Resident Fellow's suite, I bought myself a good piano, a Steinway apartment grand from about 1905 — a good vintage — and I didn't keep my light under a bushel; thus I was sometimes asked to play for weekly "beer-and-song" parties or to accompany a Branford Glee Club that perked along for a few years, being used mainly to sing carols at Christmas dinners. In general my presence in the College was supposed, I guess, to moderate undergraduate high-jinks to some extent. Over the years I came to know quite a few undergraduates fairly well.

There was one additional "duty" that turned out to be a very great privilege. In the first-floor suite beneath me lived Professor George Lincoln Hendrickson, a very distinguished Professor of Classics who had been in a sense built into the College as it was being built in 1933, just as he retired. He was already 82 when I moved in; he was a little frail but on the whole in good health, for he exercised regularly; for example, he often drove out to the fairly rigorous Yale golf course and played a little golf or just knocked a ball around the back nine. He spent his summers on Chebeague Island in Casco Bay in Maine; there was a good golf course there too, but mostly he preferred to sail his boat. One summer I visited him there, and he took me out for a sail; when we were far enough from shore for him to consider it safe, he actually let me hold the tiller for a little while.

In New Haven I was expected to keep a gentle eye on him, to encourage him to eat in the dining hall instead of cooking his own meals, which were apt to be irregular; to run small errands for him if he wished, but he drove his own car; to try to be there to help if he fell or had other small accidents. As I had studied Latin and Greek in school and Greek in college and was still trying to read Greek poetry, especially Homer and the great dramatists, I felt myself very fortunate to get to know him and talk to him about the Classics.

At one point in his career Professor Hendrickson had been Director of the American Academy in Rome; he loved Italy and knew Italian very well. After I began to study Italian and had worked my way through Boccaccio, I wanted to read Dante's *Divina Commedia*, and I asked Hendrickson if he would be willing to read it with me. He agreed, and we read it through over a period of a year and a half, one canto a night when we could get together, a very great experience for me. After that we started in on the *Odyssey*, but not much later he died, at the age of 98.

Professor Hendrickson's middle name was Lincoln because he was born a month after Lincoln's assassination in 1865. He completed his doctorate at

FIG. 6–12. Professor. G. Lincoln Hendrickson, in November 1963, about a month before his death at 98

Johns Hopkins and while there he lived through the great blizzard of 8 March 1888; he also studied in Germany, and he had some wonderful tales to tell. I used to encourage interested undergraduates to join us at dinner and so forth; one time, when we were joined by Seymour Fink, an undergraduate and an excellent pianist, Hendrickson told us about having heard Jenny Lind sing in Berlin. He added, like a careless afterthought: "Brahms was conducting." On the occasion of the party for his 90th birthday, he asked us who was the Vice-President during Grant's second term; none of us knew, of course, and he told us that, as a boy of seven, he had waved banners and shouted: "Hurrah for Grant; Hurrah for Wilson!"

When William Rainey Harper built the University of Chicago, beginning in 1891, he brought in for each field the most brilliant senior scholars whom he could attract with John D. Rockefeller's millions; he also brought in a group of brilliant younger scholars. But about 1905 some of these had to move on; at that time John Dewey moved to Columbia and Hendrickson came to Yale. The first Master of Branford College, Clare Mendell, was in 1933 not only Professor of Classics but Dean of Yale College, but in 1905 he had been a devoted graduate student of Hendrickson's. He told me that, when the first group of College Masters met to choose Fellows, he as Dean of Yale College was given the first choice, and that his first choice was Hendrickson, for whom he then arranged the Fellow's suite where I knew him. (During the War Dean Mendell took leave from Yale to work for the Navy, and Dean Buck became Master of Branford.) I came to know Mendell particularly well because I would often take Hendrickson out to Mendell's lovely home in the country for Sunday afternoon tea and supper; from Mendell I learned a great deal about Yale — the College and the University. It was Professors Hendrickson and Mendell who nominated me to be a member of The Club.

Becoming a Fellow of Branford College introduced me to many faculty members throughout the University, both senior professors and younger men like myself; for me, some of the most delightful to know were the musicians. Along with my brother Prentice, I had heard and admired the music of the American composer Quincy Porter (mainly on records, to be sure). Right after the Second World War, he was appointed to the Yale faculty, and he became a Fellow of Branford at the same time that I did; we quickly became good personal friends. Dean Buck, our Master, was also very fond of music, and Quincy and his wife Lois, a fine violinist (Quincy played the viola), put together a "Branford Quartet" with other string players from the School of Music; it became the core of an annual series of Branford Concerts. When Quincy became Master of Pierson College, the concerts became the Branford-Pierson concerts, but they kept right on. To be sure I wasn't good enough to take a regular part in these concerts; occasionally I did turn pages for the pianists. Musicians always like to have parties after they've played a concert, to help them relax, and Dean Buck would often arrange such parties at the Master's house; I quickly got his permission to offer the party after one concert each year in my Fellow's suite, and in that way I came to know many fine musicians.

At one such party in my rooms, Dean Buck brought with him a Yale alumnus who had been appointed an Associate Fellow of the College, the President of the Cummins Engine Company. It happened that he owned a Stradivarius violin, which he had just had repaired in New York, and he had brought it to New Haven; naturally our violinists all wanted to see it and play on it, so he brought it over to my party. As they were fiddling away, I sat down at my piano and struck up the *Brahms Violin and Piano Sonata in A Major*, which I had studied (and even knew by heart, but that time I used the score), and three of them — Lois Porter, Quincy Porter, and the President of the Cummins Engine Company — played the three movements with me. I think it was that evening that established me with the musicians as someone who could hold his own with them, though not of course a professional musician.

Quincy, Lois, and I were very good friends until his sudden death in 1966. Following that, I got into the way of being Lois' regular escort to musical and other affairs; I became very fond of her, and after a while, perhaps not a long enough while, I proposed to her; she thought it over and declined. No man likes to be told that he is unacceptable, and I made up my mind to wait a year and try again. When the day rolled round, I went to Lois — and told her that I now understood she had been right to refuse me; from then on we were great friends and I was her regular escort until her death in 1989.

Another pair of fine musicians whom I met through the Branford Fellowship were Keith and Rachel Wilson. Keith arrived at Yale and became a Branford Fellow just when I did, and we became very close friends; he had been hired to be the Director of the Yale Band (Football, Marching, Concert). He was not only an excellent band director but an accomplished clarinetist, and he was welcomed, to his considerable surprise, into the company of the many fine professionals in the School of Music. Rachel too was a fine violinist and took her part in informal concerts, especially those in Branford College. Later Keith became Director of the Yale Summer School of Music and Art in Norfolk in the cool hills of northwestern Connecticut; under his direction it quickly became an outstanding summer musical festival. Whenever I was in or near Connecticut during the summer (which was not always), I made sure to go to

Norfolk every Friday for the concert; as I always got invited to the party afterwards and then hardly wanted to drive back to New Haven, sometimes I would sleep in my camper on the parking lot, and sometimes Rachel Wilson would let me sleep on a bed in the "White House," the mansion of the Battell Estate on which the Norfolk Summer School was held. A couple of summers, moreover, I found geological field work to do not far away, in Mrs. Knopf's country in eastern New York State just west of the triple corner with Massachusetts and Connecticut, so I stayed in or near Norfolk all summer.

Another musician in Branford College was the pianist, Donald Currier; I first met him in 1949 at a party after a concert that Howard Boatwright and he gave; Boatwright was the first violinist of the "Branford Quartet." In the 1950s Don was appointed to the Music faculty and then to Branford College; as he was a bachelor, he soon became a Resident Fellow, and during the twenty years or so that we were both Resident Fellows we came to know each other quite well. On several occasions I turned pages for him at Branford Concerts, and for one concert we worked up and played together Hindemith's *Sonata for Piano, Four Hands*. Hindemith was a Professor in the School of Music at that time, and his music was frequently played there; it has always appealed to me strongly

FIG. 6–13. *Keith and Rachel Wilson at Norfolk, CT, summer of 1977.*

because it is so well constructed, like the music of J. S. Bach, one of my chief musical heroes. Indeed I would class Hindemith at the summit along with Bach; Hindemith himself thought very highly of Bach's music and wrote a fine book about it and him. In the 1970s Don Currier moved out of the College to a house near the shore in Guilford; then in 1979 he married Charlotte Wilson. Of course I've seen them frequently at concerts and musical parties.

Another musician whom I first met through Branford College was the Australian composer Peter Sculthorpe, who came to Yale on a Harkness Fellowship that entitled him to live as a Resident Fellow in the College for the winter-spring term of 1966. When summer came and he had to leave his suite, I invited him to stay in the guest room in mine. Part of the summer I was there, but part I was on a geological tour in Europe, visiting graduate students in Norway, Italy, and Greece, some of whom were mine, but some were those of my opposite number at Princeton, Professor John Maxwell. Then in the fall Peter went off to a musical colony in New York State, and the next February he returned to Australia. During my year in Australia, 1973-74, I saw Peter several times, and a couple of times I heard his music played there, in the Sydney Opera House. I saw him there again for a short time in 1976, and of course I've heard his music from time to time, although rather seldom in recent years. I played his Sonatina as part of a recital of twentieth-century piano music that I gave a few times in the early 1970s.

The Branford Fellowship introduced me to some other remarkable scholars and thinkers. One of them was Iredell Jenkins, an Assistant Professor of Philosophy of about my age, whom I came to know very well; we soon found that our philosophical positions had a lot in common, for we both were basically "pragmatists," for whom the value of philosophical concepts depends on their usefulness in explaining the empirical, one might say scientific, concepts we deduce from the world we observe. Jenkins was also that *rara avis*, not to say contradiction in terms — a philosopher with a well developed sense of humor. Whether for that reason or not, he was not granted tenure at Yale, and he moved to the University of Alabama (where he was Chairman of both Philosophy and Religion). There he became involved in the Autherine Lucy case, an attempt to deny entrance to the University to a black student. Because he was himself a Southerner from Virginia (the name Iredell is also the name of a county in North Carolina), his stand against the Southern establishment was considered particularly dangerous, and indeed the Grand Dragon of the Ku Klux Klan of Alabama pronounced him the most dangerous liberal on the Alabama campus. To impress upon him their strong disapproval, the

Klan burned a fiery cross on his lawn; Jenkins and his wife and children went out and toasted marshmallows on it.

Bernard Walter MacGregor Knox

Another outstanding scholar whom I met through the Branford Fellowship was Bernard Knox. Knox has told us his own history very well, up to the time he came to Yale and I got to know him, in the Introduction to his *Essays Ancient & Modern* (Johns Hopkins University Press, 1989), from his boyhood in England through the discouraging years of the Great Depression and his participation in the Spanish Civil War and the Second World War (the latter leading to his becoming a U. S. citizen), up to his doctorate at Yale and his appointment to the Yale Classics Department. In 1948 he became a Fellow of Branford College, sponsored no doubt by Dean Mendell, the College's first Master, my first reference to Knox in my diary is to his being a Fellow of the College "and quite a fellow." As I already knew both Dean Mendell and Professor Hendrickson and was much interested in ancient Greek literature, I found I had much in common with Bernard, and I came to admire him greatly both as a scholar and as a person.

A few weeks after I first met Bernard, I took the Knoxes and some others to a Chinese dinner (their first, I believe) and to Sartre's *Les Mains Sales* (Englished as Red Gloves); after that we became well acquainted and saw each other again and again. In particular I was deeply impressed by his lectures and then by his books on Greek drama, especially Sophokles; one of my prized possessions is a copy of his book *Oedipus at Thebes*, with his inscription to me "whose knowledge of the arts makes me regret my ignorance of the sciences." On several occasions also the Knoxes fed me books to read; e.g., Baudelaire, Lorca, and a very witty novel (in Spanish) about how the "Good Neighbor Policy" went over in Peru.

As time went on I learned of Betty Knox's novels and short stories (published under other names) and read them with much interest. Mrs. Knox is American, but they had met at Cambridge; after he returned, wounded, from Spain, they came back to the United States and were married. When the United States entered the War, Bernard, though still a British citizen, volunteered for the American Army; in view of his very fluent French, he was dropped behind the German lines in northern France at the time of the Normandy invasion — it was this service that earned him U. S. citizenship. Bernard and his wife went to Europe for a term or so on several occasions, to Italy, England, and Greece. One term (1957), when Mrs. Knox and their son were in England, the son being in school there, Bernard moved into my back bedroom, and of course we often went together to lectures, plays, concerts, and parties, especially parties. Another term, when he was in Greece, I squired Mrs. Knox to several concerts and the like.

About 1960 Harvard received a gift to enrich its Classics program, and Bernard served on a committee to decide how to use the money. He made a very strong case for an Institute where Classics scholars could work together unhindered by classwork and so forth; Harvard accepted the idea and created the Institute for Hellenic Studies in Washington, D. C., and then persuaded Professor Knox to accept the post of Director. The Institute was set up on lovely grounds next the Naval Observatory, and he moved there from Yale in 1962. We were all very sorry to see them go, but I had the chance to visit them there several times.

The Conklin Family — George and Anne Conklin

My father bought for a summer place the cottage on Eagle Lake in the Adirondacks where he and my mother had gone for their honeymoon fourteen years earlier. I spent some fifteen summers there while I was growing up and going to college; indeed I did the field work for my Master's thesis at Cornell while staying there. Eagle Lake is not large, three miles long and up to half a mile wide, and only a few more than a dozen families had summer places there. Naturally we came to know most of those families well; the grownups and their growing children used to meet very often to swim or boat, to go for hikes, little or big, in the surrounding mountains, and for parties; each family would give parties and invite the others. There were many children in these families, one fairly large group about the age of my older brothers and a smaller, younger group to which I and my sister belonged; sometimes we were accepted by the older group, but sometimes they thought of us as a nuisance.

Two of these families were especially close to ours — the Lodge family, whose cottage was the next one to ours on the north side of the lake, away from the main road, and the Conklin family, whose cottage was on an island halfway across the lake directly in front of ours. The Lodges lived in Albany, so we saw them also during the rest of the year; the Conklins lived in Santa Barbara, so we saw them only in the summer. Each family had three brothers and a younger sister; the Lodges also had an older sister, Gladys. I and the three younger sisters belonged to the younger age group, though Doris Lodge was just old enough, or sophisticated enough, to be accepted into the older group. The first wedding I ever attended was that of the oldest Conklin son, Charles, held on the island.

Mr. Conklin was especially good to me, for he permitted, and indeed encouraged, me to practice the piano on the second floor of his mainland boathouse, a necessary adjunct to the island but not much frequented, so that my practicing rarely disturbed anyone else. During several summers I practiced there for three hours nearly every morning, and what piano technique I have I acquired during those summers.

After I went to work for the U. S. Geological Survey, first in the summers and then steadily, I got to Eagle Lake only for a few days, if at all, in the summer; hence I saw little of the members of the other "Lake" families. On one trip to Washington in those years, I spent most of a weekend with the senior Conklins, their second son George, "very handsome in his white summer uniform," and their daughter Margaret.

In 1949, by which time I was on the Yale faculty, I made contact with George Conklin, who by then was an architect practicing in Hartford and living with his wife Anne and their two daughters in a village west of the city. I went to visit him a few times, and one time I saw his parents and his sister Margaret there.

In 1952 George Conklin moved with his family to New Haven, and he designed and built a home in the suburbs; soon we began to invite each other quite often for dinners and to theatre and other parties. It was evident from the first that George, Anne, and I were compatible; we greatly

FIG. 6–14. *Jane (Mrs. Prentice J.) Rodgers, John Rodgers, and Anne (Mrs. George W.) Conklin; taken by George W. Conklin at a restaurant in Guadalajara, Mexico, February 1988.*

enjoyed one another's company, and conversation was spontaneous and delightful. Whenever my father and mother came down from Albany to see me, we would call on the Conklins; at a party I arranged for my father's 75th birthday, I had them come too, as a surprise for him. Similarly, when my brothers and sister came to New Haven, we would go to see the Conklins. Then there were the weddings of their two daughters in 1968 and 1970; my brother Prentice and his wife Jane came down for the latter. I saw the Conklins also at Eagle Lake whenever I went up during the summer to visit my parents there, until my father's death in 1957 after which my mother sold our cottage.

Already in 1963 I learned that Anne Conklin was an artist, for I attended "a small art show for beginners" that included her work. She specialized in metal sculpture; often she just took pieces of junk metal from the dump and converted them into sculptures of animals. At a show of her work in 1976, I became entranced with a "Family Conclave" of birds made out of old gutter supports mounted on metal "twigs," and I bought it; later I bought three other clever pieces of hers, e.g., a turtle made from an old stove door. At that show I also bought a painting by George of a beach in Costa Rica, where they used to go for winter vacations.

About 1980 George Conklin built a new summer place on a point on the south (road) side of Eagle Lake; the island house passed to his oldest brother Charles but later it burned down. Beginning already that year they encouraged me to come visit them there, and it wasn't long before I was going up for a few days every summer. Very often we would go on automobile rides around the Adirondacks — e.g., Keene Valley, Elk Lake, Long Lake — and sometimes over into Vermont, to Middlebury and vicinity; some of the earlier years we would also take a short hike or two. Several times I was able to visit our old cottage on the other shore; the Thompsons, who'd bought it from my mother, loved it as much as we did, and I was happy to see the way they kept improving it over the years.

About the time my brother Prentice retired, in the late 70s, he acquired a second home at Ajijic, a sort of resort village on Mexico's largest lake, Chapala, south of Guadalajara; soon I got the habit of visiting him and Jane there from time to time. After his death in 1980, she continued to live there much of the year, though she kept their place near Albany. Several summers also she came up with me to visit the Conklins on Eagle Lake; the four of us hit it off exceedingly well. In June 1986 she arranged for George and his family to use the place in Ajijic for a vacation; while there, George painted a picture of the view over the lake. When I saw that painting at the Conklin art show the next year, I bought it and, when I took Jane to the closing day of that show, I gave it to her as a birthday present. Then early in 1988 she had George, Anne, and me come to Ajijic for nearly two weeks, and we had a glorious time together. A week after we came north, she came back to Albany for an operation on her hip; a few days later she died in the hospital of a heart attack. It was a terrible shock for the Conklins and me, so soon after our happy days in Ajijic.

When my nephew Jonathan (see below) came to New Haven, first in the 70s as a graduate student, then in the 80s on the staff of the Yale Library, of course I introduced him and his wife Anala to our old family friends, the Conklins. Often during those years we would go to dinner or a party there, or we would have them come to our party. Much of that time I still drove my own car; after I sold it I used to rent a car for trips, as when I took my sister Louise along on my visits to the Conklins at Eagle Lake in 1993 and 1994 (in 1993 I visited them at the Lake three times!). But after a bad fall early in 1995, I gave up driving. The next three summers, however, Jonathan drove east from Michigan to New Haven, where he commonly had library business, and kindly took me up there to visit them. It turned out that Jonathan fit as neatly into our happy group as had his mother Jane.

7 — Abroad

The International Geological Congress of 1948 in Great Britain

In the summer of 1933, after my Freshman year at Cornell, the International Geological Congress met in the United States; there were field trips all over the country, and a set of thirty guidebooks was published for them. I knew about the Congress, for Dr. Hartnagel was leading an excursion to see the classical stratigraphy of New York State; I asked if I could go along, but I was strongly discouraged. Instead I went to Nevin's summer camp in Pennsylvania, which at that time made a much more useful part of my education. I did buy the complete set of guidebooks, however, and I read them all through with care; reading them gave me a thorough grounding in the geology of the United States. As a beginning college student I may not have understood all I read, but that reading put me far ahead of most of my fellow Geology majors, an unfair advantage no doubt but one I exploited fully.

In 1937, the Congress met in the Soviet Union; despite vague thoughts of going, I made no effort to do so, for I was to spend the summer working for the U. S. Geological Survey, the summer job that never came off. Professor Dunbar did go; he had a splendid and fruitful time, he came to know and admire, and be admired by, outstanding Soviet geologists and paleontologists, and he returned enthusiastic about the Soviet Union, at a time when that was by no means a popular point of view. In terms of American politics, Dunbar was a "rock-ribbed Republican from Kansas," and his enthusiasm for the Soviet Union was incongruous, but he never wavered in it; he often gave lectures, both academic and "popular," trying to overcome the then-current attitude of suspicion. During the McCarthy epoch in the early 50s, many of us were worried that Dunbar, in view of his open advocacy of the Soviet Union, would be seriously hurt, but apparently Senator McCarthy had the fixed idea that the Harvard faculty were the dangerous "pinkoes" and that Yale blues needed no investigation.

The next International Geological Congress was to have been in Great Britain in 1940 or 1941, but the Second World War intervened. After the War, despite the economic difficulties, the English and Scotch geologists decided to convene the Congress in 1948, and this time I arranged to go, signing up for one excursion in northwest Scotland in August and one in southern Wales in September. Both were splendid experiences, during which I not only saw new and fascinating geology but came to know (and be known by) some outstanding European geologists, with many of whom I kept in contact for the rest of our lives.

A major goal of our trip in Scotland was to see the Moine thrust in the Northwest Highlands, one of the first major "overthrusts" to be worked out in the later nineteenth century; another such thrust fault worked out at that time was in the mountains of Sweden and Norway. Along the Moine thrust medium-grade metamorphic rocks, rocks that had been subject to metamorphic heat and pressure well down in the Earth, had been pushed from the southeast up on top of sedimentary rock strata formed at the surface of the Earth and never deeply buried; the contact is reasonably sharp though marked in places by a small thickness of crushed, milled-down rock (mylonite) that formed as the one rock body was pushed over the other. Moreover the volumes of rock involved are huge; the upper rock body cannot be less than kilometers thick, tens of kilometers wide, and hundreds of kilometers long in the north-northeast—south-southwest dimension.

To see the evidence for this colossal displacement was one major purpose of the excursion, but I was also deeply interested in the sedimentary strata below, for I already knew that their fossils were very much like those of the same age in certain places in eastern North America, as in northwestern Newfoundland, in the Champlain Valley, and elsewhere in the western Appalachians; I had worked in the latter regions. When I got to see them, I found that not only the fossils but the rock types and even the succession of strata were remarkably like those I knew in the eastern United States. Thus I was brought back to the hypothesis of Continental Drift which, as I have mentioned, was generally denigrated, when not ridiculed, by most of the older geologists I knew, except for Nevin who never let us simply dismiss the hypothesis or ignore the evidence that seemed to support it.

It was on this excursion that I met Richard McConnell, a geologist working for the British Colonial Surveys; at that time he was working in Tanganyika. We hit it off well; we even broke off from the main party a couple of times to see more geology or just to climb the nearby mountain, Ben More Assynt. A decade later, when he was Director of the Geological Survey of British Guiana, we collaborated on a short paper on stratigraphic terminology.

The post-Congress excursion in Wales was equally fruitful, for we saw many "classical" localities of lower Paleozoic strata of the same age as those I had studied in the United States, although in this case not much like them in rock type; they are more like some in eastern New England and Maritime Canada, with which I was then unfamiliar.

On this excursion I became friendly with a young Welshman named David Evans who was in general charge of the arrangements for the trip. When we moved from Fishguard in southwestern Wales to Builth Wells in east-central Wales, it turned out that the hotel had slightly underestimated the number in our party, and it became necessary for a couple of geologists to share a bed. Evans asked two Britishers to do so, but one of them, an ardent Scotch nationalist named Archie Lamont (accent on the a), refused on the ground that he was as much a foreigner as "that young American whippersnapper who calls himself a Professor" — me, for at that time I held the title of Assistant Professor, a title not used in Britain. Evans therefore came to me and asked me to double up for a couple of nights with a young British paleontologist who was to show us his work the next day. That was how I became acquainted with the outstanding British geologist and paleontologist Alwyn Williams, and I am really grateful to Lamont for his unpleasant intransigence. The next morning, when I came down with my geological hammer in my belt, the hotel clerk told me it was a good thing I hadn't had it on me the night before; "I would have beaned the fellow," he said. After the two nights, Williams flew to the United States to work with G. Arthur Cooper, the well known American paleontologist.

Years later David Evans became the Lord Energlyn.

Another good turn Lamont unwittingly did me by his attitude was to bring me to the favorable attention of the two leaders of the second half of the excursion, who were joining us just then: Professor Owen T. Jones of Cambridge University and Professor William J. Pugh of the University of Manchester. Professor Pugh later became the Director of the Geological Survey of Great Britain, and Professor Jones was one of the absolute leaders of British geology at that time and had been chosen to give one of the two principal addresses at the immediately preceding Congress in London. Moreover, he had other quarrels with Lamont, so he was very friendly to me; indeed, our talks led to his submitting a major article for publication in the *American Journal of Science*, of which I was just becoming Assistant Editor. Thank you, Archie Lamont!

All in all the London Congress and its field excursions were so valuable for me, both for the geology I saw and for the geologists I met, that I vowed to attend every succeeding Congress as long as I could, and I did so, going to every Congress from 1948 to 1992, twelve in all — Great Britain, (French) North Africa, Mexico, Scandinavia, India, Czechoslovakia, Canada, Australia, France (and western Europe in general), the Soviet Union, the United States, and Japan. The international exposure these trips gave me also opened the way for many other trips, and I can now say that I have studied mountain ranges on every continent; I have

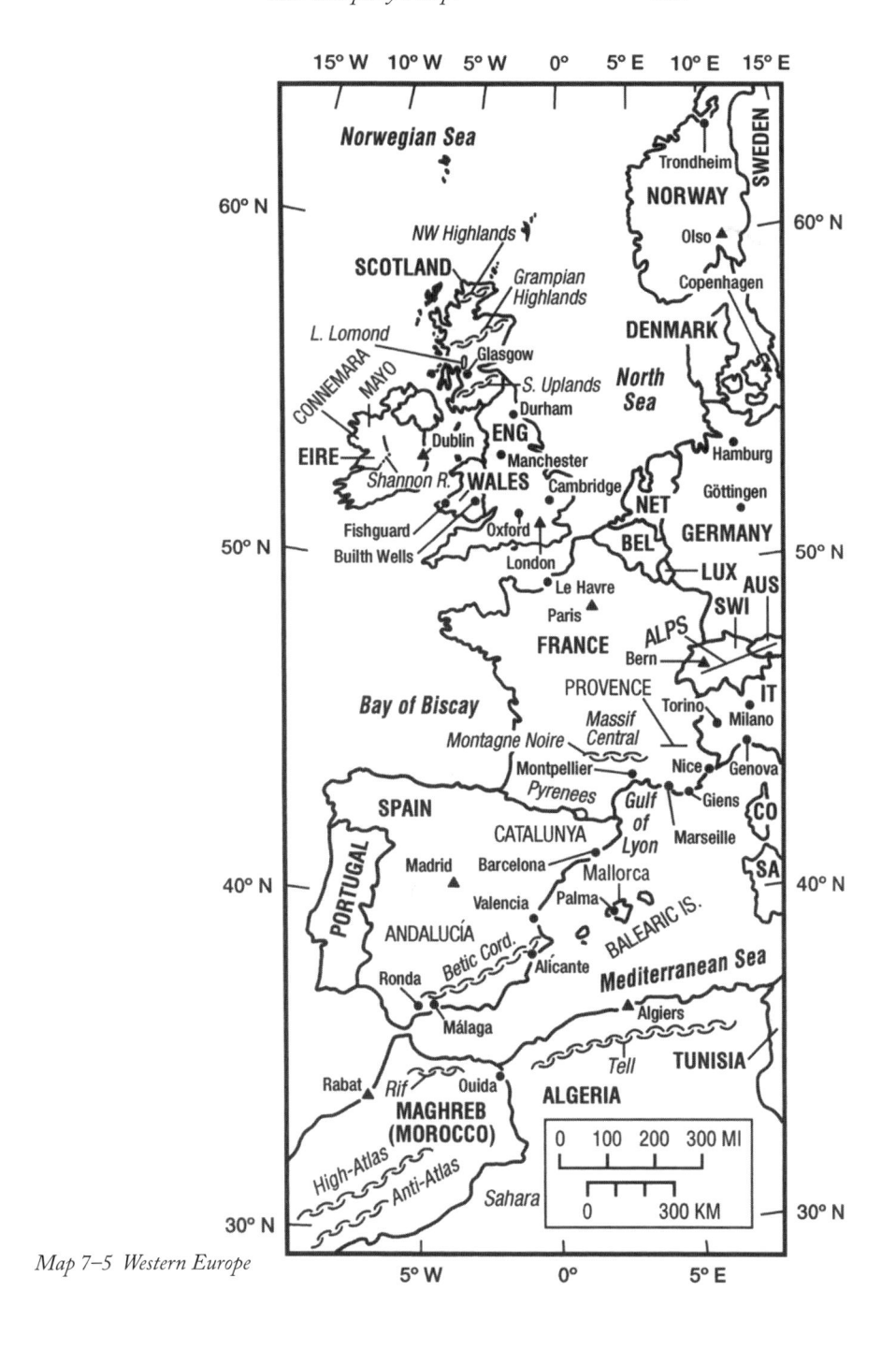

Map 7–5 Western Europe

also been able to write a series of synthetic articles on different kinds of geological (mountain) structures in all parts of the globe.

Ulbo de Sitter

I first met Professor Ulbo de Sitter, of the University of Leiden in The Netherlands, on the excursion I took in Wales following the International Geological Congress in London in 1948. Our geological styles are a lot alike, we hit it off well, and soon we were corresponding and exchanging reprints. We met again at the International Congress in Algiers in 1952, and indeed he and Professor Fallot urged me to join them in preparing an international lexicon of tectonics, covering the English or at least the American language part, but I never got deep into that project.

After the Mexican Congress in 1956, we invited Professor de Sitter to come to New Haven. He gave us a lecture comparing the Alps, the Pyrenees, and the High Atlas, a chapter from the book on structural geology he had recently published, and I took him to see some of Connecticut's geology. On that trip he had some difficulty understanding how some of us American geologists, like John Rosenfeld, who led us for a day, and myself, can consider the deformation of the rocks — structural geology — and their mineral content — metamorphic petrology — like two sides of the same coin. In Europe at that time, I guess, the two subjects were completely separated; indeed they were commonly taught by different geological Institutes in each university.

After the 1960 Congress in Copenhagen, Professor de Sitter and I both took the fine excursion across the mountains of Sweden and Norway, from Östersund to Trondheim. His wife came with him on all these excursions; on this one, as we were going up one of the high mountains in Sweden by funicular and ski-lift, she and I rode up together in a ski-lift cabin, and Professor de Sitter on the ground below put on a lovely show as the outraged husband.

Getting to North Africa in 1952

On my field trip in Scotland in 1948, before the International Geological Congress in London, there were ten geologists from seven countries; two of them, Professor Elie Gagnebin of Lausanne and Dr. Georges Choubert from (then French) Morocco, spoke virtually no English, expecting to be able to get along in French. As the British geolo-

FIG. 7–15. *Field excursion in Wales, September 1948, after International Geological Congress in London, photo by John Temple. Left to right: Fru de Sitter, Prof. Ulbo de Sitter, Prof. O. T. Jones, Prof. W. J. Pugh, John Rodgers*

gist Richard McConnell had taken his doctorate with Professors Lugeon and Gagnebin at Lausanne, he was in fact an excellent interpreter, but I observed that, while he was interpreting for them, many other things were being discussed in English, and I estimated that they missed perhaps 75% of what was going on. As I had vowed to attend every subsequent Congress if I could, and as the next one was scheduled for 1952 in (then French) North Africa, I made up my mind to be fluent in French by the time I got there. I worked quite hard at it during those four years; by the time I was ready to go, I was almost fluent enough.

In 1952 then, I made my preparations to attend that Congress, which was held in Algiers, and — even more important — excursions before and after. This was my first trip to the continents of Europe (indeed Eurasia) and Africa. In 1945 and 1946 I had visited Japan, the Ryukyu Islands, and the Philippines but hadn't seen the Asian continent (there had been talk of my going on a mission to Korea, but nothing came of it). During the London Congress in 1948, I had been taken to the cliffs of Dover, but it was a very hazy day and I never saw the French coast. Thus, the typical thalassocrat, I had crossed both the big oceans but never seen the big continent. This year however I was to remedy that lack.

I prepared conscientiously, indeed perhaps too much so, taking good new store clothes for the Congress itself and good old field clothes for the excursions, the latter with my field equipment in a big duffel bag; I also had a shiny new briefcase for my papers. To get started in French, I scheduled my trans-Atlantic flight on Air France and had a delightful flight with a fine French dinner (and much alcohol; I was in fact quite sick before morning), and we arrived at the Orly airport. My flight to Algiers left from Le Bourget, but I had more than twenty-four hours in Paris between; that was my first visit there and I had a fine time, running into an old friend, John Cady, at le Café de la Paix and seeing *Carmen* at l'Opéra Comique.

The next day, when I came to the air terminal at les Invalides, the clerk asked me for my bags; I told him they had been checked through to Algiers, but he refused to believe me. I had started to talk to him in French, and we carried on the whole argument in that language; he knew perfectly well that I was Anglophone and I that he was fluent in English, but I stuck stubbornly to French, and he followed suit. As it happened I won the argument, for I spotted the bags standing a few meters behind him; he was quite annoyed.

At Le Bourget, however, we had to wait three hours beyond schedule "for technical reasons;" we could see the mechanics out on the runway "twisting the tail" of one of the plane's motors. Finally we got going, and I was seated in a window seat, for I always choose them if I can, looking directly out at that motor. A little after we got started, it began to backfire and they throttled it down; soon the copilot came out, sat in the empty seat beside me, and stared at it; then, smiling suavely, he went back to the cockpit. The other three motors were enough, however, and we arrived at the airport for Algiers, which is near the shore east of the city.

In Paris I had bought a *Guide Bleu* for North Africa, the French equivalent to a German *Baedeker*, and I had been studying it during our delay in Paris and on the flight. Algiers is built mainly on and to the east of a point projecting into the Mediterranean, on steep slopes falling off to the shore; as we approached it from the north, its lights made a beautiful sight. Back in New Haven, when the travel agent and I were arranging the trip and were trying to decide between the two best hotels in the city, we had chosen the St.-George over the Aletti because it had more rooms. Now I learned that the Aletti is close to the shore in the center of town, whereas the St.-George is on the bluff three kilometers east of the center. Moreover we should have arrived about seven in the evening, and it was now past ten. The bus from the airport brought us into town and, behold, the air terminal was *in* the Hotel Aletti. The temptation was strong to forget the (paid-for) reservation at the St.-George and stay at the Aletti, but I am Scotch and I didn't yield to temptation. Several Arab or Berber boys were milling around the baggage yelling: "bagage," "taxi;" I chose one of them, pointed out my bags, a valise and the duffel bag, and said, in as good a French accent as I could muster: "Taxi à l'Hôtel St.-George." He picked them up and, putting the heavy duffel bag on his shoulder, started off into the street. There were several taxis just outside the terminal, but he ignored them and kept on to the foot of the slope, turning onto a street diagonally up to the left. There was one car on that street, but he went right on by it and kept walking uphill.

What was I to do? At least he was heading uphill to the left toward the better part of town, not to the right toward the Casbah, the slums of Algiers, but surely he wasn't going to walk three kilometers uphill with that heavy duffel bag on his shoulder. I was far too well dressed, in a new summer suit and with a brand new briefcase; the mere fact that I wanted to go to the Hotel St.-George marked me as a rich Englishman or American and, the minute I opened my mouth, my weak French would show. The streets were almost empty, though at least brightly lighted; we passed two men at a sidewalk bar, and I seemed to detect a wondering, and sardonic, gaze. He kept on for five or six blocks, sometimes turning up steps, then back on diagonal streets, but always up to the left. Then, suddenly, he turned into a brightly lighted hotel lobby, and the clerk immediately pushed the registration card toward me, saying (in English; he had spotted me all right): "Won't Monsieur register?" Clearly the boy was a runner for that hotel, engaged to bring people there whether that was where they wanted to go or not.

The first thing I did was to tip the boy liberally — in French francs instead of Algerian, but they were equal in value then, and he didn't seem to mind — and watch him disappear into the night; the second was to abandon the French language. It was a perfectly good hotel, as I found out later, and I could have stayed there, but my Scotch was up, and I explained to the clerk that there'd been a mistake and what I really wanted was a *taxi* to the Hotel St.-George. After a bit he got me one; the taxi driver seated me inside but put the cylindrical duffel bag on top of the cab. As we went along, every so often he would put his hand up to feel if it was still there, but it didn't roll off, and in due course we turned into the grounds of the St.-George. The taxi driver cheated me on the fare, but at that point I hardly cared. My registration was perfectly in order, so I registered and went to my room and to bed, but I was pumped so full of adrenalin that I doubt if I slept a minute all night.

I had all the next day in Algiers before I was scheduled to take my train to Morocco to join my first excursion. In the morning I went downtown (too well dressed) to find out what I could about the Congress, but nothing seemed to be open yet. In the afternoon I dressed down and took a long walk along a high boulevard with fine views over the city and the sea, as far as the upper edge of the Casbah, the old citadel on the projecting point, then down along its edge to the shore. As I walked past the Hotel Aletti, I saw my boy of the previous night sitting on the curbstone;

I walked within three meters of him, but he never recognized me. It had been dark after all, and I had walked behind him all the way.

Bernard Gèze (1913-1996)

After Algiers, anticlimactically, things went very smoothly. I enjoyed the train trip from Algiers to Oujda in eastern Morocco, where our excursion was gathering. There I met the leaders and members of our excursion, also people who were there to join other excursions. One of them, Willem van Leckwijck, a Belgian geologist whom I had met on my excursion in Wales in 1948, said to me, anent ours: "Vous verrez la tectonique de boue (you will see the tectonics of mud)." For that, and for what it taught me, see my article on Exotic Nappes: *American Journal of Science*, v. 297, p. 174-219, 1997.

On our excursion we saw the geology of the Rif, the mountain range in northern Morocco, at that time partitioned between French and Spanish zones, in theory protectorates of the Moroccan monarchy. Only five geologists had signed up to take the excursion — Professor Voigt from the University of Hamburg, who talked good French, three French geologists, and myself — but they ran the excursion anyway. It was run entirely in French; as we went along we had from four to eight guides, all French except for Spaniards who joined us in the Spanish zone. Thus I had a splendid opportunity to practice my own French; it had been almost good enough when I arrived, and within a few days it was quite satisfactory and I could hold my own in geological arguments, though I had more trouble when the subject was politics or people.

Two of the French geologists taking the trip made little or no concession to my weak French — if I couldn't follow their rapid French, so much the worse for me — but the third, Professor Bernard Gèze of l'Institut National Agronomique at Paris, was careful and thoughtful all during the trip, and I came to like and admire him very much.

After I got home from the Congress, I sent Professor Gèze a considerable batch of reprints of my articles and, after it appeared the next year, my map and report on East Tennessee; in return he sent me his massive memoir on la Montagne Noire, a range of hills along the southern margin of the French Massif Central north of the low corridor that runs, just north of the Pyrenees, from the Atlantic (Bay of Biscay) to the Mediterranean (Gulf of Lyon). His memoir had marked a major advance in French structural geology, indeed in some respects in European structural geology, an advance with which I was fully in sympathy.

That memoir had been his doctoral dissertation, and the field work had been done during the German occupation of France in the Second World War. Gèze had been an officer in the French Army, I think a Lieutenant, and was stationed in the Maginot Line during the War's first winter, what was sometimes called the "phony war," though it was anything but phony for Poland. Being a geologist, Gèze looked into the geology underlying the forts of the Maginot Line, and he found that beneath it were seams of iron ore, some of them mined, that sloped down from their outcrops in Germany beneath the line into France. He made an effort to bring this situation to the attention of his superior officers, but they showed no interest and apparently resented his intervention; they knew already that the French Army was the best in the world and wanted no questions asked. Gèze realized, therefore, that with such an attitude the War was already lost; when the Germans broke through and the French Army in effect dissolved, he found his way back to the south of France, whence he came. He spent the rest of the War doing field work for his dissertation, using a bicycle to get around.

The next time I met Gèze was at the next International Geological Congress in Ciudad México in 1956; we took the same excursion after the Congress, to the State of Chiapas in southeastern Mexico on the Guatemalan border. On that occasion we got to the border where the Pan-American Highway was to cross it; the Mexican part was already completed, but the Guatemalan part was unfinished because of bad landsliding just beyond. When we got there, we excursionists all walked right across, to be able to say we'd been in Guatemala; the Guatemalan border guards were quite upset by this international invasion, but our Mexican guides persuaded them that we meant no harm. As Gèze was the only Francophone on that excursion, I offered to room with him so that he would have someone with whom to talk French (although my French had slipped since North Africa while I worked on my Spanish). Thus again I saw a good deal of him, and again I found I liked and admired him.

In June 1959, when I arrived in Paris at the start of my sabbatical year devoted to studying the Alps from stem to stern, from Nice to Vienna, I met Gèze again, and we began making plans for him to show me his field areas in la Montagne Noire and near Nice in the Maritime Alps the following spring. I spent that winter, November to March, in Paris, and I saw Gèze a number of times. On one occasion he took me on a student field trip into the region around Paris, and the students on that trip taught me a little phrase by which to remember the names of the stages of strata in the Paris Basin: "Ménagez tes seins, Yvonne; l'amant brutal les secoue sans cesse aujourd'hui." Then in late April, after my trips to the Betic

Cordillera in southern Spain, to Mallorca in the Balearics, and to the central Apennines near Rome, we met in Montpellier in southern France for a week's field trip in "his" Montagne Noire; up to ten other French geologists were with us on that trip, though not all at the same time.

Gèze had shown, to the satisfaction of most geologists except for certain conservatives, that the structure in la Montagne Noire is nappe tectonics; that is to say, a large mass of originally flat, upright, rock strata there is now entirely upside down. An analogy would be if a pile of rugs on a floor had been pushed from the side until a large fold arose in the middle of it and then flopped over on one side, tripling its thickness and turning the middle rugs upside down. According to Gèze's hypothesis, however, the mass of overturned strata is kilometers thick and the east-west-trending overturned strip tens of kilometers wide and hundreds of kilometers long; in view of these dimensions one can understand the conservative objections, but Gèze's evidence was convincing to most of us. Note the similarity in dimensions to the block above the Moine thrust fault in northwest Scotland; it is no coincidence. But a big question remained, whether the fold had flopped over to the north or to the south; Gèze thought it was to the north, but two other very able structural geologists, both friends whom I highly respected, Rudolf Trümpy from Switzerland and Ulbo de Sitter from The Netherlands, suggested it was to the south. Indeed the three of them published (in French) a joint ar-

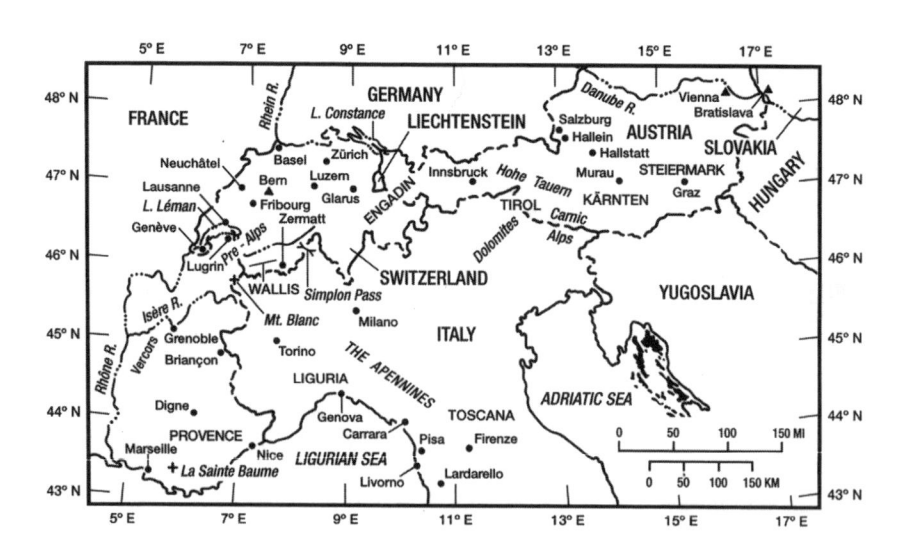

MAP 7–6. *The Alps and Surrounding Regions*

ticle setting forth the facts and the two different hypotheses, an article that has always been for me a salutary model of how to conduct a scientific controversy in a truly friendly spirit (*Société Géologique de France Bulletin*, 6e sér., v. 2, p. 491-535).

Naturally these questions were a main subject of our excursion. Gèze had based his hypothesis on the inverted order of the larger units of strata compared to their known order elsewhere, and one of the younger men on the trip, Maurice Mattauer, who later became very well known and influential in French geology, had already shown that minor features of the strata entirely confirmed the Gèze hypothesis. On the trip I was able to point out structural evidence, the shape and orientation of minor folds, that strongly favored the view that the fold flopped over to the south. At that time, structural evidence of that sort was being largely discounted in French geology, on the grounds that it led to contradictions, but I was able to convince them, especially the younger geologists on the trip, that the contradictions were spurious. Indeed, after that I wrote an article in French, with help from friends, setting forth the proper use of such evidence in structural geology, and it was published in a volume of articles dedicated to Professor Paul Fallot — intended as a Jubilee volume for his retirement but actually a Memorial after his death. I think I can say that this article had considerable influence in France; several younger men, not just those on that trip, have told me it led to a major shift in French structural geology, helping to bring it back into the forefront of modern thinking on the subject.

After that trip, Gèze, I, and some others went east into Provence, and they showed me some very spectacular geology, especially that around the great ridge of la Sainte-Baume. We also visited the dam at Fréjus, which had failed the preceding winter when its reservoir first filled up, causing a very destructive flood that devastated the town of Fréjus. It was clear to us that it was not the dam itself that failed but the foundation beneath; the foundation rock was badly weathered — rotten, one might say — and unable to support the weight of the water as it accumulated. The geologists responsible had not investigated the foundation carefully enough. We came on to Nice, where we met a student excursion from Paris and Montpellier and toured the region west and north of Nice for a week, partly in the mountains of Provence and partly in the Maritime Alps. The major interest on this trip was Gèze's evidence that the folding or deformation of the strata in the "arc of Nice" is geologically recent, certainly within the last million years and perhaps still going on; strata that had "recently" been deposited flat in lakes dammed behind rising folds are now themselves somewhat tilted.

In the following years I met Gèze a number of times in Paris from 1962 to 1988, also at the International Geological Congress in India in 1964, where we met while visiting the Red Fort in Delhi. In 1968 we met again during the first two days of the ill-fated Congress in Praha (Prague), before the tanks of the Warsaw Powers came in. Then in Vienna, the day after I got out of Praha, I unexpectedly ran into the Gèze family, who had driven out the day before; they were planning to return by Italy to the south of France, and they at once invited me to come with them. I would gladly have done so, but we quickly found that my good-sized suitcase was too big to fit into their small car with themselves and their baggage, so I regretfully saw them off and returned directly to the United States.

Paul Fallot (1890-1960)

Toward the end of the Rif excursion in 1952, when we came to the Spanish zone of Morocco, we were greeted by an older Spanish geologist, Sr. Augustín Marín, but our real guide there was Paul Fallot, Professor at le Collège de France in Paris yet so fluent in Spanish, and so fond of Spain, that he was accepted by the Spanish geologists as one of their own. He was with us for the rest of the trip, and I also saw him several times at the Congress in Algiers. In my diary for the trip I wrote of him: "Very much my ideal of a field geologist."

To be Professor at le Collège de France, in whatever subject, is one of the highest distinctions in French academic life. When in the early sixteenth century Francis I, the Renaissance King of France, and his court wanted to study the new learning coming out of Italy, they found that the scholastics at la Sorbonne, l'Université de Paris, had neither knowledge of nor interest in it. To fill the gap, Francis I established le Collège du Roi, whose Professors were required only to present each year a course of lectures on some aspect of the new Renaissance learning, lectures that would be open to anyone who cared to attend. No grades or degrees were to be issued; the professors could take students if they chose, but the students would have to obtain degrees at the University. Le Collège still exists; at the time of the Revolution its name was changed to le Collège de France, but its regulations and purpose remained the same. It was in this institution that Paul Fallot was Professor.

About 1957 I began to make plans for my first sabbatical year at Yale; by then I was fairly familiar with the Appalachian Mountain range in eastern North America, and I decided to study another well known mountain range, the Alps of Europe. I arranged for an NSF Senior Post-

Doctoral Fellowship to support me for the year 1959-60; then I wrote to Professor Fallot, asking him if he would be willing to accept me in his laboratory at le Collège and would perhaps help me plan my trip, for I knew that he was well known to and highly respected by all the leading Alpine geologists, French, Swiss, and Austrian. He replied enthusiastically, and soon he had put me in touch with a whole series of leading geologists, just how stellar a group I came to understand after I'd been in the field with them all. Furthermore he proposed that I give a series of "leçons" at le Collège, an extraordinary honor for a non-Francophone foreigner. We wrote back and forth, and soon it was agreed that I would give eight lectures in January and February 1960 on the Tectonics of the Appalachian Mountains.

I arrived in Europe in June 1959, picking up my new Volkswagen camper on the dock at Le Havre and driving to Paris, where Professor Fallot installed me in his laboratory. Then I began the long series of Alpine excursions that he had arranged. I started in Grenoble, one of the two university cities that is actually within the Alps (the other is Innsbruck), and that summer I was passed along from leading geologist to leading geologist all the way to Vienna in Austria. In October I drove back by way of northern Italy; that the summer was over was proved when I found the St. Gotthard Pass closed by snow and had to take the train through the tunnel underneath, ignominiously sitting in my camper chained onto a flat-car.

I was in Paris from the end of October to March, and naturally I saw a great deal of Professor Fallot. I attended his course of lectures at le Collège; this was his final series before retirement, and he used it for a summary of the geology and tectonics of the Western Mediterranean from the Alps to the Atlas. Also I quickly got into the habit of going to the weekly meetings of la Société Géologique de France in its rather cramped quarters on la Rue Serpente not far away; only considerably later did the Society move into its present quarters in la Maison de Géologie. There was a considerable protocol to the seating arrangements at these meetings; the major professors sat in the front rows, the young geologists listened from the back, and as a respected if young foreigner I sat in between. There were some very interesting talks at these meetings, and I continued to learn a lot. Soon I asked Professor Fallot whether I could become a member of the Society; he explained that I would need to have two parrains (godfathers), and he offered to be one and to ask Professor Pierre Pruvost of la Sorbonne, l'Université de Paris, whom I had already met, to be the other. I was very pleased, of course, for I couldn't have had two more illustrious godfathers, so I supplied him with the necessary data and left the papers with him, going regularly to the meetings.

The first meeting in January that year was the Annual Meeting; there was no geological lecture, but annual reports and so forth were to be read and the officers for the next year were to be elected. Not yet being a member, I didn't go but worked in the laboratory all afternoon. After the meeting when the boys came back to the lab, the minute they saw me they burst into laughter, saying, in French of course: "Ha, ha, ha; you were elected Vice-President!" I replied: "C'est une blague" — roughly: "You're pulling my leg" — but they kept on laughing and assuring me that I was indeed Vice-President. I worked out pretty well what had happened. The new President is always the previous year's First Vice President, unless he has died during the year, and the main question was whom to elect as the coming year's First Vice-President, but they also elected two other Vice-Presidents. One was to be Vice-Président pour les provinces; like everything else in France la Société Géologique is pretty much run in Paris, but this way the provinces would always be represented in the Society's Council. The other was to be Vice-Président pour l'Étranger, and they would elect a Belgian or a Swiss or an Italian or a Spaniard as a sort of honorary gesture (rarely did they elect a British or German). They were asking themselves whom to elect this year when someone suggested the young American in Fallot's lab, who spoke some French and would actually be on the ground and could attend Council meetings, and so they elected me. But then someone asked: "Is he a member yet?" and Pruvost spoke up to say that the papers were all ready and signed and that he had planned to bring them but had forgotten. He suggested they pretend he had done so and elect me anyway, and that was done; with parrains like Fallot and Pruvost no one was going to object. I got a nice letter from la Gérante, the lady who ran the office and indeed most of the Society's affairs, saying that at the Annual Meeting on such and such a date I had been elected Vice-President — so much was typed; then, in longhand - that at the same meeting I had been elected a member. From that time on I have always been able to consider myself a member of the French geological commnunity; the final confirmation came in 1987 when the Society awarded me its premier prize, le Prix Gaudry.

That January and February I gave my lectures on the Appalachians. I gave them in French; the first lecture was a bit shaky, but people were very nice about it and gave me courage to keep on. I got them into a good mood right at the start by telling them that there would be a sound they wouldn't recognize — i.e., the flat American r, so different from the trilled r of southern France or the uvular r of Paris — but that, if they heard such a sound, they were to remember that it represented the letter between q and s. Afterwards, to help me relax, Professor Fallot very kindly took me home to dinner, and we had a full evening of recordings of great music. I wrote out each of my lectures at the time I was giving it, and Fallot kindly corrected the French for me; then he had each lecture hectographed in 60 copies (hectographing was a means of reproducing typescript that preceded mimeographing). That French version was the embryo of my book, *The Tectonics of the Appalachians*, published in 1970.

In mid-March 1960 I started out on my travels again, but this time not to the Alps. I drove in my camper across France, around the west end of the Pyrenees, and across Spain to Madrid; there Fallot met me and introduced me to several Spanish geologists. Moreover Señor Almela, Director del Instituto geológico español, whom I had met in 1958 at a dinner at the Fallots, had us for dinner; that was set at 9:45 pm., unusually early as a special concession to us foreigners. From Madrid Fallot and I drove on south to Granada in Andalucía (where I got to see andalusite) and met Professor Fontboté, a Catalan who was then Professor at the University there; later he went back to Barcelona, where indeed he was Dean of the Faculty at the University. He showed us around that region, and we studied la Cordillera Bética as far west as Málaga, then east to Alicante — for me a very instructive tour, for Fallot knew it well. Then we came up the coast by Valencia to Barcelona, where he introduced me to Professor Solé-Sabarís, who also kindly had us for dinner.

I remember our conversation at that dinner particularly well, because it concerned the Catalan language and the status of Catalunya within Spain. At that time Spain was ruled by Generalissimo Franco, and the autonomy of Catalunya, granted by the Spanish Republic, had been revoked after the Spanish Civil War. I also remember the Good Friday religious procession in Barcelona, in which the Spanish Army, Navy, and Guardia Civil were all well represented, the iron hand in the none-too-velvet glove. Catalan newspapers, store signs, and radio broadcasts were all forbidden, but books could be published in Catalan; we were told that any book published in Catalan could count on 10,000 sales to loyal Catalans. Professor Fallot, who was quite conservative and strongly favored the Franco régime, was rather unhappy during this conversation, but I was entranced to learn so much. At another point in our trip, moreover, Professor Fallot asked me to explain American politics to him; that's no easy task, but I did so in terms of the six American Revolutions that I maintain have punctuated our history: 1775, 1800, 1828, 1860, 1896 (the last two were relative failures), and 1932 (certainly no failure); for these, see my article *The Seventh American Revolution: **Yale Review***, v. 57, p. 529-544, 1968. Naturally he didn't much like that either.

Professors Fallot and Solé-Sabarís kindly arranged for me to fly to Palma de Mallorca in the Balearic islands, and I had a fine trip there too in what is in effect the eastern termination of la Cordillera Bética. There

I had the delight of meeting and being shown around by Dr. Guilliermo Colom, an outstanding specialist in Cretaceous and Tertiary planktonic foraminifera; he also invited me to dinner in his home. Being Mallorquín, he talked the local Catalan dialect, plus Spanish and excellent French, but his wife came from Brooklyn and was happy to speak English, so we talked a wild mixture of the four languages.

During the last part of the trip in Spain, Professor Fallot developed serious lung trouble and had more and more difficulty breathing; he could no longer climb hills or even steep stairs. He was and had long been a chain-smoker but, as he was the first person I came to know with lung cancer, I didn't recognize the symptoms; I'm afraid I pushed him rather hard, but of course he too wanted to take part in all the geology. He left me to return to Paris on 10 April; I saw him a few times after I got back to France, but he died on 22 October. That my year's trip to Europe and the Alps was such a fantastic success I owe for the largest part to Professor Fallot; it was to him that I dedicated my Appalachian book, which arose out of the lectures he had me give in Paris.

The Later Fifties

8 — In North America

John P. Trinkaus - "Trink"

IN 1950 I WAS ASSIGNED to bring John Trinkaus, a young member of the Yale Biology Department, "around to lunch at the College to be looked over as a fellow, a painfully obvious procedure" as I wrote in my diary. He was duly appointed a Fellow, and we became good friends, along with others among the Branford Fellows, like Bernard Knox. Trink was always very lively and full of fun; in 1955 Keith Wilson, Director of the Yale Band (and also a Branford Fellow), had Trinkaus and Knox stage a "conducting contest" at a Band Pops concert (given mainly for the alumni) "with great gusto and hilarity."

The winter I was in Paris at le Collège de France (1959-1960), Trink was there too; we saw each other several times, and we came back on the same ship. It was in Paris that he met Madeleine, who became his second wife. In 1966 Trinkaus was appointed Master of Branford College, succeeding George Schrader, and Trink was Master for seven years. Trink's political views were always well to the left; when I got back from my five months in the Soviet Union in 1967, we had a long talk about it, and my diary records that "Trink is still pretty naïve and romantic about going there," while I was trying to make him see it more realistically.

Now it was precisely in the late 1960s that student unrest was rampant in American universities, and in several there were unpleasant confrontations between the students and the administration, the students often backed by many of the younger faculty. If things went better at Yale, it was in large part the work of Kingman Brewster, then Yale's President, who saw to it that communications were kept open and that people knew they could talk to him — and be heard.

The climax for Yale came in 1970, because New Haven had been picked for one of the four Black Panther trials that year — all the others were in much larger cities — and the students were deeply disturbed. They agitated to have classes suspended over 1 May, for a big demonstration was announced for that day and hundreds or even thousands of outside "visitors" were expected. I remember Brewster going so far as to say he questioned whether, in the prevailing mood of the country, the Panthers could get a fair trial. Conservatives among the faculty and the alumni were of course strongly opposed to any such suspension but, because communications were still open, a "compromise" was proposed and accepted; the principal architects were Brewster, aided by people like Trinkaus, and especially the young *black* faculty; the young white leftists, though they had expected to play a major role, were in fact quite ineffectual. It seemed to me at the time that both the extreme right and the extreme left were hoping for, and planning for, a violent, preferably bloody, showdown, but the students, freed of classes for those days, monitored and supervised the whole affair, and nothing violent happened, not even much "bloody" rhetoric.

Brewster came in for a good deal of criticism for his "compromising" attitude, though not from me, and afterwards he did seem somewhat more cautious. That may have been one of the reasons he didn't reappoint Trinkaus as Master of Branford in 1973; Trink was quite disappointed and unhappy about that. From then on my contacts with Trink and his wife Madeleine were pleasant but entirely social, mainly at parties and other affairs.

E-an Zen

Right after the Second World War, a number of bright young Chinese came to the United States to go to college. When in 1949 the Communists took over China, many of them decided to stay here rather than go back; a few preferred to go to Taiwan, where the previous Chinese government had set up shop. I came to know quite well two geologists in this group: Zen Ean and Xü Jinghua.

E-an Zen, as he has styled himself in this country, went to Cornell as an undergraduate, majoring in Geology, then to Harvard as a graduate student under Professor Marland Billings. I met him first in the summer of 1953 in his dissertation area around Lake Bomoseen, Vermont, and to the north and east, the northern end of the Taconic Mountains in the broad sense. By then I had finished working in East Tennessee and had come back north to work again in the southern Champlain Valley where I had mapped for my Master's thesis. Zen and I hit it off well and quickly became good friends, sharing our geological knowledge and also having similar tastes in, for example, music; we often visited each other in the field, and he came as a guest to our family's summer camp in the Adirondacks.

Before long my work in the Champlain Valley brought me into a small outlier of the northern Taconic Range, and I am sure my interpretation of the geology there was influenced by my knowing of Zen's work; to put it another way, I found that the hypotheses by which he explained the rock structure in his area also explained that in mine. Naturally I showed him what I was finding there, for we always shared knowledge and ideas freely.

It happened that a professor of geology at Laval University in the city of Québec, F. Fitz Osborne, had offered to run a field excursion for Professor Billings in the Eastern Townships of Québec province for a week in 1957, and both Zen and I were invited to come along. That trip was so successful that he ran another the next summer; at the end of that trip Zen and I took off on our own and drove all around the Gaspé Peninsula and even crossed the St. Lawrence River to see a bit of the Laurentian Mountains northeast of the city of Québec. During those trips the congruence of our ideas and of our personalities became clearer and clearer. Those trips were also very important for me, giving me a good start in understanding the Canadian Appalachians.

After completing his PhD at Harvard and teaching for a year in a college in North Carolina, Zen went to work for the U. S. Geological Survey, and soon he was involved in the geology of westernmost Massachusetts, in rocks like those I had worked in not only in the Champlain Valley but also nearer by in eastern New York in Mrs. Knopf's country, both with her and on my own. So again we had mutual interests and saw a great deal of each other.

During this period, perhaps under the influence of Senator McCarthy or others, the U. S. government decided to demand that every Chinese alien in the country declare for either the refugee Chinese government on Taiwan or the Communist government on the mainland. E-an's attitude was mainly "a plague on both your houses," but he had no use for the Taiwan group and declared for the real China on the mainland. The State Department wanted to deport him, but Professor Billings got many of us to write strong letters protesting; I was quite glad to write such a letter stating that Zen would certainly never "advocate the overthrow of the U. S. government by force or violence." He was allowed to stay, and a few years later he became a U. S. citizen.

In 1965 and 1966 E-an Zen, Jack Bird, and I made trips of a few days into areas of mutual in-

FIG. 8-16. *John Rodgers and Sidney Quarrier, Assistant State Geologist of Connecticut, at Gillette Castle, Connecticut, 6 June 1985, during a field trip for the meeting of the Association of American State Geologists at which the new geological map of Connecticut was presented.*

terest in northwestern Vermont and eastern New York. Those trips were seminal for me; from evidence I saw there I developed a new hypothesis about the relation of the Appalachian Mountains while they were being formed to the eastern edge of the continent of North America as it then existed. It was about this time that Zen and others put together the volume of articles about the geology of the northern Appalachian Mountains in honor of Professor Billings; I was asked to contribute an article for that volume, and I chose to write up my hypothesis about the former eastern edge of North America. It is I think one of my best papers; certainly it stirred up a lot of thinking and discussion by others, and it has been one of my most cited articles.

In 1968 I arranged for E-an Zen and Jack Bird to join me in Professor Andrusov's excursion through the Slovakian Carpathians, before the International Congress in Praha. How they got out of Praha after the tanks came in I don't know, but we met again at the NEIGC that October.

During the following years E-an Zen became more and more prominent in North American geology. We kept seeing each other on field excursions, at meetings of professional societies, and at *AJS* editors' meetings. He went on working for the U. S. Geological Survey; later he was appointed Professor at the University of Maryland, but he kept his connection with the Survey and ultimately returned there full time. In 1976 we were able to elect him to our National Academy of Sciences, and in 1991 he was elected President of the Geological Society of America.

Because of his work in western Massachusetts, Zen was named in the late 70s to a Survey committee to compile a new geological map of the State of Massachusetts, the first since 1917. At about the same time Connecticut too decided to compile a new state map, the first since 1906, and I was chosen to compile western Connecticut. As time went on, I was also asked to compile eastern Connecticut; in due course each of us became the chief compiler of our respective maps. We therefore met quite often to compare the maps and to ensure that they matched at the state boundary. At one of those meetings we made a bet on whose map would be published first; the loser was to treat the winner to a special ice-cream dish at an ice-cream parlor in Rutland, Vermont — i.e., neutral territory — that we both liked to visit. The dish, called a "pig's dinner", consisted of four scoops of different kinds of ice cream with four different sauces and was served in a little wooden trough. As regards the full-color maps of our states, Zen beat me by about two years, in part because my map was on a larger scale — 4 inches to the mile for me, 2 inches to the mile for him, but of course Massachusetts is the larger state — but a year or so ahead of his map I distributed a smaller-scale version of mine (an inch to the mile) in just red and black, as part of a field-trip guidebook. I therefore claimed that I'd won the bet, but he refused to concede — and of course he was right. So I gave in and bought him his pig's dinner, and one for myself; we had a lot of fun out of it.

Richard Lee Armstrong (1937-1991)

Shortly after I joined the faculty of the Yale Geology Department, Professor Flint passed on to me the job of counselling the undergraduate majors (a job later dignified with the title: Director of Undergraduate Studies), and I did that for a decade until I went off on my first sabbatical leave in 1959. In the fall of 1955, as I well remember, on the first day of the fall term an incoming freshman came to see me; he began the interview by announcing that he wanted to be a geochemist. Somewhat startled, though I had been equally sure when I entered Cornell in 1932 that I wanted to be a geologist, I advised him on the chemistry and physics courses he should take along with geology — plus languages, English, and so forth. During his first year, we realized that this freshman, Richard Armstrong, was both very bright and solid. The Chemistry and Physics Departments then held the opinion, based I fear on pretty good evidence, that Geology majors who took their courses did rather badly, but Dick reversed that opinion; later indeed the Physics Department made an effort to get him to switch to a Physics major, but without success.

The next summer Kenneth Bick, one of our graduate students, chose Dick as his field assistant for his dissertation project, the Deep Creek Mountains on the Utah-Nevada border. As part of my Alaska-to-Mexico trip that summer, I arranged to meet Ken at Eureka, Nevada, at the end of a field trip there with Dr. Thomas B. Nolan and others. On the last morning of that trip, coming out of Nolan's house I noticed two tramp-like characters across the road and was a bit taken aback when they crossed and spoke to me; they were Ken and Dick, the latter sporting a full beard, which was not so common then as later. They went with us that day, after which they took me to Ken's mountains, where we camped out each night.

When my visit was over, we headed for Salt Lake City; we had lunch in Wendover, Nevada, in a restaurant attached to a gambling hall where the tourists coming out of sedate Utah into racy Nevada could start gambling their money away. The three of us, unwashed and in dirty old field clothes, especially our full-bearded, but unlabeled, Yale freshman, provided much local color for the tourists, who naturally took us for grizzled prospectors right out of the hills.

Dick's undergraduate career was simply brilliant; indeed during those years he was able to be very helpful to several of our graduate students, and he didn't arouse their antagonism. On the other hand, one of his classmate geology majors said to me: "Why did I have to be born in the same year as Dick Armstrong?" I came to know Dick especially well because he was in my College, Branford. When Dick graduated in 1959, I strongly urged him to go elsewhere for graduate work, but he chose to stay at Yale, largely because we had recently added a geochemist to the Department, Karl Turekian, and Dick knew he could learn a great deal working with Karl. Of course we accepted him; one doesn't turn down the brightest guy in three states. At one point Dick seemed worried that I'd been miffed by his not taking my advice; I certainly hadn't been, for an able man should be free to choose his own course. But it's true that his later career might have been quite different if he had gone away from Yale for a time and we could then have called him back. In his graduate geochemical work he concentrated on geochronology, but he coupled it with field work in the Great Basin of Utah and Nevada and turned out a brilliant dissertation on the structural geology and the later geological history of that region.

During his graduate years, the Department appointed him an Instructor and, when he received his PhD, promoted him to Assistant Professor. Thus he continued to stay at Yale, except for a post-doctoral year at Bern to learn additional geochronological techniques. During this period Dick and I taught courses and seminars together, especially an undergraduate course on the Geology of the United States, dubbed "the landscapes course," in which, though it was in good part a slide show, we illustrated geological principles. It was a fun course to teach, and the undergraduates liked it. Dick was also an Associate Editor at *AJS*.

About 1970 the Geology Department made a first effort to get Dick promoted to Associate Professor with tenure, but we found that the letters we asked for from geologists outside Yale weren't very persuasive; people simply didn't know enough about him and his work, which I blame mainly on his staying at Yale. There was too a persistent question whether he wasn't simply a "clone" of Karl Turekian and me, though both of us knew perfectly well he was as independent as he was brilliant. Two years later we tried again; by that time his ongoing work had made a much deeper impression elsewhere, so that the letters were excellent, but by then the University had decided it had overdone its effort to strengthen the sciences and was feeling poor, so we were denied the tenure slot we thought we had and had reserved for Armstrong. So he had to leave Yale, after being there for eighteen years.

Armstrong's work, which had broadened since his dissertation to deal with the whole of the Cordillera — the western mountain ranges in both the United States and Canada — was by then well known, and he obtained a position at the University of British Columbia in Vancouver, where he spent the rest of his career. I saw him several times in Vancouver, the first time indeed on my return from my Australian year. He also came back to New Haven several times, as for the dissertation defenses of two graduate students whom we had supervised together. And we met at various national and international meetings; on a field trip in the Kimberley Ranges in northwestern Australia after the International Congress of 1976, we shared a tent, which however we just used to sleep on, out under the stars.

In 1990, Armstrong was awarded the Logan Medal of the Geological Association of Canada, one of the highest honors in Canadian geology. I think by that time he had become a Canadian citizen; he originally came from northwestern Washington State, and his mother was from Canada.

But the next year the word came to us that Dick was seriously ill with a tumor in the liver; it turned out to be cancer and incurable. At the suggestion of mutual friends, I called him, and we had a long conversation. He was facing death calmly and intelligently, thinking happily about the exciting and rewarding life he had led; I took the liberty of reminding him of the two incidents mentioned above, at each end of his freshman year. As it happened, neither Karl Turekian nor I were free to attend the memorial service for him in Vancouver.

Some years later, on two occasions a year apart, I had vivid dreams of seeing Dick Armstrong alive; in one he was replacing me at the piano (he never played the piano), and in the other I was just very happy to see him alive again.

Teodoro Díaz and Zoltán de Cserna

IN SEPTEMBER 1956 I attended the International Geological Congress in Ciudad México, but the rest of that summer I went on an incredible series of field excursions that took me from Point Barrow at the north tip of Alaska on 30 June to the Mexico-Guatemala border on 16 September. I have mentioned the post-Congress excursion to southeastern Mexico in telling of my trips with Bernard Gèze; in this sketch I want to speak particularly about the pre-Congress excursion in northeastern Mexico. Before that I had visited Yale graduate students in their dissertation areas in the Brooks Range in northern Alaska and in the states of Nevada,

Utah, Montana, Wyoming, and Arizona, plus U. S. Geological Survey parties in southeastern Alaska and in all the same states except Arizona, and I had stopped in or at least flown over all the other western states. I wound up the States part of the trip at El Paso, Texas, where I visited my sister and her husband and children.

On the pre-Congress excursion we worked our way southward in Mexico along la Sierra Madre Oriental, which separates the high Mesa Central from the low Gulf Coastal Plain. Our two principal guides on this trip were Teodoro Díaz, one of the leading geologists of Pemex, the Mexican government oil company, and Zoltán de Cserna, a Hungarian who was just then completing his doctoral dissertation at Columbia University under Professor Walter Bucher on some of the geology we were to see and who later became Professor of Geology at la Universidad Nacional Autónoma de México. La Sierra Madre Oriental is, more or less, the southern continuation of a mountainous belt that extends from the Canadian Rockies across Montana and into Idaho and westernmost Wyoming, where I had worked in it during the summers of 1939 and 1940, then on south across Utah toward Mexico; we were given a very fine excursion through the Mexican part of this belt. I had worked hard to master Spanish for this excursion, but actually everyone on the trip, including the Mexican guides, spoke English better than I spoke Spanish, so my Spanish saw little use.

I won't discuss the geology we saw, which has much in common with the geology I was studying in the Appalachians, but will mention a couple of amusing incidents. On one of the first days of the trip, we were taken on an oldish railway line east from the city of Chihuahua, then, in the backs of several cattle trucks, to see our outcrops. On the way out, one of the railway cars developed a hot box, which they lubricated with oily rags; on the way back, after dark, the rags caught fire, casting a lovely light out over the desert as we went along. They stopped, cooled off the box with water, jacked up the car, and changed the bearing — quite an operation. Farther south, in the mountains between Torreón and Saltillo, in de Cserna's dissertation area, we were received for the night at San Lorenzo de Parras, one of the oldest wineries in Mexico, if not the New World; we were shown through the winery and given a very fine banquet with their best wine and brandy flowing freely — some of the best brandy I ever tasted. The next morning they put us on horseback, and we rode five kilometers to see some rocks; that was a little rough. Thence we came to Saltillo and Monterrey, always in lovely if desert mountains.

In April that year I had flown to Ciudad México for a few days to help in preparing a pair of volumes that I was editing for the Congress; that was a delightful experience, especially when I was talking with the printers in their rather dialectical Spanish and was even taken by them to their usual lunch counter. At that time I had arranged that, at the end of our Congress excursion, I would drive back along the Pan-American Highway from Monterrey to Ciudad México with Señor Díaz and two other Mexican geologists; that was another delightful experience. On that trip I got more chance to practice my Spanish; also I think they had decided to find out just how far un gringo Norteamericano would go. The first day we drove south along the foot of the Sierra Madre at the upper edge of the Coastal Plain; at lunch (in a rather Americanized restaurant) they said they always started with a shot of tequila, and I went right along. That night we stayed in a truly Mexican motel — no English signs, no gringo turistas, a big cabin for four for 4 pesos, roughly $4 at that time - and had a fine Mexican dinner out under the stars with the brandy flowing freely again. The next day we climbed up over the mountains to la Mesa Central, and here we stopped in a little village not far from Ciudad México and bought our lunch at an open-air market; the woman tore meat off her roast with her bare hands and gave it to us on fig leaves, and we took tortillas off an open pile and made our own tacos, which we washed down with the excellent Mexican beer (one of them had pulque but I didn't go that far). Afterwards one of them said to me: "You're pretty brave; even we Mexicans get sick on this sometimes." I didn't tell him I was taking the diarrhea pills like mad; in fact I only developed diarrhea during my post-Congress excursion.

I met both Díaz and de Cserna several times during the Congress, and de Cserna I've seen many times at meetings in both Mexico and the United States.

Burrell Clark Burchfiel

CLARK BURCHFIEL HAS TOLD ME that, when he was an undergraduate geology major at Stanford (Class of '58), he had had no intention of going to graduate school, planning I suppose to get a job in the oil industry, which then paid fine starting salaries, at least in good years. But one of his professors at Stanford, Hugh Schenck, virtually ordered him to go to Yale and study with me. Schenck had come to know me in Tokyo, during my spell there right after the Second World War, and he may well have seen that Clark and I have compatible interests, both being fascinated with travelling to see geology in foreign parts. Anyway, Burchfiel did come, and he has certainly become one of the finest geologists I have had the honor to teach.

I have to admit, however, that as a teacher I short-changed him somewhat. He came to us in 1958, with a dissertation project in southern Nevada already picked out; it had been suggested by Chester Longwell who was still working in that region. But I was already committed to spend the year 1959-1960, including both summers, in Europe studying the Alps; thus I never did have the opportunity to visit Clark in his field area. Professor Carey, who replaced me at Yale that year, did visit him and I think helped him a lot, for Carey was an enthusiastic idea-man and could not help being inspiring to anyone, like Clark, with a passion for new ideas. On my return from that year, one of my other students said to me: "Professor Carey has taught us all about the geography of the world; now we want to learn about its geology."

Fig. 8-17. Arthur Snoke, John Rodgers, and B. Clark Burchfiel at the Annual Meeting of the Geological Society of America, in St. Louis, Missouri, 7 November 1989.

9 — In Norway

Olaf Holtedahl (1885-1975)

Professor Olaf Holtedahl was for me the Grand Old Man of Norwegian Geology. A year or so before the First World War he came to Yale, a young man with a new bride, to study with Professor Charles Schuchert, and one can understand that he had a warm spot in his heart for New Haven and for Yale people ever afterwards. I first met him and heard him speak when he visited Yale in 1946, just after I joined the Geology faculty. In his lecture he discussed the mountains of Scandinavia and northern Britain, collectively called the Caledonian chain, showing clearly how that chain continues into the northern Appalachian Mountains, as postulated by Continental Drift; moreover, he compared all those regions, at the time they were becoming mountains, to Indonesia today with its chains of islands and mountains separated by deep oceanic basins and its strings of volcanoes and earthquake centers. These were all new ideas to me then, but the more I studied the Appalachian chain, the more I found them seminal and fruitful.

At the International Geological Congress in Ciudad México, it was decided that the next Congress, in 1960, would be in Copenhagen with field excursions all through the Scandinavian countries. Of course I made up my mind to go, and I began to study Scandinavian geology; I found that Professor Holtedahl had recently published, in Norwegian, a book called *Norges Geologi*, and I set myself to learn Norwegian so that I could read it. After German, Norwegian wasn't very difficult; indeed the grammar is more like English than German. The trips of that Congress were the finale of my European year, 1959-1960, otherwise mainly Alpine.

I must now digress to explain how I came to go to so many international meetings, beginning in the 1950s. At that time, North American stratigraphers were actively arguing questions of stratigraphic terminology; an American Code of Stratigraphic Nomenclature had been published in 1933 by a committee of academic, industry, and government (state, US Federal, and Canadian) geologists, and after the Second World War the same groups decided to prepare a new version of the code. Between the wars there had also been an International Commission for a Stratigraphic Lexicon, an organ of the International Congress, presided over by an older Austrian geologist, but after the Anschluss of Austria with Germany he was unable to pursue its work, and the Commission had become a dead letter.

At the Congress in Algiers in 1952, a meeting of that Commission was called, with the evident intention of giving it a decent burial, but at that meeting Professor Raymond Moore of Kansas, one of the Americans most interested in stratigraphic terminology, gave an impassioned speech urging instead that the Commission be broadened to include both the Lexicon and Terminology. Impressed by his speech, the group present offered to elect him President of the broadened Commission; after hesitating, he said he would accept provided he could find some younger person to be Secretary and help him with the correspondence. Looking around the room, he saw me, and he invited me to take the job; I accepted, for I could see that it would bring me into contact with leading geologists all over the world, and so indeed it proved.

In the next eight years we converted the dead Commission into one of the most active in geology, and it has continued to flourish ever since. Moreover, we were able to enlist very able chairmen for our two Subcommissions, on the Lexicon and on Stratigraphic Terminology. For the Lexicon we had M. Jean Roger of the BRGM in Paris; we called each other *frères jumeaux*. We were warned in 1952 that he was a Communist, but that was actually an advantage, for he had good contacts with the Soviet Union and even with mainland China! Ultimately he was able to obtain lexicons published by both those countries and to republish them in French.

For Stratigraphic Terminology we had Dr. Hollis Hedberg, an oil geologist with a deep academic interest in stratigraphy generally who was later called to Princeton as Professor, and he ultimately put together an International Code of Stratigraphic Terminology that has been widely accepted.

The International Commission on Stratigraphy met of course at each International Geological Congress, but it also met in between, especially at meetings in Paris of the Commission for the International Geological Map of the World; when I could, I found

FIG. 9-18. *John Rodgers by Alison Krill. Begun in Norway 1990, unveiled in New Haven April 1999.*

pretexts to go to those meetings. At one of those meetings in 1958 I came to know Professor Holtedahl, just when I was assiduously studying his book, and I was able to get his advice about a dissertation area in Norway for one of my students, Edward Hansen. Moreover, in 1960 I took Prof. Holtedahl's pre-Congress field excursion, which was run from a tourist ship cruising from Trondheim in central Norway all along the northern Norwegian coast past North Cape to Kirkenes on the Soviet border and back, and we made stops to see the geology all along the way.

Hansen was only the first of a series of my graduate students who did dissertation projects in Norway, always with the knowledge and approval of the Norwegian geologists, and I got to go there again and again — six times in the years from 1959 to 1968 and again six times from 1977 to 1983. Nearly every time I came to Norway during that first period, I was able to visit Professor Holtedahl in his home on the Ringvei around Oslo and to enjoy his cordial hospitality.

One of my later students who worked in Norway, Allan Krill, and his wife Alison, liked it so well that they decided to settle there. First Allan worked for the Geological Survey of Norway; then he became Professor at the University of Trondheim. In 1990 he invited me to spend four months in his institute. At that time, moreover, his wife, who is a painter, decided to paint my portrait, in a Norwegian setting, and that portrait was unveiled in a pleasant ceremony in New Haven in April 1999. As a result of all these trips, I became familiar with many aspects of Norwegian geology and have even written articles about it.

Edward Hansen (1935-1993)

WHEN EDWARD HANSEN WAS AN UNDERGRADUATE Geology major at Princeton (class of '58), his senior thesis made a major breakthrough in the technique of reading the deformational history of rocks from features preserved within them. It had long been known that crystals of the common mineral calcite ($CaCO_3$), when subjected to deformation, developed "twins," precisely oriented buckles in the crystal structure. Later it came to be realized that, from their orientation, one could determine the orientation of the deforming stress. What Hansen showed was that somewhat less precise buckles in the even commoner mineral quartz (SiO_2), which too had long been known but were not understood, were produced in a similar way and thus could provide the same kind of information about stress. He and one of his teachers at Princeton submitted an article on this subject to the *American Journal of Science*, and we were happy to accept it for publication (v. 260, p. 321-336, 1962). At the same time, we welcomed him as a graduate student in the Yale Geology Department.

It happened that Hansen's second year as a graduate student was to be my sabbatical year in Europe, and he therefore asked if we might choose a field area for his dissertation somewhere in Europe, so that I could visit him during those two summers. Because of contacts I already had with Prof. Holtedahl of Norway, I turned to him for advice, and he helped us to choose an area in central Norway southwest of Trondheim — Trollheimen, the home of the trolls — adjacent to an area that Holtedahl himself had mapped. I visited Hansen there already in the summer of 1959, then the next two summers.

Ed Hansen was very innovative and had many brilliant ideas; I can say that I learned more from him than from any other student I've taught. Moreover, there are few to whom I have felt drawn personally as I was to him. But he was quite unwilling to accept discipline or even to discipline himself. We didn't know it at the time (1958-1961), but he was the advance guard, the "bellwether" one might say, of the student revolutionaries of the late 60s, so well known for their great ability but their unwillingness to apply it as their teachers and other elders thought they should. Ed did a splendid piece of field work and came up with many innovative ideas, but it was very difficult to get him to write them up in acceptable form; he kept thinking of new things to work on, and he kept delaying in order to perfect what he had. We finally did get a satisfactory dissertation out of him and were able to award him the PhD, but even then he kept putting off getting it into publishable form. The Geological Survey of Norway had supported him with field expenses the first summer, but they never did get a proper report on his work. After a long delay, he put together a whole book, **Strain Facies**, setting out his new general principles and conclusions and using his Norwegian work just to illustrate them. When that book was published, it was rather harshly reviewed by members of another "school" that already had its own principles and were not pleased when new and different ones were advanced. Thus the worth of Hansen's book was not recognized at first, but in due course structural geologists discovered it, and it became widely and favorably known.

Hansen was a superb teacher, but only on a one-to-one basis, and he was very helpful to each of my other graduate students who worked in Norway, also indeed to their undergraduate field assistants, who then went on to graduate work elsewhere. But he was not a good instructor in formal courses; he could not discipline himself to do the necessary hackwork for such courses.

Ed was also an excellent draftsman with a flair for seeing how to illustrate his ideas; indeed he was an artist, and he had an "artistic temperament." After he obtained his degree, we tried to help him find a position worthy of his talents, but he didn't make that easy; *twice* in those years he accepted a teaching position in the spring but then wrote during the summer that he wasn't coming, that he had found another job, one closer to New York City where he wanted to retain artistic connections. Unfortunately in one of those jobs he ran into an unpleasant situation; he felt strongly that the head of his department was treating other young faculty members unfairly; he consulted me about it and I had to agree, and later I obtained further confirmation. At the end he resigned and then decided to abandon geology altogether and to make his living in commercial art in New York. I heard nothing from him after that; I guess I'd tried to be a sort of "Dutch uncle," but he'd come to think of me as a "father-figure" whom he could hate. One of my other "Norwegian" students who taught in the New York area kept in touch with him, however, and even got him to help geology students when Ed himself was no longer active in geology. It was from that former student that I heard of Ed's death in 1993.

10 — The Alpine year (1959-1960)

Trips in the Western Alps, 1959

WHEN I ARRIVED IN PARIS early in June 1959, Professor Fallot had already arranged for me to meet several French geologists there, and we planned the first part of my excursions in the Alps. For the French Alps my main guides were Dr. Jacques Debelmas of l'Université de Grenoble and Dr. Marcel Lemoine of l'Ecole des Mines at Paris. After five days in Paris, I drove off to Grenoble, seeing all new country for me. The geologists at the University there, though busy with exams, gave me guidebooks and instructions on what to see in that region, especially the "Subalpine chains", and Dr. Debelmas in particular took me out for a day and gave me my first view of the classical geology along the valley or cluse of the Isère River.

Then I took off on my own, exploring the various groups of mountains that surround Grenoble. First was le Vercors, a large plateau-like area that had been an important center of the French Resistance during the German occupation in the Second World War, and the site of several unpleasant confrontations. That day I stopped for lunch at a little inn high in the mountains. When I asked the proprietor, in my heavily accented (one might even say Teutonic) French, if I could have lunch, he looked at me and at my VW camper with red French tourist plates, and he said: "Etes-vous Hollandais?" I am sure that, if I had been Allemand, he would have been désolé but the cook was ill, he couldn't possibly give me lunch, and the nearest restaurant was thirty kilometers away out of the mountains but, when I said I was Américain, he took me right in. But the question was so neatly put.

After exploring the region around Grenoble, I drove northeast to Lugrin on Lac Léman (the Lake of Geneva), where I found Dr. Lemoine and his family at their summer home right on the lake, and they put me up. Then for nine days Lemoine showed me around the French Alps, from the lake south past Grenoble to the region near Digne at the southwest edge of the Alps beside the mountains of Provence. In particular he explained to me the complicated geology around Briançon, on which he was expert; it was indeed a clue to geology all through the western Alps in both France and Switzerland, especially that of les Préalpes, both les Préalpes du Chablais south of Lac Léman and les Préalpes Romandes to its east - east and north of le Rhône above the lake. At one point, when we were in les Préalpes du Chablais looking up at Mont Blanc in the

High Alps to our south, he said, à propos of the hypothesis that the rocks of les Préalpes had slid by gravity northward to their present position when the High Alps rose up: "Mont Blanc shrugged its shoulders."

After visiting Lemoine at Lugrin, I drove around the west end of the lake, taking the trip by cable-car to the top of Mont Salève, an isolated mountain with a superb view of Genève and its lake, then northeast through Switzerland to Bern, the capital city. At this point I switched from French to German and from June to July. My main hosts in Bern were Drs. Walter Nabholz and Ernst Niggli.

Here I want to digress a little. In German-speaking universities it is common for Geology to be divided between two Institutes, one for mineralogy and petrology and one for stratigraphy and paleontology plus structural geology; sometimes there are even three, as in Vienna. The system got started I think because an Institute is controlled by a Doktor Professor, der Ordentliche Professor, under whom are Ausserordentliche Professoren and teachers of lower ranks; then, as Geology expanded, it seemed best to divide it into two Institutes, each with its own Professor. Unfortunately, this system led again and again to serious feuds between the two Professors and their Institutes, but it was not always so, I am happy to say. A particularly well known feud was that at Zürich between Professor Rudolf Staub and Professor Paul Niggli. Now Walter Nabholz was a student of Staub, and Ernst Niggli was the son of Paul Niggli, but evidently they made sure that no such feud developed at Bern; they were good friends and addressed each other as du, and the students in the two Institutes took courses in both and were not easily distinguished.

When I arrived in Bern, announced by a letter from Professor Fallot, Nabholz and Niggli were about to take the students in the two Institutes on a week-long field trip; I was invited to come along, and I was happy to accept. Actually that trip was planned to show the students the French Alps, and much of it duplicated what I had just seen with Lemoine, but it certainly did me no harm to see it again with different guides. On that trip also I came to know quite well a delightful older geologist, Professor Streckeisen, to whom I talked especially in the evenings when Nabholz and Niggli were often taken up with the mechanics of the excursion. The students on that trip were a lively bunch, and I got to know them fairly well; moreover, several of them later became leading geologists in their own right.

At Bern I was also cordially received by Professor Joos Cadisch who had written a major book on the geology of the Swiss Alps, which of course I had studied with care. He also kindly introduced me to others in his Institute and even took me as a guest to a big formal dinner of the Science Faculty of the University, after I got back to Bern.

Later in the summer I met Professor Cadisch in the Engadin, in southeastern Switzerland, and he showed me its fascinating geology. The lower part of the Engadin Valley extends into Austria, and he took me there and also over into Italy; thus at this point an American and a Swiss in a German car with French plates (my VW camper) crossed from Austria into Italy. Naturally the Italian customs officials were a bit startled, and they wanted to inspect the camper; campers were new then, and people everywhere wanted to look at mine. They were also intrigued by the trunk I had sitting on the bed in back, filled with maps: road maps, topographic maps, geologic maps. They gave us no trouble; they were just interested, and besides Cadisch was wonderful with customs people, knowing exactly how to get on their good sides and jolly them along.

Back in July, I returned from Bern to Lausanne and French and visited Professor Fallot in his summer home. He took me into Lausanne and introduced me to Professor Héli Badoux of the University, who arranged a whole series of day-long excursions with his students, and one with himself; they gave me still another view of les Préalpes and the adjacent Alps. On one of those days the student was Canadian, on another American, and we actually talked English! Then I visited Professor Jean Tercier of l'Université de Fribourg, and he made the same kind of arrangement, again in les Préalpes. As Professor Tercier was well known as a specialist in Alpine flysch (flysch is a kind of stratified rock, actually widespread in the world but first named in the Alps), the trip with him was very rewarding.

Peter Bearth

DURING THE SUMMER OF 1959 I also met Professor Peter Bearth, for me a very special person. As a boy he had been a goat-herd in the Alps of Wallis — Valais — and then an Alpine guide; some intelligent person whom he was guiding recognized his intellectual ability and encouraged (helped?) him to go on to the University. He became an outstanding student of rocks, especially unusual igneous rocks, and rose to be Ausserordentlicher Professor at Basel. But apparently that wasn't enough to support him and his family, for he also taught Physics in a local school; the wife of one of my other Swiss geological friends told me she had taken Physics from him. I don't think he ever really liked city life, however, preferring life in the mountains.

I met him in the heart of the Swiss Alps, and he took me at once to Zermatt (under the Matterhorn, though of course we didn't climb that) and showed me the complicated geology of the "Pennine" zone there and nearby. He was relieved to find that I could talk German; some years before he had spent a term at Pomona College in California and had spoken English, but by now he had pretty well lost it. He set me several "tests," not telling me of course but I could guess what they were, and evidently I passed them, for he became steadily more cordial during our time together.

While I was with him, he took me on several regular working traverses he was making in the mountains; more than once he ordered me to take an easy route around, while he clambered over the rocky cliffs to see the geology. One day he planned to make a long climb, and he was uncertain whether to stay the night before with a farmer in one valley or to camp out in an open stone hut in another, but the weather was poor, and we finally stayed in a small hotel near the Simplon Pass. During the climb we had breakfast at the farmer's wooden hut, where the cattle lived on the ground floor and the people above; clearly he felt happily at home there, and I had to be very careful to conceal my discomfort with the pervasive scent of stale urine. If he had observed that, he would probably have sent me packing at once. But he showed me some lovely scenery and some fascinating geology.

The last day, when we were about to eat lunch in a high, beautiful, isolated, and unspoiled Alpine valley, he made me promise never to tell anyone its name lest the tourists discover it and ruin it. Here I tried out on him a quite heterodox hypothesis about the geology in that region — on the Swiss-Italian border — which I'd been gestating over several days. At first he was taken aback, but he could think of no valid objection; then the more he thought about it the more he liked it. Finally he was willing to say that the idea explained a whole series of difficulties he'd had in understanding the local geology; he went so far as to suggest I write it up and get it published.

After we parted, I went on to Zürich and more field trips (including my first trip to Norway to see Ed Hansen). Later in August I visited Dr. Nabholz for two days in his field area, in the mountains around the head of the Vorderrhein. Those rocks had a good deal in common with those that Bearth had shown me and indeed provided a small test of my hypothesis, favorable as it turned out. Then during the winter both Bearth and I studied maps and reports of the region to test my hypothesis, he in Basel and I in Paris. I wrote a first draft of an article in German but asked him to be a joint author; he agreed, correcting my German of course. Professor Fallot also liked the idea, and he proposed that we publish a quick, short note in French in *les Comptes-rendus de l'Académie des Sciences* in Paris; that came out in January. Moreover, Bearth decided to present the idea in a lecture at Basel in late January, and I went over to hear him give it. But he never told anyone there what it was about; the title of the lecture gave only the locality (Lebendun), and none of them had seen the French note. For Bearth, der Ausserordentliche Professor, and Wenk, der Ordentliche, didn't much care for each other, country boy vs. city boy; Wenk had also worked in that region and was of course familiar with the orthodox interpretation. After Bearth's lecture, Wenk tried to disprove the idea, but it appealed to others who were present; e.g., Professor Streckeisen, who had come over from Bern to hear it. Someone said afterwards that it was the liveliest discussion they'd had after a lecture for some years.

The Bearths put me up that night and also a few weeks later, when I came back to give a lecture of my own. They fed me Apfelküchen "like Mother used to make," though my mother wasn't Swiss or German. On the second trip, Bearth and I took a long walk and found ourselves in agreement on many non-geological matters, despite the great contrast in our backgrounds — again country boy vs. city boy. All in all, I formed a very high opinion of Bearth. I saw him once again, in 1981 when I was at a meeting in Zürich and made a special trip over to Basel to visit him.

My hypothesis had a certain vogue for a few years, but then the Swiss geologists gave it up; Bearth himself abandoned it in his later publications. But in the 1980s geologists at Lausanne reinvented it, and then discovered our paper; in June 1992 I was invited to come to Italy after a trip to Greece and the Greek islands and see the new evidence, which I saw with Dr. Martinotti, by then of the University of Torino. So the idea isn't dead yet.

Rudolf Trümpy

Rudolf Trümpy and I began to exchange reprints in 1953; we may well have met at the International Geological Congress in Algiers in 1952, but my diary does not record it. From the first we each found the other's work of very great interest. The first time I had the opportunity to go into the field with him was in August 1959; I met him in Zürich, where he was a Professor at the ETH — die Eidgenossische Technische Hochschule, the Swiss equivalent of MIT — and he gave me six days in the field over a large part of eastern Switzerland, from Glarus around to the Engadin. In Glarus we saw the famous outcrops where Escher von der Linth laid the foundations of Alpine geology in the second quarter of the nineteenth century (Glarus is in the Linth valley).

Although a Professor in Zürich, Trümpy's home was Glarus; a Swiss always considers himself a citizen of the canton where he was born, or even more where his ancestors came from. Professor and Mme. Trümpy very kindly had me to dinner in Glarus several times; once however they were going out to dinner, and I was able to highjack the party. They'd met when he was teaching in l'Université de Lausanne, so when she was present the language was always French, but otherwise Trümpy insisted on talking English with me — he had worked for an oil company in Venezuela, and his English and Spanish were nearly as colloquial as his German and French. With his graduate students on the other hand he talked schwyzerdutsch, the Swiss variant of German, which I never mastered; the only words in it that I can now remember are auf Wiederluege, "till we meet again" — note the root close to the English look. And in the Engadin I encountered Romansch, Switzerland's fourth official language, a Romance language different from French and Italian; one time there I was seated with four people talking Romansch and, because they were discussing a loud party from the previous night that I too had witnessed, I could even follow some of what they said.

About this time, the Geological Society of America was commissioning and publishing review articles on various geological subjects, and they had asked Trümpy for such an article on the Alps. My friend Preston Cloud was chairman of the relevant committee, and he suggested that, as I was in Switzerland, I might review it for Trümpy. I did so, and it was a masterpiece, as I reported to Cloud. Later I was talking about it with my French friend Marcel Lemoine, who I knew had seen it, saying it was the best description of Alpine geology in the English language. "Yes," he said, "and in French too." (It was published in the *GSA Bulletin*, v. 71, p. 843-907, 1960.)

I saw Trümpy several more times during my Alpine year. He was in Paris when I gave my first lecture at le Collège de France in January 1960 (and he got Professor Fallot to give him one of the hectograph copies of each lecture as they were made). In 1969 we met at the 100th Anniversary of the Hungarian Geological Survey in Budapest; in 1972 he turned up at the Northeastern Section of the Geological Society of America in Buffalo, for he was then spending a couple of weeks at Lehigh University. Later that year he was one of a group of Francophone friends who had shown me around Europe, for whom I ran an informal trip through the U. S. Appalachians before the formal pre-Congress excursion through the Canadian Appalachians, run in connection with the International Geological Congress in Montreal; he also took the formal excursion.

Digression: The formal excursion was run both before and after the Canadian Congress, and Dr. William Poole of the Geological Survey of Canada had asked me to join him in guiding it. It is quite an honor for a United States citizen to be asked to help guide an official excursion in

Canada, but I know why it happened. Canada is officially bilingual and hence, as an officer of the Crown, Dr. Poole should have been able to talk both French and English. But, coming from British Columbia, he had little French — or need for it — and he asked me to join him because he knew that I was both reasonably fluent in French and reasonably well acquainted with the Canadian Appalachians. End digression.

After that I kept running into Trümpy at international meetings: at the Ophiolite Symposium in Moscow in 1973 and on the following excursion to the Tien-Shan and the Lesser Caucasus, at the International Congress in Australia in 1976, at a GSA Penrose Conference in the Blue Ridge of Georgia in 1978, at the International Congress in Paris in 1980, at meetings in Switzerland in 1981, at the International Congress in Moscow in 1984, in Chengdu in China in 1985, at the Annual Meeting of the Geological Society of America in Orlando, also in 1985, where he was awarded the Society's Penrose Medal, and finally at a meeting of *la Società geologica italiana* in Milano in 1990. In 1981, moreover, we had him come to Yale as a Visiting Professor for two months; he gave us a fine series of lectures on the Alps (in English, but then I've given lectures in German in Zürich), and we took him on short field trips from Vermont to Maryland and to that year's GSA meeting in Cincinnati. It is said that, if two people have met on three continents, they are world travellers; clearly Rudy and I both qualify.

Christof Exner, Alexander Tollman, Eberhard Clar

QUITE A GROUP of fine Austrian geologists showed me around Austria from late August to mid-October 1959. First I saw the Northern Calcareous Alps, the northern Alpine range of Austria, spectacular mountains including the beautiful Hallstättersee (lake), whose scenery bowled me over. I was introduced to this range by Professor Heissel of Innsbruck but then traversed it for a week on my own. I was particularly intrigued by the geology of the salt deposits around Salzburg; e.g., Hallein, Hallstatt, for salt in Celtic is *hall-*, like *hal-* in Greek, as in the mineral name *halite*. For part of that I had the privilege of being taken around by Oberbergrat Schauberger, the chief salt geologist of Austria; he took me deep into one of the mines and had me drink from what he said was the most mineralized spring in Europe. Nor did I neglect to hear a lot of Mozart at the Salzburg music festival; among other fine concerts I heard *The Magic Flute* given as a marionette show, which fit the unreal plot neatly without spoiling Mozart's wonderful music.

Then I met Dr. Christof Exner, a very able petrologist, who for nearly a week showed me *die Hohe Tauern*, the highest range in the Austrian Alps, and also took me to an important meeting of Austrian geologists in Murau. At that meeting a major controversy in Austrian geology was aired for four days and, although I was pretty confused at first, I came to know fairly well the conflicting hypotheses — and the conflicting hypothesizers: the bright but brash young man Alexander Tollman, whose hypothesis I came to accept, having been bright and brash myself at his age, the old conservatives, the man who loves to start a fight, the field geologist with an acid wit but the best evidence, and best of all the calm and serious older professor, Professor Eberhard Clar, who gave me the clearest picture of the problems. Moreover, he himself gave me two days afterwards to see more geology. Back in Salzburg, three different geologists, including Schauberger, took me around.

From there I drove across the mountains to Graz in Steiermark, where Professor Flügel and others at the University showed me around; Flügel took me over into Kärnten for three days, and we looked particularly at the Carnic Alps on both sides of the Austrian-Italian border. After that I came into Vienna, where I met Dr. Exner again, and he was very kind and helpful.

In Vienna there happened to be a mineralogical meeting, and I got in on a couple of days of their excursions, on which I met Professor Wieseneder, whose main concern was the minerals of sediments, and a bright and lively young petrologist named Zirkl. Then Professor Clar, who had just been in Czechoslovakia, arranged a three-day excursion back into the Northern Calcareous Alps for Professor Dmitri Andrusov from Bratislava — a "White" Russian who left Russia at the Revolution and had lived in Czechoslovakia since then — for whom I came to have a very high regard.

Back in Vienna, Professor Clar had me give a lecture on the Appalachians (in German, but I didn't do very well), and I also saw Dr. Exner and the others. Then I took off to return to Paris, going around by northern Italy and stopping to see a bit of geology here and there.

The next March I saw Professor Clar again at a meeting in Würzburg in Germany, and again he was, or tried to be, the calming influence in a hot debate over the ideas of the brash young man. Then much later, in 1976 during my month in Göttingen, I went down to a meeting of the Austrian geologists at Hallstatt — again that beautiful lake! — where the geological arguments were quite different from 1959 and 1960 but the geological personalities were exactly the same. There I was assigned to be Prof. Clar's roommate, and again I greatly admired his knowledge, his clarity, and his wisdom. I met Tollman again at several International Congresses from 1968 — before the tanks came in — to 1992.

Livio Trevisan (1909-1996) — Trips to Italy in 1960

I GOT TO SEE ITALY and its geology a number of times during my first sabbatical year, 1959-1960 — my year for the Alps. During the two summers I made several trips into the Italian Alps, especially into the Dolomite Alps in the Tyrol. In this case the mountains were named for the rock, not the rock for the mountains as usually happens; dolomite itself is named for the scientist, Déodat de Dolomieu, who at the end of the eighteenth century discovered its difference from ordinary limestone. During the spring of 1960, on the other hand, I made three trips to see the Apennine Mountains, the backbone of the Italian peninsula, one east from Roma, one in Toscana around Firenze (Florence) and Pisa, and one around Genova in Liguria.

The April trip from Roma I made by myself, hiring a car and driving for three days right across the Apennines of Latium, Umbria, le Marche, and gli Abruzzi; I put 1,250 kilometers on the car in those three days, to the astonishment of the rent-a-car people when I brought the car back. The June trips out of Genova were made partly with Professor Conti and Drs. Fierro and Terranova of the University there and partly with Dr. Lanteaume, whom I'd met in Fallot's lab, and students of his westward toward France, where the northwest end of the Apennines merges with the south end of the great western curve of the Alps.

The May trip, in Toscana, I made for a definite purpose, to see a rock called argille scagliose or scaly clays; I have described the rock, the problems it raises, and the various hypotheses to explain it in my article on Exotic Nappes, *American Journal of Science*, v. 297, p. 174-217, 1997. These matters were the subject of new and exciting work and ideas by the Italian geologists right after the Second World War, and they were brought to our attention in America in a series of articles by Professor John Maxwell of Princeton University. Indeed I wasn't the only American geologist curious to see the evidence for these ideas; when I got to Firenze I found two other American geologist friends who were there for the same reason. Professor Giovanni Merla of Firenze, one of the main proponents of the new ideas, was tied up during the five days I was there, but Drs. Passerini, Valduga, and Losacco took us on field trips, also including visits to Carrara and its famous marble quarries and to Lardarello, where the Italians exploit subterranean steam to produce electricity to run the Italian railroads.

After that I went on to Pisa, where Professor Livio Trevisan and his assistant, Dr. Piero Elter, also gave me five days to explain their ideas about the argille scagliose, which were rather different from those of the

Florentines. Prof. Trevisan and I hit it off at once; it turned out that he played the violin, and we spent a happy evening together playing violin-and-piano sonatas by Mozart and Brahms. I also remember a pleasant Sunday drive down the coast past Livorno (Leghorn), during which the car motor suddenly developed a very bad knock; when we got a mechanic, he found that a small rock had got caught between the oil-pan and the drive-shaft. We called it la vendetta dei sassi, the revenge of the rocks, and went on with our drive.

The Sixties

11 — In the United States

John M. ("Jack") Bird

I FIRST MET JACK BIRD early in 1962 when he was a student of Professor Shepard Lowman's at RPI (Rensselaer Polytechnic Institute) in Troy; he took me out for a day to show me his dissertation area near Nassau, New York, in the hills east of the Hudson River at Albany. He was working in rocks of the Taconic sequence, named for the Taconic Mountains on the border of New York and Massachusetts. These rocks underlie most of New York State east of the Hudson from north of Hudson Falls to Poughkeepsie and extend over into southwestern Vermont, westernmost Massachusetts, and northwestern Connecticut. Their geology has posed problems for a long time; during the nineteenth century they were the subject of a very bitter, personal controversy that became famous in United States geology. That controversy died down toward the end of the century, but in the twentieth century a new one erupted, and people took sides again.

It happened that Professor Lowman and I were on opposite sides of this new controversy, so when I went in the field with Jack Bird, knowing that he would be influenced by Lowman's views, I was careful not to attack them head on. What I did was simply to talk about the problems raised by the rocks he was showing me, reviewing the ways the two opposing theories explained them. I didn't need to do more, for Jack knew his rocks well; before long he saw that they provided support for my side of the argument, and in time he became one of its strongest advocates. In the long run I think we won that argument, though a few geologists may still have doubts about it.

Shortly after he completed his doctor's degree, Jack took a position with the Earth Sciences Department of the new State University at Albany, and before long he was Acting Chairman of the Department, the other members of which were then as young as he was. Knowing that I came from Albany, he had me appointed to several successive visiting committees for the Department. Thus I got to meet not only him and his colleagues but many of the higher officials right up to the President.

In those years New York State was making a determined effort to build, from scratch, a system of universities that would rival California's outstanding system, which had been built up slowly over the preceding decades. It seemed to me, however, that New York thought all that had to be done was to go out and buy a system. Four campuses were established:

Stony Brook (on Long Island), Albany, Buffalo, and Binghamton, all except Stony Brook being based on small older colleges; e.g., the State Teachers' College in Albany. As a result of my visits, I came to the conclusion that none of the high brass at Albany really knew what they were doing — with the signal exception of the head Librarian, for whom I had much respect.

At that time E-an Zen was already working in western Massachusetts and hence was dealing in part with the same rocks as Jack and I; Jack, E-an, and I got into the habit of taking joint field trips to see one another's significant outcrops and localities and to visit other relevant places. Several of these trips led to fruitful hypotheses, which we then presented for other geologists to argue about. On those trips I found Jack to be a careful observer and at the same time a shrewd, even bold, thinker in explaining his observations.

In 1966 Jack, as one of New York State's Taconic geologists, came along on the field trip in Newfoundland that pretty much consolidated the evidence for a similar "Taconic-type" hypothesis there.

In 1968 Jack Bird, E-an Zen, and I made our memorable trip with Professor Andrusov through the Slovakian Carpathians, and of course he was one of the hosts for the banquet we gave for the Andrusovs in Praha, the evening before the tanks came in.

Jack's situation at Albany seemed to drag on and on, but he succeeded in making a couple of spectacular senior appointments: Professor Akiho Miyashiro, one of the leading theorists on metamorphism, and Professor John Dewey. A bit later indeed, Dewey and Bird published a seminal article, one of the first to ask what were the implications for continental geology of the "new global tectonics" (now plate tectonics) then being worked out in the oceans. But during those years Jack became more and more dissatisfied at Albany, and finally, when Professor Jack Oliver was rebuilding the Geology Department at Cornell University, which had been in the doldrums since shortly after I left — for the price they had paid for getting rid of the feud there was mediocrity — Oliver persuaded Bird to join the Cornell Department.

Personally I have always found Jack Bird a delightful companion. He has a quick, irreverent temperament that expresses itself especially in very clever but risqué (not to say dirty) stories of the kind that bear frequent repetition. To be sure I always take care, when I repeat them, to give Jack the full credit.

John Dewey and Stuart McKerrow, also Richard Bambach

I MET John Dewey and Stuart McKerrow together in the summer of 1964, when I went to see Richard K. Bambach in his dissertation area at Arisaig, Nova Scotia. Dick Bambach was a graduate student in paleontology at Yale, working under Dr. Lee McAlester, but he took my graduate structural geology course and did very well. His dissertation was on the fossil clams of the well known Silurian section at Arisaig; of course I was in no position to pass on its merits, but clearly it was very good. In studying the previous literature, especially the previously described species, he found that several such species differed only in their proportions and in the angle between their long dimension and a crossline nearly perpendicular to that. He then observed that the rock slabs containing his specimens were affected by a fine parting — what geologists call slaty cleavage because it is what causes slate to split into thin slabs — and that the proportions and the angle varied regularly with the angle between the long dimension of the specimen and the fine parting. He therefore concluded that the deformation or change of shape that had induced the parting or slaty cleavage had also distorted the fossil clams; hence all the apparently differing forms were just distortions of one species. It was a very neat, well documented example of a general principle in structural geology; when he showed me his evidence, I urged him to publish an article about it, and he did.

Another thing I remember about Bambach as a graduate student was being invited to his apartment to watch the returns for the U.S. Presidential Election of 1964 — Johnson vs. Goldwater; we shared our glee at the result.

I've seen Bambach repeatedly over the years; somewhat after completing his degree he joined the Geology Department at Virginia Polytechnic Institute, where Professor Byron Cooper was building up an outstanding department. Indeed he published his article on the distorted clams in a volume of articles dedicated to Professor Cooper (*American Journal of Science*, v. 273-A, p. 409-430, 1973).

In 1964 Dewey and McKerrow were visiting Nova Scotia at the invitation of Professor Arthur Boucot, then of MIT; it was Dewey's first visit to North America. In 1966 both Dewey and McKerrow came to a field meeting in western Newfoundland to examine the evidence for, and against, an unconventional interpretation that Ward Neale of the Geological Survey of Canada and I had proposed for a large body of rocks there, which we thought had the same structural relations as a similar body of rocks in the Taconic region of easternmost New York State and

Yale, so I knew him well; he wasn't my student there but he took courses from me. To be sure, the hypothesis was then equally controversial for the Taconic region, but most people, including I think Dewey and McKerrow, came around to our point of view for both bodies. On that trip Ward and I were accused of having little yellow feathers sticking out of our mouths.

Dr. McKerrow came to be associated with the Department of Geology at Oxford University during those years, whereas Dr. Dewey was associated with Cambridge University, where he obtained his doctoral degree. In January 1968 I met Dewey when he was in the United States, and he kindly invited me to a field excursion in western Ireland that spring, being run by Dr. McKerrow and himself. So I flew over to Dublin where I met their trip, and we bused across the Shannon valley, the central plain of the island, to Mayo and Connemara where we had a fine field trip. Even the weather cooperated, for we had almost no rain; in fact there had been a sort of drought, and the Emerald Isle was mostly brown, even in April. Then we bused back to Dublin, Dewey and I flew on to London, and he took me up to Cambridge and showed me around, putting me up there for three days. It happened that Harry Whittington, a Briton who had been a graduate student of Dunbar's at Yale at the same time as myself, had recently become Professor of Paleontology at Cambridge, and he and his wife Dorothy (whom he had met and married in New Haven!) put me up for two days more, so I got a fine view of Cambridge and vicinity.

Shortly after that, Dewey was called to be Professor of Geology at the State University of New York in Albany, part of the efforts of Dr. John M. ("Jack") Bird to build up that relatively new department. Dewey was there through the 1970s, so I saw him quite often; we saw each other at conferences and on field trips.

In 1970 I was named a Foreign Member of The Geological Society (of London but, as the first geological society ever formed, it didn't need to specify); later I was called an Honorary Member, then an Honorary Fellow. In the early 1980s I crossed the Atlantic several times for meetings of the Society. One time Dr. McKerrow had me as his guest at Oxford and then took me to the Society's general meeting in London where I met many outstanding British geologists. A year later John Dewey was being awarded the Lyell Medal of that Society, and I went over to see that and to congratulate him; by that time Dewey had returned to England as Professor of Geology at the University of Durham. At that meeting I asked him if he would accept me as a visitor in the spring of 1984, and he kindly agreed.

I spent three months in Durham; my stay there was very pleasant as well as rewarding geologically. Dewey had arranged for me to have an apartment in one of the Colleges there (Trevelyan), not unlike my apartment in Branford College at Yale, and I took part in the college life; I even gave a recital of Haydn and Mozart piano sonatas. Also I went on student field trips into northern England, plus one fairly extended trip into the Highlands of Scotland, and I visited other universities and went to meetings in London. Actually Professor Dewey, who was as much of a tripper as I was, wasn't always in Durham while I was there; one time he was in Beijing! where I only got the next year.

That summer was the International Geological Congress in Moscow; on the way back from that I went to a meeting in Glasgow, of which I was an organizer as it concerned the Caledonian-Appalachian mountain belt on both sides of the Atlantic. After that I took short trips to Durham and to Loch Lomond, and went on Dr. McKerrow's excursion into the Southern Uplands of Scotland.

During that trip I developed the first symptoms of my prostate trouble, and after I returned to New Haven I had my first prostate operation, at the end of 1984. Unhappily my stay in the hospital was considerably

FIG. 11–19. *Harold Williams and John Rodgers at meeting in honor of Williams, Grand Falls, Newfoundland, August 1994.*

lengthened by a blood clot in my lung (pulmonary embolism) and a severe case of paranoia that I developed. It took the form of delusions of persecution (complete with persecutor!); when I was thinking clearly, I knew quite well they were only delusions, but they kept coming up in my thoughts, involuntarily it seemed, for several months. Finally I went into psychoanalysis to dislodge them; probably on that account the delusions finally left me. More recently, however, the paranoia has taken the (for me much more agreeable) form of delusions of grandeur. Indeed the present book, though first conceived in another context (as indicated by the title), may well be their monument.

Later Dewey was called to Oxford as Professor of Geology. I continued to see both Dewey and McKerrow now and then; the last time was again at a meeting in Newfoundland held in 1994 to honor the outstanding Newfoundland geologist Harold Williams, whom we all knew well.

Xü Jinghua (Kenneth J. Hsü)

KEN HSÜ, like E-an Zen, is one of the bright young Chinese who came to college in the United States during the window between the Second World War and 1949, the year the Communists took over mainland China. He went first to Ohio State University, then to the University of California at Los Angeles, where he wrote his doctoral dissertation on an area in Switzerland under the direction of Professor John Crowell. For a few years he taught geology in the University of California at Riverside; one of his undergraduate students there was John Suppe, whom he sent on to us at Yale for graduate work. Hsü was with us in May 1966 for the first days of the memorable trip during which Suppe chose his dissertation area in the "Franciscan" rocks of northern California, to whose fascinating problems Hsü had introduced him.

Soon after that, in 1967, Professor Hsü was called to the Geologisches Institut of the ETH in Zürich, where he has spent the rest of his career. Not much later he was Co-Chief Scientist for the Mediterranean cruise of JOIDES (the Joint Oceanographic Institutions Deep Earth Sampling program). Ken has been at least as much a world traveller as I, and we have met not only in the United States and in Europe but elsewhere in the world — Moscow, Papua-New Guinea, Istanbul, and China.

By 1985 it had become possible for eminent non-Communist Chinese to return to China, and Hsü began to do geological field work there. His research concerned a large terrain, called Banxi, of unfossiliferous sedimentary rocks, in part mildly metamorphosed, in the region south of the lower Chang Jiang (Yangzi River) and extending far to the west-southwest — a part of a major mountain range in south China that may be called the Yangzi fold belt. Lacking fossils, the Banxi had been assigned a quite old age, but Hsü claimed that it is younger, moreover that it doesn't lie beneath fossiliferous strata in the region but was emplaced — thrust — laterally over them for tens if not hundreds of kilometers. This idea was quite unpopular among the older Chinese geologists, but some younger ones liked it.

At Istanbul in 1985, Ken Hsü presented a paper about his work on the Banxi rocks, and I became much interested; it gave me "the ideal excuse for going there." The next year, 1986, had already been chosen for my exchange visit to China, and Ken saw to it that I was invited to the field excursion that September on which he planned to demonstrate the evidence for his ideas; we started at Hangzhou in Zhejiang province and visited Jiangxi and especially southern Anhui. On that trip, I for one became convinced that the so-called Banxi terrain includes two quite different groups of strata that needed to be separated; to one of them Ken's theory could apply, to the other not. Later several discussions of his idea were published, some rather polemical; I contributed one, and at the end Ken and I published a joint letter setting out the two-Banxi hypothesis more clearly and suggesting that the answer could be found only by more field work. Ken later told me informally that he considered our joint note the best thing yet published in the debate.

At about this time, Professor Hsü published a book called *The Great Dying*, referring especially to the extinction of the dinosaurs and several other forms of life at the end of the Mesozoic era or geological Middle Ages (often called the K-T boundary), although actually his book concerned several other such events in geological time. At first glance, he seemed to be denying organic evolution; he was in fact quoted approvingly in the creationist literature, which infuriated him. He did want to attribute much of it, especially the great extinctions, much more to chance than to "natural selection" and "survival of the fittest," but I think he opposed those doctrines because he felt that they had been used, in the form called Social Darwinism, to bolster "white" supremacy, especially perhaps British supremacy (Darwin having been British), against which he reacted so strongly because he had been brought up in a part of China then dominated by a variety of British "colonialism."

During his years in Switzerland, Hsü naturally became familiar with the geology of the Alps; he published a book on the geology of Switzerland in which he developed a general theory of mountain building or deformation based largely on the Alps. In March 1997 he visited Yale and gave us a lecture on his theory; I even wrote in my diary that "he wasn't anywhere near as dogmatic as I'd feared he would be." For my part,

I hold that mountain ranges are much more varied than his theory suggests, but our different hypotheses are just that and, like any hypotheses, they must compete with each other in the intellectual "market place," the decision, if any, being left to later generations of geologists.

John Suppe

John Suppe came to Yale as a graduate student in geology in 1965, recommended to us by Kenneth J. Hsü, his professor when he was an undergraduate in the University of California at Riverside. I remember that in his first years he was very slow of speech, almost embarrassingly so, but we soon learned to wait as long as necessary to hear what he had to say because of the uncommon understanding and insight he displayed.

The next summer, 1966, Suppe and I went on a series of connected field trips in coastal California to choose a dissertation area for him. He had already made up his mind to work in the "Franciscan formation," a group of rocks named for San Francisco because they are its bedrock. They are widespread in California, especially northern California. We started from Los Angeles with Professor Hsü and worked northward; many geologists joined us for parts of the trip, especially in and around the San Francisco Bay area. After Professor Hsü had left us, we went out with some of my friends in the USGS who disagreed strongly with Hsü's ideas concerning the Franciscan. I was well impressed by Suppe's reaction to this controversy (he was only a graduate student, remember): calm, mature, concerned chiefly with obtaining evidence for and against the various hypotheses. In the long run it was Suppe who chose his area, and he chose well; the evidence he was able to obtain there led him to conclusions that proved to be valid in many other parts of the "Franciscan" region. At the very end of our trip, he persuaded me to take our last day off for a tourist trip on a scenic railroad crossing the Coast Ranges to the sea, providing relaxation — almost comic relief — after ten days of serious attention to geology.

John didn't hurry his dissertation but took the time to make it outstanding. After he received his PhD, he was appointed Assistant Professor at Princeton, and less than ten years later he was named Full Professor there. Moreover his calm, slow-seeming but eminently sensible approach to problems soon made him "the glue" of the Princeton department, which before then had had a history of deep divisions: "hard-rock" vs. "soft-rock."

Quite soon after going to Princeton, Suppe chose the island of Taiwan ("Formosa") for his geological research because, as he has shown, it is in effect a mountain range in the process of being formed, progressively from north to south, as the crustal plate of the Philippine Sea pushes against the east margin of the plate containing the diagonal contact between Asia and the South China Sea. In the process, the thick sedimentary rock sequence that has been accumulating in recent geological time in the Manila deep-sea trench west of the island of Luzon is being compressed and forced upward to mountainous heights. Suppe showed that the process began some 4 million years ago at what is now the northern end of Taiwan and has worked southward, and the mountains now rise four kilometers and are still rising, though being worn down at about the same rate by erosion in the rainy tropical climate.

Not long after he started work on Taiwan, Suppe asked me to write a letter of reference for his application for a Guggenheim Fellowship. I was happy to do so, but I imposed one condition; namely that I would come to visit him. He got it all right, and we arranged for me to spend three weeks with him in February 1979. In those three weeks we covered the island from end to end, even to the south tip where the recent coral reef is currently being bowed gently upward as the island grows southward.

My visit to Taiwan only increased my desire to see mainland China as well, and I succeeded in doing so three times in the later 1980s. But John had become in a way committed to Taiwan, politically as well as geologically; he has not, I think, visited or wanted to visit mainland China. He learned to speak Chinese well, and so did his wife and children, who spent that year with him. His work there has been outstanding, adding much to our store of knowledge on how mountain ranges form. When Professor Schaer of Neuchâtel asked me to join him in arranging a special course on mountain ranges for the Francophone Swiss universities, I urged him to include Suppe and Taiwan. John's lectures there were very well received, and the article he wrote for the book we put together out of that course was excellent; I quoted it shamelessly in one of my recent articles on mountain structures around the world, and I even lifted one of his figures — with his permission of course.

Suppe is also well known for the theoretical studies by himself and his students on how rock strata are folded during the deformation that produces mountain ranges. His stature in the geological profession has risen steadily over the years. He became Associate Editor of the *American Journal of Science*, and in 1995 he was elected to the National Academy of Sciences of the United States. His most recent "field area" has been the planet Venus: "Venereal" tectonics as revealed in satellite photographs.

12 — Abroad: Greece & the Soviet Union

*Pendelis Tsoflias, Demetrios Papanikolaou,
Spyros Lekkas and Alexandra Zambetakes-Lekkas*

A<small>NCIENT GREECE HAS ALWAYS MEANT</small> a great deal to me intellectually; I feel sure I owe this, like much else in my life, to my mother. On the mantelpiece over the fireplace in the living room of our home in Albany stood a handsome clock on which was the Greek word *Agora*, the name of her college society or "sorority" at Wellesley. While I was still a boy, she encouraged me to learn the Greek alphabet and even to work my way through White's *First Greek Book*; then during my last year at the Albany Academy, I and two other boys took the elementary Greek course given by "Professor" Charles Goold, by then old and I think officially retired. With him we not only studied elementary Greek grammar but went through the whole first book of Xenophon's *Anabasis*; Goold told us we had got farther than any other elementary Greek class he had taught.

Mr. Goold also taught French, and he had an effective way of driving home certain grammatical points. For example, anyone who missed the significance of a past participle that agrees in gender with a preceding direct object, as in qui l'a blessée — who has wounded her (not him) — was required to bring him an orange, which he then put on a stand made of erasers with the inscription "Mort pour le participe passé." In his Greek class he kept reminding us that there is no future subjunctive tense; what looks like one is really an aorist subjunctive. So one time I tricked him into mentioning the future subjunctive — I think he was hoping to trick me into agreeing to its existence — I demanded my orange, and I got it.

At Cornell, I took (not for credit) a course in Homer's *Iliad*, and it entranced me; I learned great swatches of it by heart, and I can still recite the first 50 lines from memory and many later lines. (After I got into Greek, I dropped Latin like a hot potato.) After that I worked on my own, reading principally the lyric poets and the great dramatists; of these too I have some bits in my memory. Since college I haven't worked hard on ancient Greek, but I have never allowed it to slip away entirely.

Naturally I became acquainted with all the well known episodes in Greek history — such as Marathon, Thermopylai, the Peloponnesian War, and the career of Alexander the Great — and Greek heroes, places, and ideas seeped into my mind. As I became more and more concerned with philosophy, I studied Greek philosophy: the Pre-Socratics (in Burnet's great book), Plato, and above all Aristotle, to whom my scientifically inquisitive mind was most attuned. For all these reasons, Greece, ancient Greece at least, became for me "a home of the soul," and I kept dreaming of going to see Greece some day.

My first opportunity came in the summer of 1966. That summer Professor Maxwell, my opposite number at Princeton, and I visited together several of our graduate students (his, mine, or first mine, then his) in Norway, Italy, and Greece. We entered and left Greece through Athens of course, and we spent a couple of days there both before and after our trip north to visit his student Jay Zimmerman. Thus I was able to get a first look at the city and its great monuments, for example the Akropolis with the Parthenon, and also to attend a couple of concerts given in one of the great open-air theatres built in ancient times, even to hear one of the plays of Sophokles (though it was translated into modern Greek!). Going north to see Zimmerman, we drove as fast as we could, taking only one day en route, but coming south we took an extra day and were able to visit other famous spots, such as Delphi. But this trip, only eleven days in all, simply whetted my appetite to see more of Athens and of Greece.

MAP 12–7. *Greece and Adjoining Countries*

Zimmerman was studying the Vourinos mountain complex in northern Greece, which interested me greatly because it has much in common with certain complexes elsewhere, notably one in western Newfoundland for which, as mentioned above, Ward Neale and I had earlier proposed an unconventional, not to say outrageous, hypothesis based on the equally controversial hypothesis about the Taconic region in easternmost New York and adjacent New England. Indeed the conventional interpretation of the Vourinos, which Maxwell and Zimmerman at that time accepted, had been cited to me as evidence against our idea for Newfoundland. To be sure an earlier student at Princeton who had worked on the Vourinos complex, Eldridge Moores, had already suspected that the controversial idea was correct there, but he had had no support from his professors.

According to the conventional idea, the rocks of the Vourinos complex, igneous rocks but of an unusual character, forming what later was called an ophiolite suite, were intruded where they now appear and hence are in their proper place, sitting on top of a thick sequence of limestone, an ancient carbonate bank, rather as if an igneous intrusion of those unusual rocks were to punch up through the middle of the Great Bahama Bank. According to the unconventional idea on the other hand, the rocks are not at all in place but have been pushed laterally up onto the carbonate bank from the floor of an oceanic basin tens, maybe a hundred, kilometers away, during a major but long ago mountain-building (orogenic) episode. Such a situation may be being prepared today where the great Sahul carbonate bank along the northwestern coast of Australia is approaching and being pulled down beneath the ocean floor of the basins around the nearby Indonesian islands, notably Timor. Well, Maxwell and Zimmerman took me to see this complex and, during the very first of the five days we spent there, I found evidence for the unconventional idea; that evidence convinced me, and before long I was able to convert them too.

One of these days, "As we had to cross the [Aliakmon] river, John Orban and I simply stripped and swam across it, then wandered around in the altogether looking at the rocks on the other side — frightfully Greek!" John Orban was an undergraduate at Princeton whom Maxwell had brought along to assist a graduate student of his in Norway but who came with us.

My short trip in 1966 only made me want to come back to Greece. At the beginning of 1979 I took a term's leave for a trip around the world; after visiting Taiwan, I came on to Greece where I spent three months (plus a week on Cyprus). A few years earlier la Société Géologique de France had taken a two-weeks' field excursion through much of central and northern Greece, and I had with me a copy of the excursion guidebook. I spent a week in Athens, looking up geologists with whom I had corresponded and being introduced to others; they were all extremely cordial. My principal hosts were Dr. Pendelis Tsoflias at the Polytehnical Institute and Dr. Demetrios Papanikolaou, Dr. Spyros Lekkas, and his wife Dr. Alexandra Zambetakes-Lekkas, also a geologist, at the University of Athens. They kindly arranged day trips and also invited me to join longer trips they were already planning all over the country.

My first trip was on my own, however; I rented a car and simply followed the French guidebook through northern Greece. Later I went on four trips into the Peloponnesos (the island of Pelops), the large southern peninsula of Greece south of the Gulf of Corinth. On one of these trips, Dr. Lekkas asked me along because he was to guide a group of Americans from Syracuse University (in New York State, not in Sicily), and he knew I could help by translating from his French to their English.

On these trips, I didn't confine my attention to geological outcrops but sought out ancient cities and ruins, visited famous battlefields, and enjoyed the glorious mountain scenery. Moreover I had with me, in Greek and English, *Pausanias' Guide to Greece*, a "Baedeker" written in the second century AD for the many Roman tourists who visited Greece in those years.

During my visits to Greece, languages were an important matter. My knowledge of ancient Greek didn't extend to speaking it, and in any case modern Greek is nearly as different from ancient Greek as Italian from Latin. A majority of the Greek geologists I met spoke French, and some spoke English (I'm sure they all could read it). On one of my trips into the Peloponnesos, two German geologists from the Free University of Berlin were with us; they were looking for a dissertation project for a Greek student of theirs. As for me, I acquired enough modern Greek to get along, though here again English or French would often serve and German turned out to be useful in northern Greece. And I learned to read it; during my long stay in 1979, I was avidly reading the modern Greek poetry of Kavafy (as he Englished it) or Kabaphes, an outstanding poet from the Greek community in Alexandria, Egypt.

One of my colleagues at Yale, Professor George Veronis, has relatives in Crete, and he had put me in touch with a Greek friend of his who ran the Viking(!) Tourist Agency in Athens, which arranged tourist trips into the Greek islands, so I signed up for one of them. It was a glorious trip and took us to Mykonos and Delos, Paros, Ios, Naxos, and above all Thera or Santorini, a great caldera now filled with seawater produced by an immense volcanic explosion in about the fifteenth century BC, late in the time of the Minoan civilization, which it may have helped to destroy. I also signed up for a trip to Crete to visit the ruins of Knossos, after which I rented a car and drove from one end of Crete to the other studying its geology, for the French excursion mentioned above had gone there too.

I had hoped to combine my trip to Crete with a trip to the islands of Samos and Rhodes, but by this time summer was approaching and there were more tourists than beds on those islands, so that further visits there had to be forbidden. Instead, when I came back to Greece that August, Dr. Papanikolaou invited me to join him on a six-day trip to far northeastern Greece, to the Rhodope Mountains along the Bulgarian border.

In 1982 I had the chance to get back to Greece; I was asked to give a lecture at the University (a standard lecture I give on mountain ranges in the Soviet Union; I gave it in English and it was translated), and they gave me a short trip across central Greece. In May 1988 I spent ten days at a meeting of the Geological Society of Greece in Athens and on field trips before and after, in the Peloponnesos and in northern Greece. I was even asked to chair one of the sessions at that meeting. In 1992 I went to a very similar meeting; this time the second trip went to the islands of Khios and Lesbos in the northeastern Aegean, quite new country for me.

Finally, in August 1994 I took a Cornell Adult University Cruise through the Mediterranean Sea that emphasized geology, especially volcanic geology, because the President of Cornell, Frank Rhodes, a fine geologist, was one of the leaders. After seeing Vesuvius, Stromboli, and Etna, we sailed on to Greece — not neglecting to stop on the island of Ithake for which Cornell's Ithaca is named — traversed the Gulf of Corinth and the Corinth Canal, notable because of the obvious earthquake faults in the (geologically speaking) very young strata on its walls, where more earthquakes are by no means unlikely, again visited Thera, and went on to Ephesos on the eastern (now Turkish) coast of the Aegean Sea, then came back to see Athens and once more took a trip, though this time mainly archeological, into the Peloponnesos.

Five Months in the Soviet Union with Soviet Geologists:
Dmitri V. Nalivkin, Vladimir V. Menner,
Aleksandr Peyve, Aleksey A. Bogdanov

AT THE FIRST TWO International Geological Congresses I attended — Great Britain in 1948 and North Africa in 1952 — there were very few geologists from the Soviet Union. Evidently they were scared to be seen alone with Westerners; their interventions, at Council and Committee meetings for example, were "party-line." The only exception I heard of was in Algiers, where A. J. Butler, who had been General Secretary of the London Congress, got the chief Soviet delegate to go out with him on what appears to have been a wild drunken party, and he reported that the Soviet was in fact very open and friendly. But in

1953 Stalin died, and at the Mexican Congress in 1956 there were many more Soviet geologists, and they were clearly anxious to make contacts; they sought us out, gave us reprints, exchanged addresses, and the like. It was in Copenhagen in 1960, however, that I really came to know several of them.

Even before 1960, at meetings of the International Commissions on Stratigraphy and the Geological Map of the World in Paris in 1958, I met Akademik D. V. Nalivkin, then a senior academician. He was very cordial to me because he and Professor Dunbar had become great friends in 1937, during an excursion to the Ural Mountains at the International Congress in the Soviet Union that year. Also he knew of the stratigraphy book that Dunbar and I had just published. As Secretary of the International Commission on Stratigraphy from 1952 to 1960, I had learned of the Russians' great interest in stratigraphic terminology and their very definite views on the subject (to us they seemed dogmatic). During that period I got hold of a pamphlet in Russian: *Stratigraphic Classification and Terminology*, prepared by the Interdepartmental Stratigraphic Committee, USSR (1956), and translated it into English; then I sent the translation to Akademik Nalivkin asking him to have it reviewed. After that review, my translation was published in the *International Geology Review* (v. 1, no.2, p. 22-38, 1959); it was then republished in Moscow, in the second edition of the original Russian pamphlet in 1960.

Naturally these matters were discussed at meetings of the International Commission at the Congress in Copenhagen in 1960, at which the Soviet point of view was represented by Professor V. V. Menner; in my diary I mention his "good humor and a spirit of scientific toleration that I hadn't expected and have admired." He and I worked together in translating at those meetings, he handling translations between Russian and French and I between French and English. Moreover, some of Menner's students were just then translating the Dunbar and Rodgers textbook, **Principles of Stratigraphy**, into Russian; it was published there in 1962. Nalivkin too was at the Congress in Copenhagen, and both he and Menner were very friendly and helpful when I asked them about the possibility of my coming to the Soviet Union in a few years' time.

On my post-Congress excursion that year, a splendid excursion that crossed the mountains of Sweden and Norway from Östersund to Trondheim, I met another Soviet geologist, Aleksandr Peyve; although he had very little English and my Russian was still inadequate, he had a translator with him, a geographer named Lange, and I made a special effort to get to know him. I was amazed to learn that for Peyve the chief tectonic movements are horizontal, like pushing rugs sideways on a floor, as in folded mountain ranges, or moving blocks laterally past each other, as along the San Andreas fault of California. Thus Peyve was a "mobilist," friendly to such ideas as Continental Drift. Up to that time we in the West had come to believe that V. V. Belousov represented Soviet tectonics, for he had been the only Soviet structural geologist to come to meetings in the West. According to him the primary movements are all vertical, the horizontal movements being secondarily produced by gravity-sliding off uplifted blocks onto downdropped ones; thus he was resolutely fixist. Later indeed I learned that, in the Soviet Academy of Sciences, Peyve was *Akademik* (full academician) but Belousov was only *Chlen-Korrespondent* (corresponding member); in a classless society such distinctions can be important.

Only later did I come to know Belousov personally; before that I had only heard him lecture, in English, and I had found him very stiff and rigid, quite unyielding about any part of his own theories. When I did come to know him, I found him charming and undogmatic, as indeed he had been represented to me by some Westerners who knew him well; his platform stiffness and rigidity vanished entirely, and he had a delightful sense of humor, except perhaps when his pet theory was in debate. After that I could understand why so many Russian geologists who had been his students held firmly to his theory. Curiously, when I met another famous and very influential geologist whose ideas I could never accept, Hans Stille, I found that he too was warm and charming; I am sure that helped to extend his influence.

To continue digressing, in later years I also came to know Akademik Peyve quite well. Then in 1972 he came to the United States, and early in May I took him on a field trip for four days into the Appalachians of Pennsylvania and Maryland. In Pennsylvania we were guided by Lucian Platt, in Maryland by William Crowley, both former students of mine who had recently made important break-throughs in the regional geology. We were accompanied on parts of the trip by the State Geologists, each in his own state, and by various Yale faculty and graduate students.

Later that year both Peyve and Belousov came on the excursion in the Canadian Appalachians that Dr. William Poole and I ran after the International Congress in Montreal but, as they barely spoke to each other, they specifically asked not to room together; Peyve roomed with me on the trip and Belousov with Dr. Poole. End digression.

In 1962, at a meeting in Paris like that in 1958, I met Professor A. A. Bogdanov of the Moscow State University (MGU), and with him too I discussed my hopes for coming to the Soviet Union. He was very helpful and told me to write him if I ever had the opportunity to come.

Preparing for the International Geological Congress in India in 1964, which was held in December instead of the usual August to avoid the rains and the hot season, I decided to fit it into my first round-the-world trip, so I arranged to stop in Moscow on the way for five days, to mend fences for my trip to the Soviet Union in 1967, which was already in the planning stage. I was held up for two days in Paris, however, by bad fog on the airport in Moscow; the weather was unseasonably warm, and indeed, when I got there, the Muscovites were all complaining about it. Professor Bogdanov met me at the plane; in the three days I still had I was shown much of the city and taken to a concert at the Moscow Conservatory and to an opera at the Bol'shoy Theatre, but the fog had deprived me of another opera and of a ballet — Swan Lake! I did give a lecture, on New England as a part of the Appalachians, at the University's Faculty of Geology, of which Bogdanov was Dean — a faculty fifteen times the size of Yale's Department of Geology with 2,000 students! Although my Russian was coming along, I gave it in English, after a halting apology in Russian, and it was translated, a sentence or two at a time. Professor Bogdanov introduced me to several geologists on his faculty, especially those interested in problems that interested me; among them was Dr. Maria Raaben who was pioneering the use of fossil algae to date and subdivide an early part of the geological record that had no other fossils, a method then rather frowned on in the U. S. I persuaded her to write an article about it for the *American Journal of Science*; it was published in 1969 (v. 267, p. 1-18) and helped to change people's minds. Two days later I flew on to India, along with some twenty Russian geologists going to the Congress. In India I came to know fairly well several geologists whom I first met on that flight, especially Professor Azhgirey over a bottle of vodka he had brought along, and the younger Nalivkin, son of the academician.

Learning Russian — As mentioned above, while at the Albany Academy I studied French, Latin, German, and ancient Greek. Then before the Mexican Congress of 1956, I studied Spanish and really had very little difficulty learning first to read and then to speak it; having had both Latin and French, I found it fairly easy. As a result I got rather a swelled head about languages and decided to take up some more. First I took up Portuguese, and by chance the Portuguese grammar I got from the library was by the same authors as the Spanish grammar I had used — the same lessons, the same vocabularies, even the same exercise sentences; there was one extra lesson, for the pluperfect tense, which still exists in Portuguese but in Spanish has become the second past subjunctive. I've never tried to speak Portuguese, however. In each language I learned, I made a point of reading great literature — Cervantes in Spanish, Camões in Portuguese — and I worked through the *Oxford Book of*

Verse for each. Then I tackled Italian; that wasn't quite so easy, but fairly soon I was reading Boccaccio and then Dante. Later I also tried to speak it, but I never did well and I never tried to give a lecture in Italian; Spanish words and even phrases kept creeping into my Italian sentences when I was talking, but the Italians were pleasantly indulgent.

Still very cocky, I took up Russian, and my head came right back down to size. English is of course a mixture of Teutonic roots, which lead one into German and the Scandinavian languages, and Latin roots, which lead one into the Romance languages, but that doesn't help one with Slavic languages except for a few simple words like mother — *mat'* — and milk — *moloko*. Nevertheless in a few years I had nearly mastered Russian, and of course my five months in the Soviet Union in 1967 gave me the necessary fluency. When my graduate students complained to me about having to learn foreign languages, I just told them that the first four are the hardest; they never liked that.

To the Crimea

My visit to the Soviet Union in 1967 was on an exchange between the two Academies of Sciences, though at that time I wasn't a member of the U. S. Academy; I was therefore a guest of their Academy and the beneficiary of superlative hospitality. My main host was Menner, who since 1964 had become Akademik, and when I was in Moscow I spent most of my time in his Academy Institute. On my arrival my Russian wasn't quite good enough, but it soon became adequate; indeed before I left I gave nine lectures in Russian, in five different cities on five different topics.

When I was there, geology in the U.S.S.R., indeed science in general I think, was done by three different groups, and the relations between them tended to be formal, weak, and sometimes unfriendly. There were the Institutes of the Soviet Academy of Sciences, which had the highest prestige. There was the All-Union Geological Research Institute, VSEGEI (a part of the Ministry of Geology), which would correspond to the U. S. Geological Survey if all our State surveys were its branches. There were the Geology Departments of the Universities, but they apparently had the lowest prestige, as their principal job was supposed to be teaching, not geological research. I was lucky to have "ins" into all three groups, through Menner and Peyve, Nalivkin, and Bogdanov, so I saw a full sample of the geological research being done.

Right at the start I was lucky to run into Dr. Michael Churkin, a PhD from Columbia University then working for the U. S. Geological

Survey in Alaska. He was in the Soviet Union to confer with their geologists on geology across the Bering Strait — Chukotka vs. Alaska; one must not forget that Alaska was part of the Russian Empire until the United States bought it in 1867, just one hundred years earlier. Churkin's parents were Russians who were living in Mukden in 1905 when Japan replaced Russia as the "protector" of Manchuria; later they emigrated to California, and Churkin spoke excellent Russian but no French, up to that time my principal means of communicating with the older Russian geologists. It happened that Churkin, with his wife and two sons who were with him, was *driving* from Moscow to the Crimea beginning the next day! and they kindly invited me to go with them. They had driven in from Germany in a bright red, new Volkswagen station-wagon, which naturally attracted everyone's attention; e.g., the police, who always had to look at it and inspect its papers but who made relatively little difficulty. The trip took three days, and there could have been no better way to see and appreciate the great Russian plain or steppe.

In the Crimea, which has a backbone of mountains, the only mountains in the great Russian plain between the Carpathians and the Ural, we were by courtesy of Professor Bogdanov his guests at the summer Geology field camp of the University of Moscow, whose Director, Oleg A. Mazarovich, was very cordial and helpful. I was there for two weeks being shown the geology of the Crimean mountains, which I later learned are like a pocket edition of the Greater Caucasus. In Moscow I had met Dr. Muratov, who had given me a copy of his book *Geology of the Crimea*, an excellent treatise written in admirably straight-forward Russian (too much scientific Russian is written in a prose that apes the most complicated variety of scientific German), and indeed I had been reading it on the trip down.

One day during our visit Churkin and his older son, Mazarovich, and I drove around to the village Verkhorech'e, where we parked Churkin's bright red car and climbed the mountain behind to see the geology. When we arrived, we could see that a marriage was being registered at the village hall, and those with cameras took pictures of the groom, in a trim Western suit, and the bride, in a bright Ukrainian peasant dress. When we came back down off our mountain, we met the brother of the groom, weaving through the streets, and he loudly insisted we come to the wedding, so we did. Actually it was the wedding banquet; the bride and groom, flanked by their parents, sat at a sort of high table, and everyone else was below, happily milling around. Of course the first thing for us to do was to drink a toast to the happy couple; as they had run out of wine glasses, they brought us tumblers, which they filled with vodka till they were running over. For a major toast like that, one must drink the whole glass;

MAP 12–8. Maps of Parts of the Former Soviet Union

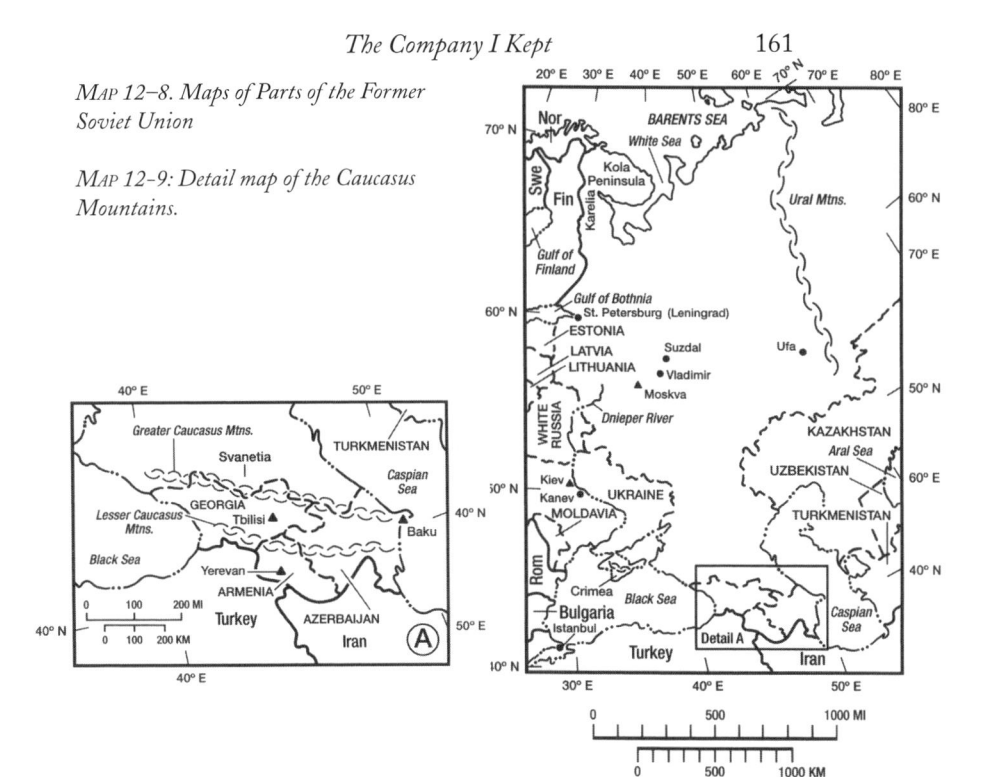

MAP 12-9: Detail map of the Caucasus Mountains.

one can stop midway and wave it about, but on no circumstances may one set it down till it's empty. We took our time, saying nice things while waving the glasses — it was wonderful how my Russian improved with the vodka — but we did our duty. Then they wanted to fill our glasses up again, but I got them to fill mine with white wine instead of vodka. Soon we were as happy as the other guests; the bride's brother and I swapped war stories (he'd fought the Germans and I'd fought the Japs; Russians and Americans are brothers), her father and I embraced several times, and I danced a sort of trepak with the local (grass?) widow. Somehow we got back to camp. I heard later that the visit of the American geologists to the wedding in the Crimea had become a sort of legend among the Soviet geologists.

Toward the end of our stay at the camp, Professor Bogdanov showed up, for it was after all the summer camp for his geology faculty, and it was agreed that I would return to Moscow with him. But he had business to do in Kiev, so I went there with him and spent three days in that lovely and very historical city, the first center of civilization in Russia.

Moscow and Kazakhstan

I SPENT MOST OF THE NEXT TWO MONTHS in Moscow, waiting for further plans to be completed, and I met a whole group of able geologists working in all corners of the Soviet Union, who told me about their field areas and gave me their books to read. I also got into the habit of going to the Bol'shoy Theatre and standing on its steps looking for someone with a ticket to sell; I rarely failed to find one, and I got to a number of wonderful concerts, operas, and ballet performances. One time indeed a lady had two tickets to sell and wouldn't sell them separately, so I bought both and then turned around and sold the extra one to someone else. Another time when I was standing there, a Lieutenant in the uniform of the Soviet Navy came up to me and asked, in Russian of course: "Where is the Hotel Metropol?" It was just across the square, as I told him, for I'd eaten dinner there more than once, but I added: "But I'm a foreigner (inostranets) here myself." "So am I," he replied; "I'm Lithuanian." In the uniform of the Soviet Navy!

Sometimes when I was talking Russian, I had the distinct impression that my rather good Russian pronunciation, learned from the records beforehand, combined with my limited Russian vocabulary made people think of me as an intelligent child who could use a lot of help.

Several of the Russians had me for evening parties (vecherinki), including a fine one at the Bogdanovs. By that time I'd met both their sons: Aleksey Bogdanov, a biochemist who had in fact stayed a couple of nights in my suite at Yale in April 1967 during his "post-doc" at Harvard, and Nikita, a geologist whom I'd met when I first got to Moscow in June 1967 and who later stayed in my suite when he was in the States in 1968. I invited their father to come on the trip through the U. S, Appalachians that I ran in 1972 for my Francophone friends, so that he too could stay in my suite, but he died in 1971. Moreover, people kept giving me presents; one of the best, from Professor Bogdanov, was an atlas of road maps of the Soviet Union, by far the most useful set of maps I encountered there. I also have a later edition, bought another time I was in the Union.

During that spell in Moscow, Menner had been working to get me, a foreigner, to Kirgiziya in Central Asia but had apparently not been able to break through the red tape. In the meantime, Professor Bogdanov decided to have me visit a field party in central Kazakhstan, so in early August I was taken there for about two weeks. We flew to Akmolinsk or Tselinograd, the "Virgin City" because it was the center of the "Virgin Lands" program of the 1960s. Thence we drove in a truck to the field camp. Central Kazakhstan is a region of small bumpy hills scattered over a flattish plain, so the scenery was only moderate but the geology quite interesting. Again Bogdanov flew in near the end of my stay there. At the end we went by truck to a big collective farm, which we had visited before, and by local plane back to Akmolinsk, then a regular flight back to Moscow. Because the telegram they'd sent the day before took twenty-four hours to reach Moscow, nobody had reserved me a hotel room, and Sasha Belov, one of the younger men of the Institute, had to take me home to his apartment in a big concrete dormitory building west of the city; fortunately his wife and son were off at camp, so I didn't crowd him, but I got to see how many of them live.

The Ural Mountains

DURING THE LATTER PART of my long stay in Moscow, I'd been reading about the Ural Mountains; I already knew that they are a lot like "my" Appalachians, but on reading I discovered some quite astonishing parallels, and I began to urge my hosts to arrange to get me there. When I got back from Kazakhstan, arrangements were well along for a really big tour, not only to the Ural but to Central Asia and the Caucasus, for Akademik Peyve had arrived in the meantime, and he was very good at cutting red tape. Several geologists who knew Ural geology came in to talk to me, some with exact directions on how to get to critical localities for deciding between two hypotheses about the rock folds there, the same two hypotheses in fact that I'd spent much of the last two decades arguing about with Byron Cooper in the Appalachians. Moreover the evidence seemed to be coming out on my side of the argument, whether Ural or Appalachian.

Our senior leader on that trip was Dr. Boris M. Keller of the Moscow Institute, whose dissertation had been in the region we were to visit; he flew out with me to Ufa, west of the southern Ural, for they almost always had someone from the Institute to fly with me on my trips around the Union. He was rather a conservative in the argument, but one of the local geologists who joined us was M. A. Kamaletdinov, a Tatar geologist who was in charge of drilling for oil on the west flank of the Ural and who had already published evidence, and I had read his article, which clinched, for me at least, the other hypothesis. They put on an eight-day field trip in that part of the western Ural, stopping each night at a different place where the people in the truck that accompanied our jeep had set up camp, generally under pine trees by a rushing stream; moreover the whole trip was arranged just for me. We saw a great deal, and virtually all my guesses, based on parallels with the Appalachians, were confirmed. I was so impressed with young Kamaletdinov that, when I got back to Moscow, I sang his praises as loudly as I could, and later I heard that he got two good promotions, first from the trest or government oil company for whom he'd been working to the Geological Institute of the local Bashkirian Academy of Sciences, then again when that Institute was made a filial of the main Geological Institute in Moscow. I met him in 1973, then again in 1984 at the International Geological Congress in Moscow, where we had a nice reunion.

I gave two lectures in Ufa, both in Russian if not very good Russian, but I'd so much rather make my own mistakes than have a translator make them. As soon as I got there they asked me to give one comparing the Ural with the Appalachians, but I begged off, as I hadn't seen the Ural yet, so my first lecture was about the two hypotheses for the Appalachians; of course the implications for the Ural were clear enough. Then when I got back I did have to give a lecture comparing them, but by then I knew enough to do so intelligently. But that morning I was taken to my press conference for the local newspaper, *Sovetskaya Bashkiriya*, an idea thought up by my main local host, S. A. Fattakhutdinov. It took place in the Chief Editor's office; I was seated in a nice Morris chair in front of his desk, and reporters and photographers lined the walls. The questions were quite general at first — e.g., what did I think of Bashkiriya — but I was well primed for this, for Dunbar had told me much about his trip there in 1937, and I'd picked up a lot during our tours of Ufa, and besides I'm for mother and against sin. But then they started asking political questions, for this was the period of our war in Vietnam, and they asked me about my young colleague in Political Science at Yale, Staughton Lynd, who had recently gone to Hanoi in defiance of our State Department. At that point my Russian failed, I couldn't understand the question, and my host rescued me, as we had prearranged. Later they even showed me the text of what they intended to print and let me make a few changes; what American newspaper would do that? Still later I was given a copy of the article as printed, in the middle of which is a picture of me sitting in that Morris chair looking thoroughly relaxed; how they got such a picture I will never know. After that my own lecture was a bit of an anticlimax.

Central Asia

From Ufa we flew on to Tashkent, where we were met by Dr. Valentin S. Burtman, the leader for the next part of my excursion; I had already met him at the Institute in Moscow and come to admire his work. He guided us round the western Tian-Shan for a week, showing us the evidence for the nappe structure he had worked out there. I was so pleased with his work that I talked him into writing a big article about it for the *AJS*. Moreover, when he wrote it and sent it in, in English!, in 1972, it was in fine shape and required a minimum of corrections; by 1973 we had sent him the galley proof to correct.

Digression: When I left in 1973 for my sabbatical year in Australia, I left strict instructions to publish Dr. Burtman's article as soon as possible after the proofs got back, and in Australia I kept telling people about the fine paper soon to appear. When I got back in the fall of 1974, however, it still hadn't been published and I was pretty upset, but they gave me a soft answer about the proofs having been lost in transit and there was nothing I could do about it. Some seven months later there was a meeting of the Journal Editors with Yale's Committee for the Journal; the Journal is wholly owned by Yale, and the Committee is supposed to make sure the Editors don't go senile. But that meeting suddenly turned into a testimonial to *me*, telling me I wouldn't be allowed to resign as Editor. This all seemed like a broken record to me, for almost two years earlier I'd suggested that, after twenty-five years wielding the power of an Editor — if it's publish or perish, I was deciding who perishes — it was time for me to resign; they had then held a similar meeting, very publicly refusing to let me go. But now at this new meeting, my colleague Brian Skinner, Chairman of that Committee, after repeating the same old arguments turned to me and said: "And to prove it, here's your book, in honor of your *first* twenty-five years as Editor" - the *Rodgers Volume*, v. 275-A of the *American Journal of Science*. Among the many fine articles in that volume was Burtman's; they had talked him into waiting a full year to appear in it. I can say in all modesty that it's a very fine volume, for I had nothing whatever to do with putting it out. End digression.

MAP 12-10: *Central Asia*

On Burtman's trip we slept out every night, in the open when the weather permitted, as it often did. One day, from a camp of other geologists at 2,600 meters, we rode on horseback to about 3,600 meters (over two miles) to look up at summits in the Alay Range at 5,000 meters (a good three miles). On that trip also we camped by a lake called Iskander-Kul, because Alexander the Great got there. At the end of the excursion we came into Samarkand, a wonderful city that was the capital city of Timur or Tamburlane, and we had a couple of days to be tourists.

The Caucasus

From Samarkand we flew back to Tashkent, and I flew on, over deserts and the Caspian Sea, to Tbilisi, the capital of Gruziya, Soviet Georgia, between the Greater and the Lesser Caucasus. The difference between the Greater and the Lesser Caucasus is somewhat like the difference between the Eastern Rocky Mountains, those of Colorado and most of Wyoming, and the Western Rocky Mountains, those coming down from Canada across western Montana into Idaho and westernmost Wyoming and on into northern Utah.

At Tbilisi I was met by Dr. Tsagareli, a Georgian geologist whom I had first met on the plane to India in December 1964 and then had met again, recognized, and greeted by name in June 1967 in Moscow. The next day, before we started on that day's field trip, he took me around to the Government Palace and introduced me to Dzotsenidze, a geologist who had worked on volcanic rocks in Georgia but who was now the President of the Georgian Soviet Socialistic Republic. Moreover Dzotsenidze decided to join us for the day, so we transferred to the Presidential limousine and drove north into the foothills of the Greater Caucasus. When Dzotsenidze left us that evening, he said he had to fly to Moscow the next day on business — was it for a meeting of the Central Committee of the Communist Party? The other three days of that excursion we spent mainly in the foothills of the Lesser Caucasus, reaching the east end of the Black Sea.

The following day, in Tbilisi, I gave a lecture on the Appalachians; I gave it in Russian — Tsagareli introduced me as "the American who doesn't speak English" — but I prefaced it by thanking Tsagareli in three words of Georgian, learned for the occasion, and they broke into applause; I doubt if the Russians ever do that. Then that night they gave me a splendid banquet in a private dining room in the restaurant on top of the mountain that rises out of the city, reached by funicular, and I was seated at the right hand of President Dzotsenidze, while six or seven fine Georgian wines were served us.

Then I spent nearly a week in Armenia, again a mixture of field trips and sightseeing, with Mt. Ararat looking down on us, though from the Turkish side of the border. One particularly interesting spot was a metallurgical plant some 5,000 years old, complete with an altar and a place to observe the stars, to insure success in the smelting.

Georgian hospitality is proverbial, even among the very hospitable Russians (at least they were always very hospitable to me), and the Georgian wines are the best in the Union, so my visit to Georgia was a memorable one. The Georgians are very proud of their country and of their history, but they express their chauvinism with such a light touch that the visitor wants to go along. Armenia is quite different; the Armenians too are very proud of their country, but their "patriotism" seems to be mainly impressing on you their historical difficulties, the centuries of domination by the Turks; their intense nationalism gets rather tiring. Erevan has fine museums and libraries with priceless manuscripts; on the outside wall of one they showed me a great map of the Armenian Empire of the eighth century, reaching to the Mediterranean. When I suggested that Armenians must then have dominated several other peoples, they hotly denied it.

During that trip I was reading a lot of Russian literature: poetry — notably Pushkin and Aleksandr Blok — novels by Turgenev, and plays and short stories by Chekhov, of whose writing I became particularly fond. When I got back to Moscow, I had the opportunity to see a couple of his plays at the Moscow Art Theatre where they were first performed; by that time my understanding of spoken Russian was better and I got a good deal, though by no means all.

Moscow and Leningrad

A<small>FTER</small> A<small>RMENIA</small> I <small>CAME BACK</small> to Moscow for my last month in the Soviet Union, and there I went to work writing an article on the Appalachians for the Institute's journal, *Geotektonika*, one of the best geological journals in the Union, and preparing a series of three lectures they'd asked me to give. I prepared both the article and the lectures in Russian, rather to their astonishment; Nikita Bogdanov, Professor Bogdanov's geologist son, was I think a bit put out as he'd expected to translate both for me, but by then I had already given four lectures in Russian, though not in Moscow. Of course my written Russian required a lot of correction — some of my blunders were quite amusing — but I felt the would-be translators tended to pad out the writing unnecessarily with clichés and paraphrases, rather in the style of bad scientific German. Amusingly, my Russian article was then translated back into English and published in the

United States, in the translation of *Geotektonika* regularly published by the American Geophysical Union.

During that month I went to Leningrad on the Union's crack train, the Red Arrow, for ten days. Most of the days I spent at VSEGEI, mainly being talked to by one geologist after another about the geology he'd been studying in some corner of the Union. That helped to fill out my knowledge of its general geology; also very helpful was their Museum, which contains displays exhibiting the geology of each major geological region. Akademik Nalivkin was there, for he was the grand old man of VSEGEI, and he was very cordial, which made everyone else very cordial too; he came to listen to my lecture, again on the Appalachians and the two hypotheses. They liked that so much they asked me for another! which I gave a couple of days later on structure like that in the Taconic region.

Needless to say, in Leningrad I also took in a lot of sights, concerts, and operas, and above all the Hermitage Museum, which is remarkable not only for its splendid collection of paintings but for the opulence of its rooms. I also visited the sumptuous Issakovskiy Cathedral, built by the nineteenth-century tsars more for their glory than for God's. My guide for much of this was Akademik Nalivkin's son, also a geologist; he was shocked when I told him the cathedral didn't seem religious to me, as for him I suppose it quite epitomized religion as it was under the tsars and patriarchs before the Revolution. I also got to see their Museum of the History of Religion and Atheism in the Kazan Cathedral, very tendentious — but well done.

During these trips in 1967 I visited five different mountain ranges in the Soviet Union. When I got home I plotted them up on a map of the Union, which I superposed on a map of Anglo-America — Canada and the United States — at the same scale and latitude but turned right for left because we started on the east coast and worked westwards but the Russians started at the west and worked eastwards. Looking at the map, I realized that I'd hardly been halfway across their country; it embraced after all one seventh of the land area of the Earth, a fifth more land than Canada and the United States combined. In 1969 I remedied that; in 1973 I got still farther east.

1969: Lake Baykal

During a pleasant lunch with three Soviet geologists in Moscow in October 1967, I learned that an informal specialist group of geologists called AZOPRO — l'Association pour l'Étude des Zones Profondes — was planning to hold a meeting on Lake Baykal in 1969, and I resolved to go if I possibly could. The leader of that group was Professor Paul Michot of Liège in Belgium, and it happened that he and I had a rather special bond. During the meeting of the International Commissions in Paris in 1962, I had played hookey from one of the geological sessions and gone to hear a performance of Debussy's opera *Pelléas et Mélisande* based on the play by the Belgian writer Maurice Maeterlinck; during the intermission I ran into Professor Michot, who was playing hookey from the same meeting, and naturally we became good friends. Now I wrote to him asking how I could become a member of AZOPRO, and he replied that I need only send him $10 (U. S.) once in a while, when he needed it for postage. Thus I got all the circulars for the Baykal excursion, and I signed up for it.

In August 1969 then I flew to Moscow, where I met many of my friends from 1967, especially at a *vecherinka* in Akademik Menner's apartment. Furthermore, Professor Bogdanov, his wife, and Akademik Peyve were on the same excursion to Baykal: it was a superb trip. We flew to Irkutsk and were taken to the Academy's Limnological Institute on the lake; they gave us a ten-day cruise on the lake in their research vessels. Lake Baykal isn't the largest lake in area in the world — that is our Lake Superior — but it is the deepest and therefore has the largest volume of fresh water. It is not like any of our Great Lakes but much more like Lakes Tanganyika and Nyasa or Malawi, the second and fourth deepest. They are in the East African rift valleys, fault troughs that have formed where the part of Africa from the Gulf of Aden to Mozambique is getting ready to drift away and become a sort of super-Madagascar. Baykal is in a similar fault trough along an east-west line of breaks where China, with Tibet, is sliding eastward relative to Siberia and the rest of Asia because India is pushing under Tibet and forcing it eastward, raising the Himalaya Mountains in the process — or so we geologists think.

One of the high points of this trip was to visit a quarry not far from the southwest end of the lake where Professor Korzhinskiy, an outstanding Soviet petrologist, had worked out certain significant principles that just then were coming to be recognized and accepted by North American petrologists; moreover Korzhinskiy was with us and demonstrated his principles in the quarry. Another high point was to climb up an alluvial fan at the mouth of a stream coming out of the mountains along the west side of the lake, to see where a very recent earthquake fault (a century ago?) cut across the fan, dropping the lake or trough side down relative to the mountain side by a meter or more.

Early that year, Walter Sullivan, Science Editor for the *New York Times*, had reported in the *Times* on the serious danger of pollution of Lake Baykal by wastes from a paper mill recently built on its eastern shore, getting his material from articles in the Soviet press; the location on the Trans-Siberian Railroad and close to vast spruce forests and a large supply of fresh water — the lake! — was "ideal" for such a plant. The Director of the Limnological Institute, Dr. Galazyy, when asked about it, pointed it out on the opposite shore, and said that the problem had already reached a quite high level in the government and should soon be resolved. Four years later I got to Lake Baykal again, and Galazyy told us that it had been resolved by building a pipeline to carry the wastes around the south end of the lake and dump them in its outlet, the Angara River.

Before and after seeing Baykal, we visited Novosibirsk and its Academic City, headquarters of the Siberian Branch of the Soviet Academy of Sciences. A high point of that visit was to see specimens of the diamond-bearing rock of northern Siberia, a dark green rock in which were embedded fairly small but perfect octahedra (double four-sided pyramids) of diamond.

In 1969 I again got to Leningrad for a couple of days; again I visited VSEGEI, especially its Museum, and the Hermitage. Then I flew out to Copenhagen and on to Spain; to Madrid, where I visited El Prado and saw its wonderful paintings, above all the Goyas. Thence I went on to Oviedo on the north coast, in Cantabria, where my host was Professor Manuel Julivert; I had met him in Praha the year before, and we had arranged this visit then. He and his assistant Alberto Marcos took me around the Cantabrian Mountains, a curious hairpin range; moreover I got two fine articles for the *American Journal of Science* out of them (v. 270, p. 1-29, 1971; v. 273, p. 353-375, 1973).

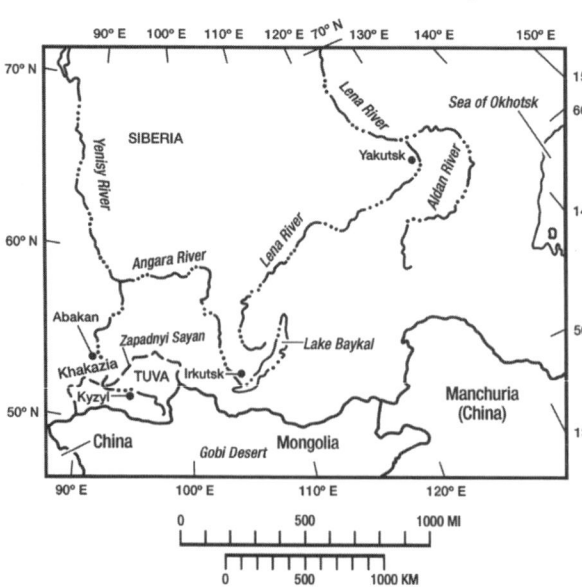

From Spain I flew back to Switzerland, where I spent a few days in Zürich, making a trip to Luzern to go up Mt. Pilatus and look down on the lake. After that I had ten days in Hungary attending the 100th Anniversary of the Hungarian Geological Survey in Budapest and going on a field trip to the hills near Lake Balaton. I also got to see three Bartok works — a ballet and two operas — at the Budapest Opera.

MAP 12-11: *Lake Baykal*

The 1970s & After

FIG. 13–20. *Willie Ruff's Branford seminar on Afro-American Music, 18 October 1972. Bessie Jones, the principal speaker at the seminar, is visible behind John Rodgers.*

13 — In the United States

Willie Ruff and Dwike Mitchell

I DO NOT NEED to chronicle the lives of Ruff and Mitchell, as they have been beautifully told by William Zinsser in his book *Willie and Dwike* (Harper & Row, 1984) and by Willie himself in his autobiography *A Call to Assembly* (Viking, 1991). I would like to say however that for the last quarter century of my life they have been two of my very closest friends.

Music was of course my means of coming to know them. They met in the Army in 1948, in the band at the then all-black Lockbourne Air Base near Columbus, Ohio; in 1955 they formed the Mitchell-Ruff Duo, which is still giving concerts over forty years later, almost certainly the longest-lasting combo in the jazz world: Mitchell on the piano and Ruff on the string bass and the French horn, in jazz yet. I first became aware of Willie Ruff in the early 1950s when he was an undergraduate student in the Yale School of Music, which took undergraduates then; Willie was there on the GI Bill after his years in the Army, in which he'd enlisted at fourteen by lying egregiously about his age. I particularly remember a Branford concert in which he and Robert Cecil, another fine horn player, were playing Mozart's *Musical Joke* with the Branford Quartet; during the Trio of the Minuet, in accordance with Mozart's explicit instructions in the score, they opened up a checkerboard and started a game while the string players kept playing away in front of them.

In the fall of 1970, when Willie returned to Yale as a member of the Music faculty, I recognized him as soon as I saw him and greeted him by name, rather astonishing him I think, and that was the beginning of our friendship. A year later I talked John Trinkaus, "Trink," then Master of Branford College, into making Willie a Fellow of the College as a sort of "legacy" from his part in those earlier Branford concerts. Moreover Trink then arranged for him to be a Resident Fellow, and in July 1972 he moved into the suite over my head. That fall term Willie taught a seminar in Afro-American music, not just jazz, for the undergraduates in the College, and he made me co-instructor, though I never understood why, for I contributed nothing except that the seminar often met in my suite to use my piano. It was at meetings of that seminar that I came to know his partner Dwike Mitchell, and I also met other famous jazz musicians like Dizzy Gillespie and Lucky Thompson.

It happened that the suite upstairs was reserved for someone else for the spring term of 1973, so Willie moved into my back bedroom; we both were away on trips of various lengths that spring, but we saw a lot of each other, and we began playing horn-and-piano sonatas together informally: Mozart, Beethoven, Hindemith. When I went off to the Soviet Union and on to my Australian year, he continued to live there. Somewhat after my return he moved back upstairs, but also he bought himself a small place in northern Alabama, where he had grown up, and he spent considerable time there.

Both Willie and I have a very great admiration for the music of Paul Hindemith. Although I saw Hindemith every so often during the years that he was teaching at the Yale School of Music, I never knew him personally, and he wouldn't have known who I was. Willie on the other hand took courses from him as a student in the School, and Hindemith, while teaching him a great deal about the whole history and theory of "Western" music, strongly encouraged him to keep on with his jazz career. After I got back from Australia, Willie and I began to work seriously on Hindemith's music, first the big *Horn Sonata in F*, then the *Sonata for Waldhorn in E Flat*, and I also worked up the *Second Piano Sonata*. We practiced together all through 1975, and in December we gave our Hindemith recital, consisting of those three sonatas.

At about this time we got into the habit of having Mitch stay in my back bedroom when he came up from New York to rehearse with Willie; thus he too became a good friend. Then in 1977 I began going to New York now and then to visit him, as we became better and better friends.

During 1976 and 1977, Willie began to study Hindemith's long and seldom played opera, *Die Harmonie der Welt (The Harmony of the World)*, which is built on the life of Johannes Kepler and his discoveries. At one point in the opera, Kepler's daughter asks him about the Man in the Moon, and in reply Kepler sings a long aria setting forth his three laws; the poor girl, understanding none of it, goes back to look at the Moon. Willie was then led to ask whether Kepler's challenge to the musicians of his day to realize in music the "Harmony of the World" (*not* the Music of the Spheres) that he had discovered — a challenge that had never been met — could now be addressed with modern computers and tone-synthesizers. Needing someone with some mathematical and astronomical background, he came down to talk to me, for he was still living over my head when he wasn't in Alabama, so I went to work calculating the necessary parameters. We then looked for a computer expert to help us convert the data into sound; the first one we found who understood what we wanted was Dr. Laurie Spiegel, and she was able to put the music on a tape which had its first public demonstration in April 1977. We presented it several times in New Haven in the next few years and also elsewhere, as at Amherst.

Then with the help of a graduate student at Princeton, Mark Rosenberg, we turned out a record (later a cassette), which Willie, with his characteristic enterprise, published on a new label, the Kepler label, later used also to publish records and cassettes of music by the Mitchell-Ruff Duo. We got some good publicity for our realization of Kepler's "Harmony;" we published an article in the *American Scientist* (v. 67, p. 286-292, 1979), Walter Sullivan wrote it up for the Science Section of the *New York Times*, on its front page!, and Harold Schonberg, the music critic of the *Times*, reviewed it, stating however that it's not really music. That depends of course on one's definition of music, but I'm inclined to agree with him, for no human mind chose the ratios of the vibration-frequencies that determine the tones. Anyway the Kepler matter took much of my time in those years, and it still comes up now and again. For example, in 1996 Willie and I presented our Kepler cassette and talk at the Whitney Center, where I now live.

In 1980 Willie started to teach a seminar in rhythm, and each year he invited me to give a talk about "rhythm in space" — crystals and their structure — which was great fun to prepare and teach. The first years he combined my talk with one by Professor Evelyn Hutchinson, biologist

FIG. 13–21. *Willie Ruff, John Rodgers, and Dwike Mitchell in Columbus, Ohio, 19 May 1994*

and limnologist and one of my greatest intellectual heroes, who talked about biological rhythms, and also about physical rhythms like the seiches in lakes.

All these years I went to hear the Mitchell-Ruff Duo whenever they gave a concert in New Haven, and a couple of times I heard them play in New York. Sometimes indeed I transported them, and Willie's bass, once to a wedding party where they were playing and I was allowed to crash. In 1989, at the end of a geological excursion in Oregon and northern California, I came down to the San Francisco Bay area and heard a fine concert they gave at Stanford University with the San Jose "Pops" Orchestra. After that Mitch and I rented a car for two days to see the hills and mountains north and east of the Bay, and we drove to the tops of Mts. Tamalpais and Diablo, a new experience for Mitch, who isn't sure he likes heights. The next day, on our flight back East, we even looked directly down on Mt. Diablo where we had been the day before.

In 1994 I arranged for the National Academy of Sciences to invite the Mitchell-Ruff Duo to play the Handler Memorial Concert, given every year (alternately jazz and classical) on the evening before the Academy's annual meeting in April. The Academy members gave them a standing ovation, and afterwards many eminent scientists thanked me warmly for having proposed the concert. The next month I further arranged for them to play at the reception following the wedding of my great-niece, Sarah, née Rubinstein, Dubinsky, as my contribution to the

FIG. 13–22. *John Rodgers and his nephew, Jonathan H. Rodgers, on 19 May 1994*
photograph by Ann & Paul Schliffer

festivities (the first wedding in that generation of our family). The wedding took place in Columbus, Ohio, a city of which Willie and Mitch are fond because they first met and played together in the nearby Lockbourne Air Base. Later that year I flew down to Alabama and visited Willie in his home there; then we drove back to New Haven together, following "my" Appalachians.

Jonathan Henry Rodgers, Anala Schultis Rodgers

OF MY EIGHT NEPHEWS AND NIECES, five are the children of my older brother Prentice and his wife Jane, three of my sister Louise and her husband William Ackerman; my oldest brother had no children, and I am a bachelor and hence "have no children to speak of." Among them, the one I've known best has been Jonathan, my brother Prentice's third child and second son. As Prentice, alone of us four siblings, continued to live in Albany after graduating from Amherst College, I saw him and his family very often, every time I went back to visit my parents there; my diary records my seeing them nearly every Christmas through 1966, the year my mother died.

Jonathan went to the Albany Academy; his record there was undistinguished, though he always did well in languages. He was unable to get into Amherst where his father had gone, but he was accepted at Hobart; he didn't take college very seriously, however, and in his sophomore year, having spent as much time drinking beer as going to classes, he flunked out. Now this was the period of the Vietnam War, and he was eligible for the draft; my brother was deeply concerned about his son's lack of ambition, but the best job he could find for him was as a cook's assistant in the best French restaurant in town. From that experience, Jonathan learned to be a fine cook. In due course the Army took him, tested him, discovered his language abilities, and sent him to a language school to learn Arabic, then to Eritrea to monitor broadcasts from the opposing forces in Yemen's civil war. By this time he had married Anala Schultis, who is also, by the way, a very fine cook — dinners at their home, even simple ones, are always culinary delights — and indeed she went to Eritrea with him. In that job he became fascinated by the south Arabian dialects he was hearing and translating, and he made up his mind to go back to college and study Arabic languages; Anala backed him in this resolve and, being a nurse and thus always able to find employment, she worked to help him to do so. He went on the GI Bill to the State University of New York at Binghamton, where he burned up the course, then to graduate school at Yale, where I saw them frequently from 1972 to 1977.

Jobs for young men specializing in the Arabic languages have never been plentiful in the United States, and only after some months did he obtain a position in the library of Hebrew Union College in Cincinnati, which has an excellent collection of books and manuscripts in the various Semitic languages. He found the job challenging and rewarding, and after a while he took a course in the Library School of the University of Kentucky to increase his usefulness to Hebrew Union College. I visited them in Cincinnati twice during 1981, the second time for the meeting of the Geological Society of America at which I was awarded the Penrose Medal. At a party during that meeting, Jon Rodgers being with me, I ran into a geologist I knew named John Rogers, and the three of us had a lot of fun introducing each other to various friends as they came by. Moreover, John Rogers had worked in Arabia, and he and Jon Rodgers had a pleasant time discussing the Arabic language.

In 1983, the Yale Library called my nephew to be one of their specialists in Semitic languages, and he moved to New Haven; thus again I saw a lot of him, Anala, and their growing family of four children. Already during their first stay in New Haven I had introduced them to my old friends George and Anne Conklin, and during the second stay we saw more of them, as for parties and concerts, for we were all fond of good food and company and of the music of Willie Ruff and Dwike Mitchell as well as more orthodox musical fare. A further bond was kieshunds, for Jon added one to his canine family after seeing one the Conklins had. We would see the Conklins especially when Jon's mother Jane came down to visit, for she too was a great friend of theirs until her sudden death in 1988, right after the Conklins and I had visited her in Ajijic in Mexico.

Anala's family lived in Woodstock, New York, at the south foot of the eastern Catskill Mountains, and on one visit there Jonathan and I climbed the western part of the Black Head Range. We had "done" the eastern part years before with his father Prentice and other members of the family, and another time Prentice and I had climbed Slide Mountain, the Catskills' highest peak.

In 1987, the University of Michigan Library made Jonathan a fine offer that Yale was unable to match, and he and his family moved to Ann Arbor. After that I saw them less, but I visited them there several years, right up to 1995, and Jon came back to New Haven from time to time, as on library business, when of course he would stay with me.

14 — Later trips to the Soviet Union

1973: Ophiolites; Eastern Siberia

IN 1973 I GOT TO GO ON TWO SEPARATE EXCURSIONS in the Soviet Union. The first followed a major international conference on ophiolites in Moscow. The name ophiolite is derived from Greek and means "snake-rock." The corresponding name derived from Latin is serpentine, and the rock serpentine is commonly found in ophiolites. Geologists hold that the rocks they class as ophiolite are fragments of old ocean floor (crust and mantle) that have somehow been pushed up onto the continents where geologists can examine them on dry land; they therefore record the existence of former oceans, otherwise completely eaten up or swallowed down into the underlying mantle where two continental masses have been pushed together. The surface area of the Earth is kept more or less constant by the complementary creation of new ocean floor where two continental masses have drifted apart, as where the Atlantic Ocean has formed, in the last 200 million years, between Africa-plus-Europe and the Americas. At the Ophiolite Conference I met several of my good friends from the 1967 visit, like Peyve, Burtman, and Kamaletdinov.

On the (equally international) field trip following the conference, we flew first to Tashkent, and Burtman took us to see the mountains and the geology in Central Asia that he had shown me in 1967, but this time we saw even more. They also gave us time to be tourists in the old cities of Khiva, Bukhara, and above all Samarkand. From Samarkand we then flew to Baku on the Caspian Sea, at the east end of the Greater Caucasus, whence we came by train to Istisu, a watering resort at over 2,200 meters in the Lesser Caucasus in Azerbaydzhan; we were even greeted by the Prime Minister of the Azerbaydzhan Soviet Socialistic Republic. Here, à propos of a question about the geological relations of ophiolites, a leading French geologist quoted a conclusion of Eldridge Moores in his dissertation at Princeton on the Vourinos ophiolite in Greece, and Moores replied that, on my visit there in 1966 with his Princeton Professor Maxwell and another graduate student, Jay Zimmerman, I had found and showed them new evidence that reversed that conclusion.

After the ophiolite trip, we returned to Moscow. The Russians had thought that they could take a small group of Americans to the southern Ural to see the evidence for a new and hotly disputed interpretation in the geology there, an interpretation that I favored. They were even crediting me with having thought of it first, but a small minority of Russian geologists had already proposed it; all I did was get the other Russian geologists to take it seriously, and they ultimately accepted it. But that trip had to be cancelled, I think because the area was too sensitive to permit foreigners to visit there, and I therefore had two weeks in Moscow before the next excursion. I spent them as I'd spent my stays in Moscow in 1967, going to operas, concerts, and ballets, and being wined and dined by my Russian friends. They even took me on a two-day trip, complete with picnics and a night in the first Russian motel, to Suzdal and Vladimir, two lovely, old, and well preserved towns near Moscow. And I succeeded in giving one or two parties on my own, such as taking the Peyves to see Chaykovskiy's opera *Pikovaya Dama (The Queen of Spades)* at the Bolshoy Theatre.

The second excursion was into eastern Siberia to study the strata there that record a particularly important change in the history of life — the beginnings of the multicellular animals that make shells and hence are preserved as easily observed fossils. This transition, which was about 550 million years ago, has been studied in many parts of the world, as in Canada, the United States, Iran, Morocco, and Australia, and specialists from all over the world were present. From Moscow we flew to Irkutsk, where we had time enough to see Lake Baykal again, then to Yakutsk on the Lena River, then in Army helicopters! to the Aldan River, a major tributary of the Lena, where we were met by a river steamer that took us to our camp, with wooden-floored tents and a small dining hall that had been built specifically for our excursion. (When the Soviets decided to do something, they did it up brown.) Then for five days the ship took us up and down the Aldan to look at the rocks in cliffy outcrops along its banks. After that, returned to Yakutsk, we boarded a bigger river steamer, chartered for us, and were taken some tens of kilometers up the Lena River; then for a week we drifted downstream, a little each day, studying the even higher cliffs along that river. I had stomach trouble on that trip, but I managed to climb several of the cliffs.

After that excursion, we flew back to Irkutsk and then Moscow; after a couple of days there, I left on the next leg of my trip, the beginning of my Australian year.

1984: International Geological Congress in the Soviet Union
Excursions to Southern Siberia and the Greater Caucasus

As at all the International Congresses, I carefully chose my excursions for the Congress in the Soviet Union to be as long as possible, and as rewarding. My excursion before the Congress was into the mountains along one part of the southern margin of the great Siberian plain, the Western (Zapadnyy) Sayan. These mountains form the boundary between the Khakas Autonomous Oblast on the north and the Tuva Autonomous Republic on the south.

Digression on the system of republics in the Soviet Union: The whole Union was divided into eleven Union Republics, now for the most part independent, though linked in the Confederation of Independent States; much the largest of these was the Russian Soviet Federated Socialistic Republic or RSFSR (the words Soviet Socialistic appeared also in the names of all the others). Within the RSFSR there were several Autonomous Republics; that they were less autonomous than the Union Republics was shown by the use of languages, for in the Union Republics the local language — Ukrainian, Georgian, Kazakh, Tadzhik, etc. — appeared above Russian on official signs, such as those for cities, streets, and offices, but in the Autonomous Republics Russian appeared above the local language. The Autonomous Oblasti were one step farther down in the hierarchy.

During my trips to these "autonomous" areas, I was frequently embarrassed by the arrogant, if perhaps mainly unconscious, attitude of the Russians to the local people, whom they tended to treat as, in Kipling's phrase, "lesser breeds without the law." This sense of being a "master race" is of course by no means confined to Russians in their "empire;" one is reminded of the crack that the British were never taken in by Hitler's story about the master race, for they knew all along who was the master race. But after all the British aren't in it with the Chinese; the Chinese have known for nearly 3,000 years who was the master race. And we Americans can be just as bad, with our (not always) unconscious attitudes toward blacks and "Native Americans." One knows the nasty things that are said about "the ugly American" abroad, and I have frequently been embarrassed by American tourists, but we've no monopoly on such attitudes. I have to say however that, during my geological trips in the Soviet Union, I frequently witnessed strong and even bitter arguments between the Russians, generally from one or another Institute in Moscow, and the local geologists, and usually I had the impression that the evidence from the rocks supported the Russian point of view.

On this particular trip then, we began in the Khakas Autonomous Oblast (capital: Abakan) and worked south into the Tuva Autonomous Republic (capital: Kyzyl). Khakasia was part of the Russian Empire before the First World War and of the Soviet Union afterwards, but Tuva was part of the Chinese Empire. In 1921 Mongolia declared itself an independent republic, which it still is; Tuva, a much smaller area along the border between Mongolia and Russia, also declared its independence as the Republic of Tannu-Tuva, for the Tuva people are Turki, not Mongol, had once been under Mongol domination, and had no wish to have it happen again. In 1944 Tuva was taken into the Soviet Union, and there were monuments in Kyzyl to the Red Partisans who effected the change, but naturally none to those who fought to stay independent; I feel sure the capital city was named Kyzyl then, for Kyzyl in Turki means red. Chinese governments, at least the one in Taiwan, have never admitted that Tuva isn't part of China; on the wall of the Bank of China in Taipei I saw an outline map of China, and I know maps well enough to see that Tuva was included.

In Kyzyl there is a monument declaring, in Russian, in English, and in Tuva, that it is at the geographical center of Asia. But from the inscription in Tuva I could see that in that language the word for center is close to tuva, so that the whole thing may be simply a clever pun, though our Inturist guide denied it. End long digression.

Our trip lasted for two weeks, in late July and into August. The country is fairly dry, lying not far north of the Gobi Desert, but that year the rains, ordinarily confined to the spring, continued right through the summer, and many of the streams, which are generally dry by July, were in raging flood, so much so that several days the trips had to be cancelled or relocated. Ordinarily the grass cover turns brown in May, but our year there was green grass everywhere.

During the trip we were mostly housed in hotels in the capital cities or one other city, but for four days we were in a camp specially constructed for us, with trailers for sleeping quarters as good as many hotels, batteries of showers and privies, a nice dining-room attached by a plastic corridor to the kitchen tent, waiters in black tie (no coats, for it was warm) with napkins over their arms.

The last day of the excursion we were taken on a river steamer sixty kilometers up the main branch of the Yenisey River, which heads in the mountains along the Mongolian border, flows across Tuva and Khakasia and then through Siberia to the Arctic Ocean. We had already been shown the great dam they were building on the Yenisey where it comes through the Western Sayan.

We then came back to Moscow for the Congress itself, where I met many old friends and made new ones, both Russian and foreign. The most exciting person to meet was Yang Zunyi, who as Tsun-yi Yang had been my fellow graduate student at Yale in the 1930s and then had gone back to China. At first we heard he was doing very well; then he disappeared when the Communists came in. But now he was a member of the official Chinese delegation to the Congress (Taiwan was not invited to that Congress).

During the Congress also I took a very pleasant two-day trip into the Ukraine; we went by train to Kiev, then by hydrofoil boat tens of kilometers down the Dnepr River to Kanev to see some mild structure, then by bus back to Kiev and by train to Moscow. It was a delightful interlude.

After the Congress I took a 10-day trip to the Greater Caucasus, where I saw many things I hadn't seen in 1967, notably the north, Russian flank of the Caucasus and the beautiful valley of Svanetia within it. It was good too to be in Gruziya (Georgia) again. Our chief leader on this trip was Aleksandr (Sasha) Belov, who had been very helpful to me as my principal younger host when I was in Moscow in 1967, like putting me up the night I got back from Kazakhstan without a hotel reservation.

When I came back to Moscow to leave the Soviet Union, I had the opportunity to pay a call on Akademik Peyve, to whom I owe a great deal; I'm pretty sure for example that it was he who arranged for me to be elected a Foreign Member of the Soviet Academy of Sciences. I hadn't seen him before in 1984 because he was quite ill, but at this point I did get to see him; he died not long after.

From the Soviet Union I came back to Great Britain and especially Scotland, to a meeting in Glasgow and some field trips.

In 1989 I went to the Soviet Union one last time (my sixth) because I had the chance to take a field excursion into a corner I hadn't previously visited, the northwest corner — Karelia and the Kola Peninsula west of the White Sea. There was interesting scenery to see and geology to study, but the main purpose of the trip was to visit the super-deep drill hole then being drilled and cored by the Soviets to a depth of fourteen kilometers (nearly nine miles). When we got there, we were shown samples of the core and even given little disks of core from eleven or twelve kilometers; also we received handsome diplomas from Pluto (in Russian), welcoming us to his realm, and hoping he'd see us there again some day.

On the way back from that trip I went again to Britain, to make a tour of Wales with Robert Tucker, a former Yale graduate student then working on especially accurate techniques for dating rocks; he was in Wales to collect samples from classical localities to establish the exact ages in (millions of) years of several marker points in geological history. An upset during that tour led, after I got back to New Haven, to my second prostate operation, which followed an operation for hernia brought on by carrying too many heavy bags from hotels to buses to airports.

Dmitri Andrusov

At the International Geological Congress in India in 1964, it was decided to hold the next Congress in Praha (Prague) in 1968, with excursions in Czechoslovakia and neighboring countries "behind the Iron Curtain." I decided to concentrate at that Congress on the Carpathian Mountains, which form a great loop eastward from Vienna, where the Danube separates the Slovakian Carpathians from the Austrian Alps, around to the Iron Gate, where the Danube separates the Romanian Carpathians from the Balkan Mountains of northeastern Yugoslavia and Bulgaria. When the advance circular for the Congress arrived, however, I learned that the leader of the official excursion in the Slovakian Carpathians was a geologist whom I considered a hopeless conservative (doubtless he considered me a dangerous radical), whereas I knew that Professor Dmitri Andrusov of Bratislava, whom I had met and come to admire on the trip arranged by Professor Clar in 1959 into the Austrian Alps, was very well acquainted with the Slovakian Carpathians and that I was much more likely to sympathize with his point of view. I could also guess that Professor Andrusov had not been asked to lead an official trip because he was "White" Russian, neither Czech nor Slovak.

I therefore wrote to my Austrian friends asking if they thought Professor Andrusov would be willing to run an informal, pre-Congress field trip in the Carpathians for a few American geologists, who would arrange to pay for it. They wrote back that he was actually in Vienna about the time my letter arrived and that he would be pleased to run such a trip. The matter of how to pay for it was left informal, but it was suggested that we might provide Western funds to cover a vacation in France for Andrusov and his wife. I then arranged for two good geological friends, E-an Zen and John M. ("Jack") Bird, to accompany me on the trip; in the meantime I signed up for the official post-Congress trip to the Romanian Carpathians.

In 1967 Premier Dubcek (a Slovak, by the way) began to liberalize the policies of the Czechoslovak government making, as many will remember, a strong impression on the Western world. By the summer of 1968, the Dubcek summer, Czechoslokia had become quite attractive to Western tourists. When the time came, I flew down from Norway, where I had been visiting a graduate student, to Vienna, where I met Zen, Bird, and Andrusov, and also the Austrian friends who had helped to arrange the trip. The next day, without the Austrians, we crossed over to Bratislava, Slovakia's capital, and Professor Andrusov, and for part of it Mme.

Andrusova, gave us a splendid two-week excursion from there to Kosice near the eastern end of the country as it was then; between the Wars, Slovakia had extended even farther east to include Ruthenia, but later in 1968 it lost Kosice as well. Afterwards, during the first days of the Congress in Praha, we were happy to give a banquet for the Andrusovs, to thank them for their kindness in arranging the trip, and we were able to supply funds for their French vacation. In Bratislava, at both ends of this excursion, I met Professor Andrusov's chief assistant, Dr. Erwin Scheibner.

From Bratislava E-an Zen and I took a full day to ride the train to Praha. It was a gray day, but we had a good time following the geological maps; we came through Brno in Moravia, then into Bohemia and so to Praha and the Congress.

I remember well that, at the opening ceremony of the Congress, the Lord Mayor of Praha told us to look at the monuments of the city's great days, and also at those of its evil days; none of us knew that another such day was imminent. Two nights later the tanks of the "Warsaw Pact" rolled in; the Soviet government and its tributaries could not accept Dubcek's liberalization and decided to crush it. There must have been 10,000 Western tourists in Praha then, not counting the geologists at the Congress, and I remember a conservative American friend of mine bemoaning the presence of so many hippies scattered over Wenceslas Square; two days later I got him to admit that hippies were better to have there than tanks.

At first, after the tanks came in, the Czechs tried to keep the Congress going, but soon they learned that the invaders were using that as evidence that things were "normal," so they scheduled a closing ceremony. Many of the Western geologists, especially those with cars, had left by then; the Czech people were very helpful, and no one had any trouble crossing into Austria or Germany. But I stayed for the ceremony; it was quite impressive. They told us they had hoped to award several medals to geologists present, including some Russians, but couldn't, for the medals were in the building of their Academy of Sciences, to which they were denied access. The Russians were present but pretty much sat on their hands; they had all taken off their badges, which gave their names and country. Then speaker after foreign speaker condemned the invasion, even the Cuban delegate, though the Cuban government was already pro-Communist.

What I learned from that episode, however, is that power is power; we were all outraged and bitter about what had happened, but there was nothing whatever we could do about it. I don't know what I would have done if I'd been young and a Czech, but such things had happened in Bohemia several times in the past, most recently in 1939 when Hitler marched in; there were few overt incidents, but many young Czechs talked to the young Russian soldiers in the tanks, for they all knew Russian, and when they left there were chalk swastikas on the tanks, and many graffiti on the walls equated 1968 with 1939. In fact a few young Russians were so disturbed that they sought asylum in Western embassies or even committed suicide; the invaders then realized they had made a mistake to bring in young soldiers, who had been told of course that they would be welcomed, and they replaced them with seasoned troops. That was however the only real mistake in a brilliant military operation that will no doubt go down in the annals of War and be studied with care by War Colleges all over the world.

There were of course many Russian geologists at the Congress; many of them were good friends whom I'd met during my five months in the Soviet Union the previous year and had greeted at Praha with bear-hugs and rusty Russian. The reactions of the Russians to the invasion were various. Gorbunov, the "commissar" of the Soviet delegation (and no friend of mine), seemed at first a little pleased and proud, but soon he became quiet and even took off his badge like the others. Bogdanov wanted to forget the whole business and just go on discussing geology. Old Nalivkin I met wandering around the streets with his son and muttering: "All governments are bad; all governments are bad."

After the final ceremony, I was able to take one of several Swiss buses that had been sent in to evacuate Swiss citizens; as most of them had already left by car, the Swiss offered places to other Westerners. The buses arrived in Wenceslas Square early in the evening, but of course the drivers needed a rest and some dinner; by the time they were ready to go, the tanks had been rearranged and blocked the exit, but their commander was easily persuaded to move his tanks, and we left. We drove through the night; many of the road-signs had been deliberately taken down or misdirected, but we had no delays, except for a wait at the border to check money and passports. We arrived in Vienna at four in the morning; we were taken to the Red Cross and sacked out on cots in a big dormitory, like any other refugees.

I spent a few days in Vienna, trying to decide whether to go on my post-Congress excursion to Romania but, if another country was to be invaded, it would certainly be Romania, so I simply turned tail and flew home. Romania was not invaded, and my Romanian friends were quite unhappy that I hadn't joined them, for the excursion was run as planned.

In 1972 I invited Professor Andrusov to join the informal excursion through the United States Appalachians that I ran for my Francophone friends before the Congress in Canada, but he was unable to get permission to leave Czechoslovakia.

FIG. 14–23: *Lake Imandra on the Kola Peninsula, USSR, 13 September 1989 — by Jan Zoubek*

After the invasion, Erwin Scheibner, Andrusov's assistant in Bratislava, simply left the country; apparently that wasn't difficult even for Czechoslovak citizens in the first days after the invasion. He and his wife Vera got to Switzerland, where Rudolf Trümpy helped them and got Erwin the offer of a good job, but the Scheibners decided Switzerland wasn't far enough away, and they emigrated to Australia! Erwin wrote me from the Geological Survey of New South Wales asking me to write a letter of reference for him; all that I could say was that I'd met him twice, though only in the office, but that his superior, Andrusov, for whose judgment I had great respect, thought very well of him. In fact Andrusov was much annoyed with Scheibner for leaving; like others I have known who actually lived through the Russian Revolution, he tended to think of other revolutions and political upheavals as rather minor events, which I suspect, relatively, they were.

Anyway Scheibner got the job, and before long he brought a lot of new ideas, "the new global tectonics," into Australian tectonics, which had been rather stodgy; predictably, Australian tectonicians divided into those who were glad to have him and his new ideas and those who were unhappy about it. From my point of view, Scheibner was one of the best things that happened to Australian geology in those years. When I got to Australia in 1973, and again in 1976, he was fully established, and he was very friendly and cordial, evidently crediting me more than I deserve with his opportunity there. Thus Rudy Trümpy and I were both his houseguests during the 1976 Geological Congress in Sydney. In 1978 he came to the United States, and we had him give us a lecture at Yale; I saw him here again in 1982.

Jean Sougy

In 1958 or 1959 Robert King, Phil King's brother, asked me to review a short paper by a Frenchman named Jean Sougy, who was presenting a quite new interpretation in the geology of West Africa, in Mauritania and vicinity. According to him, a belt of deformed rocks that, being well worn down, was thought to record a quite old mountain chain is in fact considerably younger, about the age of "my" Appalachian chain in eastern North America. I was much excited by this idea, and the evidence looked sound, for if it were true the Mauritanide chain would be the eastern side of the Appalachians, split off later when the Atlantic Ocean opened and the Americas Drifted away from Africa and Europe. So I urged King to see that it was published, and it was (*Geological Society of America Bulletin*, v. 73, p. 871-876, 1962). When I got to writing the relevant chapter of my book on the Appalachians, I cited that paper and a later article of Sougy's in discussing the trans-Atlantic or "African connection" of the Appalachians.

In May 1970 I went to a geological meeting in Rabat, Morocco, that was preceded by a two-week field excursion into the Anti-Atlas Mountains, a lower range south of the High Atlas in central Morocco at the edge of the Sahara Desert. Already in 1952, before the International Geological Congress in Algiers, I had taken an excursion in Morocco, but into its northern mountains, the Rif. Other excursions at that time had visited the Atlas and the Anti-Atlas, however, and I had talked to friends who took those excursions and had read the relevant guidebooks, so I was pleased to have the chance to go. It was on this excursion that I met Sougy and we started comparing notes on our respective mountain chains; he also gave a fine paper at the Rabat meeting.

In 1972, before the International Geological Congress in Canada, I ran an informal trip through the United States Appalachians for Francophone friends, including Sougy; he also took the formal pre-Congress trip in the Canadian Appalachians that was run by Dr. Poole and myself, and indeed he found some fascinating parallels between the rocks in his Mauritanides and those in our Appalachians.

Professor Sougy also came to North America to attend two Penrose Conferences sponsored by the Geological Society of America, one in 1975 in Saint John, New Brunswick, and one in 1978 in the Blue Ridge at Helen, Georgia, each with field trips in the vicinity. In 1979 I met him and his son, who had been with him at Helen, in Norway in August during a *Réunion Extraordinaire de la Société Géologique de France*, and on an extended field trip through New England in September, before a big meeting in Blacksburg, Virginia.

In May 1980, when Sougy was visiting at Cornell University, he called me and invited me to come to Marseille (l'Université d'Aix-Marseille III, St.-Jérôme, where he was Professor) for a term or so, perhaps in 1982. That summer also I attended the International Geological Congress in Paris, and he had me come down to Marseille for a few days, to lay plans for my later visits. He even took me to his home at Giens, near the western end of the Riviera, for a very pleasant weekend.

My last night in Giens I had a crazy dream: There was a lad with a rattlesnake, with which he was playing (Sougy and I had discussed rattlesnakes during the day); after a bit the snake sounded its rattles and bit the boy on the big toe. I was naturally upset until I realized, or the boy told me, that it was just a mechanical rattlesnake; one pressed the head, and it — the head! — rattled and bit whatever was there. So I asked the boy if they ever made one with real poison, and at that I woke up.

On that trip also, Sougy proposed that he and I run a Penrose Conference on the "African connection" of the Appalachians and that we run it there in Giens on the Riviera, to be the first Penrose Conference run outside North America. It sounded like a great idea to me, and we followed up on it, though it didn't actually happen until January 1984.

Then in September 1980 Sougy had me come back to Marseille to be a member of *le jury* for the defense of a French doctoral *thèse*, the first of many for me. The candidate, Jean-Pierre Lécorché, was one of Sougy's chief assistants at Marseille and in his Mauritanide work, and the thesis was of much interest to me.

The defense of a French doctoral *thèse* is a formal, and formidable, affair, whether for a *Doctorat d'Etat* or a *Doctorat du Troisième cycle*, though the former is more formidable. A jury of six or seven members, of whom two must be from outside the University conferring the degree, reads and criticizes the thäse beforehand; then the candidate presents a public lecture of an hour or more, with *le jury* sitting at a table at the front. Then they question and criticize him for an hour or two — I've seen it run to two and a half hours — after which they retire for ten minutes or so to make their decision. I have however never witnessed a negative decision; it's always passed with "mention très honorable". When they return, the Chairman of the jury, the Professor under whose guidance the work was done, announces that the candidate is *d'ores et déjà* (from that moment onward) *Docteur des Sciences* (or *du Troisième cycle*, as the case may be); in other words it is the jury that actually confers the degree. I have been been on nine such juries and have witnessed a couple of others.

At the beginning of 1982 I spent three months in Europe, at Marseille and at Neuchâtel where I helped Professor Schaer arrange and run a course of lectures on mountain ranges for the Francophone Swiss universities. In 1983 I went to Europe three separate times; during the first spell I gave lectures at Marseille on the geology of North America — in French. In both 1982 and 1983, much of our time was taken up preparing for our Penrose Conference which we ran in January 1984. Sougy had arranged it at a workingman's vacation resort at Giens — les Villages Vacances Familles — where their staff took good care of us. We ran a field trip to see the local geology, and very luckily we had a beautiful day for it (between rainy days).

In 1984 also I crossed the Atlantic three times: for the Penrose Conference, to attend the International Geological Congress in Moscow and the accompanying field trips, and to serve on *le jury* for three more *défenses de thèse* at Marseille in two days; and finally, in 1987, to be on *le jury* for the doctoral defense of Pascal Affaton.

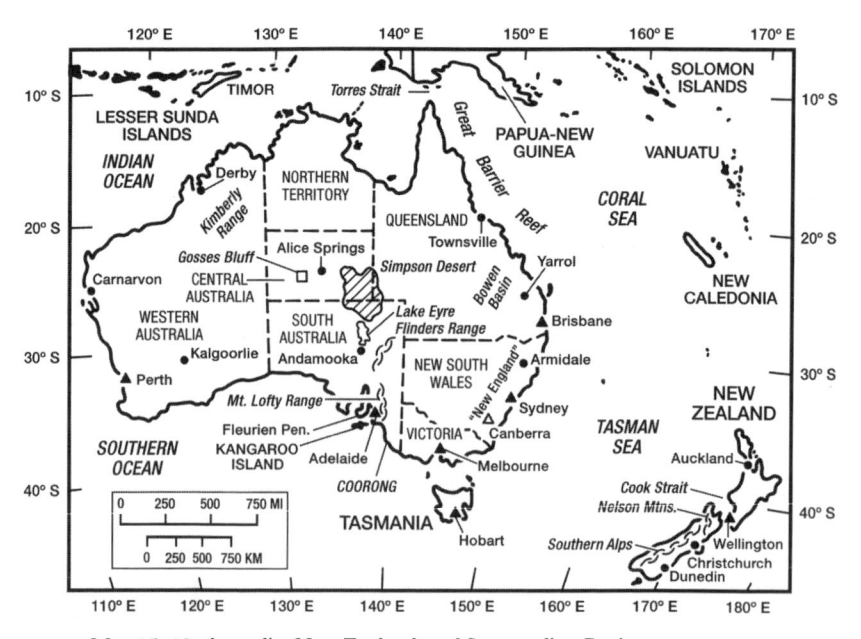

MAP 15-10. *Australia, New Zealand, and Surrounding Regions*

15 — In Australia and New Zealand

Keith Crook and Anne Felton -
My Year in Australia (1973-1974)

I MET KEITH CROOK when I arrived at the geology field camp of the University of Moscow in the Crimea in June 1967; indeed I was assigned to be his roommate there until he left five days later. Keith was fluent in Russian, having been in the Soviet Union for some months, and he had been living in the student dormitory of the University of Moscow. He told me that, talking to the students there, he found that not one of them was the son of a peasant or a working man; they were all the sons of professors or other intellectuals or, above all, of party officials. I knew that nepotism had been a way of life in Czarist Russia; evidently things didn't change that much under the Soviets.

Right away Keith strongly backed the idea I already had of coming to Australia for a year; that year, as it turned out, was my next sabbatical leave, 1973-1974. I saw him again when I returned to Moscow in July and, as a sort of preparation for my trip, he let me read through the page proof of the book, *The Geological Evolution of Australia and New Zealand*, by Professor Brown, Dr. Campbell, and himself, all from the Australian National University (ANU) in Canberra. Then in November 1972 Keith visited us in New Haven "with his wife Miss Anne Felton (sic)" as I wrote in my diary at the time, and we made further plans, for by then my visit to Australia was imminent.

In July 1973 then I flew from Moscow via Bombay and Singapore to Australia, crossing the continent diagonally from Derby on the northwest coast to Sydney. In particular we flew over the Simpson Desert and its red sand dunes, which made me think I had flown into a painting by the outstanding Australian painter Russell Drysdale. Once in Sydney, I went directly to Anne Felton's apartment to spend the night, as we had prearranged; she worked for the Geological Survey of New South Wales in Sydney, whereas Keith was on the faculty of the ANU in Canberra. The next day I flew on to Canberra, where I was met by Professor Brown and Dr. Crook and taken to my room in the University House; I lived there while I was in Canberra during the first half of my Australian year.

It happened that my first full month in Australia coincided with a major conference on Gondwanaland, the vast Continent composed of Australia, India, Africa, South America, and East Antarctica before they split up a couple of hundred million years ago and started drifting to their present dispersed locations. (In North America, a tiny sliver is hidden under central Florida.) Beside the conference itself in Canberra, three field trips were scheduled in various parts of Australia, and I signed up for them all.

Hence early in August, after two weeks in Canberra and going on a couple of short field trips from there, I flew off to Perth in Western Australia and joined a week-long field excursion up the west coast to and beyond Carnarvon. An amusing thing about this trip was being taken around in a big four-wheel-drive bus, reported to be the only one in Australia (in the world?). Also we spent several nights in large sheep stations and watched the sheep being sheared. The next week's field excursion was in the general vicinity of Sydney (the Sydney basin). After the conference was the third trip, in southeastern Queensland (the Bowen basin).

After that, in early September by now, I didn't return to Canberra but flew around via Sydney and Adelaide to Alice Springs in Central Australia, where I was met by a former Yale graduate student, Alastair Stewart, and his partner, Russell Shaw, both of whom worked for the Australian Bureau of Mineral Resources, their Geological Survey, and they took me around the Center for two weeks, partly in the area that Alastair had mapped for his doctoral dissertation at Yale. Most nights on this trip we slept on camp cots out under the stars, and I was happy to be able to consolidate my knowledge of the southern constellations. One day we went to see Gosses Bluff, a ring of hills about a kilometer across, standing isolated in otherwise nearly flat desert, that records where a meteorite or asteroid struck the Earth some 140 million years ago; we slept out beside it. It is holy for the aborigines, because the yellowish and reddish rocks of which it is composed make it resemble a kilometer-long "wichity grub," an edible caterpillar that is one of their sacred "totem" animals.

From Alice Springs I then flew east-northeast to Townsville, on the east coast of north-central Queensland, where I was met by another former Yale graduate student, Arthur Bloom, by then teaching at Cornell but on leave at Townsville to study the Great Barrier Reef; I also saw Keith Crook there. I spent over two weeks in, or rather mainly out of, Townsville, being shown the geology of that part of Queensland. Among my guides were two very bright young Australians, Gary Arnold and Michael Rubenach, with very different things to show me.

So finally, after more than two months of field trips all around the country, I got back to Canberra for a while. But even then, I went off on a twenty-day field trip around northern New South Wales with Keith Crook and, off and on, many others, including Professor Bruce Hobbs of

Monash University in Melbourne, a young American named James Granath who was studying there, Dr. Lawrence Frakes, an American who had decided to settle in Australia and found a position at Monash, and Dr. Barry Webby from the University of New South Wales in Sydney. From time to time on these trips, or between them, I gave lectures as requested.

By now, late November, it was time for my first trip to New Zealand, and Larry Frakes kindly drove me to Sydney. There I saw not only Keith Crook and Anne Felton but also Erwin and Vera Scheibner, whom I had first met in Bratislava just before the International Geological Congress in Praha, the one where the tanks came in.

I got back to Canberra just before Christmas, and just afterwards — mid-summer, don't forget — Keith and Anne kindly invited me to join them and family for a few days' vacation, camping out on a beach north of Sydney. Then, only a few days into the new year, I took a longer trip. I flew up to Bali and spent four days there, meeting friends of musical friends and learning something about Balinese music, then on to Kuala Lumpur in Malaysia to visit with my friends the Weinmans. Earlier Mrs. Weinman had been Managing Editor of the *American Journal of Science* for fifteen years, but Dr. Weinman was a specialist in tropical diseases; hence he took his sabbatical leaves in places like Thailand and Malaysia, and she naturally went with him. I spent nearly a week with them, and Prof. Hutchison of the University there gave me a two-day field trip, before I flew back to Australia.

But again I didn't go directly back to Canberra but went instead to Armidale to visit the University of New England — Australia's New England is the northeastern part of New South Wales — whence Professor Larry Harrington, Dr. Bruce Runnegar, and others showed me the geology right up to the Queensland border. After that I did return to Canberra, but only a little more than a week later it was time for me to move to Adelaide for the second half of my Australian year. Keith Crook and Anne Felton very kindly drove me from Canberra to Adelaide, showing me on the way the geology from southeastern New South Wales across Victoria into South Australia.

When we arrived in Adelaide, Professor Roye Rutland, my main host there, was on vacation in New Zealand and we were greeted by Dr. Brian Daley, a paleontologist concerned with some of the very earliest shelly fossils; I had met him in 1967 in Moscow where he was conferring with Russian experts on the same fossils. He took us at once on a four-day trip to the Fleurieu Peninsula and Kangaroo Island, the southern and southwestern continuations of the Mount Lofty Ranges east of Adelaide. After that Keith and Anne drove back to Canberra, but Dr. Daley took me to Adelaide and indeed put me up for four days until I could move into rooms in St. Mark's College at the University, where I stayed while I was in Adelaide, sometimes in a student room, sometimes in a guest room. Two of those four days moreover he took me out on short trips to see the fascinating geology of the Mount Lofty Ranges.

In Adelaide I met and was the luncheon guest of Mr. and Mrs. Skinner, the parents of Brian Skinner, whom we had appointed to Yale as Professor of Economic Geology in 1966 and then elected as Department Chairman in 1967, when I went off for my five months in the Soviet Union as part of my second sabbatical year. Mr. Skinner was a banker, and he was happy to hear that I too was the son of a banker, like his own geologist-son. The Skinners showed me Adelaide, and I also met Brian's brothers, businessmen like their father.

So I settled in at Adelaide, in both the College and the Department of Geology, and spent my time partly reading about New Zealand in preparation for my second trip there and partly about the Flinders Ranges, which extend north from the Mount Lofty Ranges far into the interior of South Australia; they were one of my main interests in Australia. I also learned about them by talking to the geologists at the University and in the Geological Survey of South Australia who had worked there, and I got a first three-day trip there early in March, before my second trip to New Zealand.

As I started the New Zealand trip, I flew to Sydney and spent two nights with my old friends Keith and Rachel Wilson of the Yale School of Music, who were there for part of his sabbatical year. One evening the Wilsons, Keith Crook, Anne Felton, and I had dinner together and then went on to a concert at the brand-new and splendid Sydney Opera House; the next morning I flew to New Zealand. While in Sydney I also saw Peter Sculthorpe, the Australian composer whom I'd met in New Haven in 1966.

When I got back from New Zealand, I was in Adelaide only two nights before Professor Rutland, Dr. Robert Nesbitt, and I flew over to Tasmania, to be shown its geology. We were met by Professor S. Warren Carey, who had built up the Department of Geology at the University of Tasmania, in Hobart, into one of the best in Australia.

Sam Carey warrants a digression. He was a very innovative geologist, a maverick indeed and consciously so, with some very good ideas and others that most of the rest of us considered crazy. When I took my first sabbatical year (1959-1960) to go to Europe, I got an NSF Senior Post-Doctoral Fellowship to pay my way, and Yale therefore had my salary to appoint a Visiting Professor. After careful consideration and consultation, and largely on the basis of a very innovative early article of his, we invited Professor Carey. Moreover, he made trips all over the United States and Canada, lecturing everywhere in his inimitable now-you-see-it-now-you-don't style (he had put himself through college by working as a magician) and North American geology has never been the same since. For he ended, once and for all, the condescending dismissal of the idea of Continental Drift that had characterized North American geologists. He also helped to lay the foundations for the theory of plate tectonics, "the new global tectonics" as it was called at the time, which revolutionized tectonic thinking during the 1960s. About 1955 Carey apparently anticipated the new global tectonics in a manuscript that was rejected for publication as too speculative; I haven't seen it, but I'm told that it included both the creation of new crust at the mid-ocean ridges, forming the oceans, and its destruction or at least swallowing at belts of compression, where new mountain ranges are built. But curiously, in later years he reneged on the latter and recognized only the creation of new crust, and he became a strong advocate of the theory of an expanding Earth, going so far as to claim that its radius has about doubled in the last five hundred million years, implying of course that its volume has nearly octupled and therefore that its density then was nearly eight times what it is at present. It is this aspect of the theory that makes most of us unwilling to accept it, preferring to balance the creation of new crust, on which we agree with Carey, by the destruction of old crust, on which we disagree. In any case, the best thing I ever did for North American geology was to go away for a year, so that Carey could spend the year here.

That first day in Hobart, Professor Carey showed us his department, and he gave us a fine dinner party at which we met both his colleague Maxwell Banks and the Tasmanian Government geologist, Ian Jennings. Those two, with many others, notably Emyr Williams and Keith Corbett, but not Professor Carey, gave us thirteen days of field trips all around the island of Tasmania, seeing its very complicated geology. During the latter part of those trips, the similarity of some of the rocks in western Tasmania to rocks I knew in the Taconic region on the border of New York and (our) New England led me to a very heterodox hypothesis, heterodox for Tasmanians at least. I kept it to myself, however, till after we got back to Hobart. I had three days in Hobart, though one of those we went on a field trip; I talked to lots of poeple and gave two lectures; in the second lecture I sprang my new idea. My diary reports that: "It met the proper amount of skepticism, but certainly they didn't seem offended; in particular they seemed to like" one part of it. I never heard, however, how the idea fared after I was gone.

From Hobart in Tasmania I flew to Melbourne in Victoria where I was met by Professor Hobbs and Dr. Frakes of Monash. I spent six days in Melbourne (two of them were field trips) and visited both Monash and the University of Melbourne, giving lectures at each and even, at Monash, an informal seminar on the geology of Tasmania, after having been there only two weeks! At the University of Melbourne my host was Professor Owen Singleton, "the late Owen Singleton" I called him (behind his back), for he always seemed to be late. The day he took me out in the field we left the next-to-last outcrop as darkness fell, and he showed me the last outcrop, a cliff on the shore, by the light of the three brightest stars in the heavens (there was no moon that night), though then he had the driver take the car around and shine its headlights on the outcrop from 200 meters away. That day we got back to town at 11 pm.

So then I came back to Adelaide, but after two days, during which Professor Rutland put me up, he, Dr. Nesbitt, Dr. John Cooper, and I flew out to Perth for a five-day field trip to and around Kalgoorlie in interior Western Australia. Here we were around mines, but mostly we looked, in surface outcrops, at the complicated geology of very old rocks. Our chief guide was John Platt, a Britisher who nevertheless had taken his doctorate at the University of California in Santa Barbara.

Back in Adelaide Professor Rutland put me up for six days while plans to show me the northern Flinders Ranges came unstuck but then got stuck together again. Dr. Peter Haslett took me on a week's trip there, a splendid trip in mostly clear but cold weather; I slept out under the stars most of the nights but retreated to his tent when it clouded up (it never did rain hard).

In the northern Flinders Ranges originally flat strata have been folded up, not into a neat pattern of parallel folds all trending one way, like most of the fold belts I've known including the southern Flinders Ranges, but more irregularly, almost a checkerboard pattern of ups and downs. In the "up" areas, the lowest rocks visible, below the more regular strata, are strikingly broken up or "brecciated" and have apparently been squeezed laterally out from under the "down" areas, but the cause of that is quite controversial. Such an arrangement is called a diapir — rocks piercing through from below — but in general, as in the oil fields of Romania where the word was coined, it is related to the presence of beds of rock salt, which is plastic and so is easily squeezed from the "down" areas to the "up" areas, but it's not commonly accompanied by brecciation. It wasn't at all clear whether salt was involved in this region, probably because these rocks have been close to the Earth's surface for a long time (in contrast to other diapiric areas), so that any salt has been leached away, but we did find evidence of its former presence in the form of molds of salt crystals. But the brecciation is less easily explained. Possibly it formed when the salt was leached away, as Dr. Haslett thought, but in the broken-up rocks there were many small bodies and fragments of a dark igneous rock, rock that had been molten and would have been lava if it had reached the Earth's surface, and I argued that the intrusion of that molten rock was what mobilized the salt and helped to break up the other rocks. We didn't settle the argument.

One of these days we drove into Wilpena Pound, a spectacular "down" square of the checkerboard a few kilometers across, a flat area almost completely surrounded by a rocky ridge — pound because that's the word for an enclosed area in which cattle are penned or impounded, what in western North America would be called a corral.

We got back to Adelaide on the first day of June, and I was there for a month — except for two more trips. One was a two-day trip to Sydney arranged by Dr. Webby; one of the days I spent with Peter Sculthorpe, the other with Dr. Webby at the University of New South Wales, where I gave a lecture at the Geology Department.

The other was a one-day trip to the Coorong, a coastal lagoon southeast of Adelaide, a very interesting trip for me. As I mentioned when telling about my lessons in geology with Dr. Hartnagel while I was still in school, the mineral and rock dolomite (the rock is often called dolostone) has been a sort of leitmotiv in my geological life, for it is prominent throughout the western Appalachians from northwest Newfoundland to central Alabama, as in the Champlain Valley where I worked for my Master's thesis and in East Tennessee where I worked for many years. When, after I came to Yale, Professor Dunbar and I were writing our textbook, I wrote the chapter on carbonate rocks, and I devoted a good part of it to the "dolomite problem." Based on what I knew at the time, I made the flat statement that dolostone "is nowhere known to be forming today, and therefore the present fails us as a key to the past." But, while the book was going through the press, an article was submitted to the *American Journal of Science* showing that dolomite is in fact forming today, in the Coorong. The article came from Adelaide, and one of the authors was Catherine Skinner, an American who had accompanied her Australian husband, Brian Skinner, my future colleague, on a visit to his home town. They had met when he was a graduate student at Harvard and she an undergraduate student at Radcliffe; I didn't get to know the Skinners for nearly another decade.

Of course we published the article (*American Journal of Science*, v. 255, p. 561-567, 1957), but naturally I very much wanted to see the Coorong. When we got there, I took off my shoes and socks and waded barefoot in the dolomite mud in the lagoon and over algal mats that may be the present-day equivalent of certain structures called stromatolites that can be found as fossils in old strata back almost as far as there is evidence of life on Earth, 3.5 billion years.

In early July I left Adelaide for eastern Australia. The first week was a field trip with Dr. Evan Leitch of the University of New South Wales into (their) New England, the geology of which continued to confuse me. At the end was a big conference in Brisbane where I met lots of old friends; Keith Crook and Anne Felton, Erwin Scheibner, and Gary Arnold (one of the bright young Australians from Townsville), all of whom gave fine papers. The last evening I was invited to a dinner party for Professor Dorothy Hill, *la grande dame* of Queensland geology, in whose honor the whole conference was arranged. Afterwards I visited the geology field camp of the University of Queensland at Yarrol and saw the geology around it, partly with the students and partly on my own. Here again I had the chance to sleep out under the stars, though the nights were pretty chilly, including the night after my 60th birthday; it was winter of course. All in all I slept out under the stars thirty nights during my year in Australia.

My last month in Australia I was mostly in Adelaide, but even then I made trips away. I spent four days on a "dude ranch" named Arkaroola in the northern Flinders Ranges, run by a geologist, Reginald Sprigg, but he only turned up the last evening I was there; here I walked around mostly on my own, seeing the geology. Then I had the wonderful chance to fly the full length of the Flinders Ranges in a Cessna four-passenger plane, all the way to Lake Eyre, which is ordinarily quite dry but that season was full of water from heavy, indeed catastrophic rains they'd been having in the eastern mountains. On the way back we stopped for the night at Andamooka, a famous locality for gem opal.

So finally I left Adelaide and Australia; I flew across the Pacific Ocean during two 20ths of August, arriving in Vancouver whence I went up into northwestern British Columbia to visit a graduate student in his dissertation area before returning to New Haven.

I met Keith Crook and Anne Felton again at the 1976 International Geological Congress in Sydney. Dr. Erwin Scheibner, who put me up during that Congress, had me join two pleasant dinner parties, one with Keith and Anne and the other with three well known non-Australian geologists — John Dewey from England, David Gee from Sweden, and Viktor Khain from the Soviet Union.

Henno Martin

I MET PROFESSOR AND FRAU MARTIN (the accent in the last name is on the i) in Australia very soon after I came there in mid-1973, what would have been summer for them in Germany and for me in the United

States but was winter in Australia, actually more like a beautiful fall. About as soon as I arrived, I went on the three field excursions accompanying the Gondwanaland meeting, and so did they; thus I had a fine opportunity to get to know them personally and to observe Professor Martin as a geologist. Professor Martin I came to admire deeply, and I found them both delightful company.

Professor Martin taught at the University of Göttingen; when in 1976 I was invited to spend a month there on my way via South Africa to the International Geological Congress in Australia, he was retired but still very active, especially in the group there who were studying the geology of Southwest Africa/Namibia. Southwest Africa was a German colony until the First World War, after which it became a mandate of the Union of South Africa; the German presence remained very strong, however, and more than sixty years after that war street signs, etc., were in three languages: Afrikaans, English, and German.

Martin had gone to Southwest Africa in the early 1930s, the first Hitler years in Germany, for he could see that Hitler's policies were leading to another great war; he chose to go there on the advice of his mentor, Professor Hans Cloos of Bonn, who had worked there before the first War. But when the Second World War erupted in Europe Martin, despite his deep antipathy to Hitler and all his works, became an enemy alien. Acting out an idea that had at first been only a passing thought, he and a Jewish friend, Hermann Korn, who had left Germany at the same time for even more obvious reasons, decided to disappear into the Namibian desert; they prepared themselves and carried out their scheme. For two and a half years they lived there, entirely "on the land." After the war Martin told the story of that extraordinary adventure in a book, published in both German and English. I am proud to own an autographed copy of the second English edition, entitled *The Sheltering Desert*. In the end Korn became seriously ill, and Martin brought him to an outlying farm, whence he could be taken to a hospital, but the authorities then came after Martin and brought him in too. The two men were tried, and convicted, for having ignored official decrees concerning enemy aliens, but the judge then simply fined them small amounts for some of their lesser infringements, such as their failure to obtain annual dog licenses for their dog. Afterwards the Southwest African government employed them as geologists, especially on water supply in desert areas, on which by then they were obviously quite expert.

During my month in Göttingen in 1976, the Martins were very kind to me, often having me for lunch, often going with me on pleasant walks, often just discussing the state of the world and reaching rather pessimistic conclusions. On one of those occasions they introduced me to a younger geologist named Alfred Kröner, who then had a position in South Africa but was anxious to come home to Germany; he did obtain a position there and became Professor in the University of Mainz.

In 1981 Professor Kröner, with the backing of Professor Martin, arranged a field excursion in Namibia, to which they invited me; naturally I accepted with pleasure. It was a very fine excursion, taking us from Windhoek in the center of the country to Swakopmund on the Atlantic coast, then back through some of the desert country around the gorges of the Kuiseb River where Martin and Korn had hidden out for those two and a half years. The high point for me was to visit the Naukluft Ranges, about whose spectacular geology Korn and Martin had written an article that I'd read earlier and found very exciting. Frau Martin came along with us on this excursion appointing herself chief cook, evidently to be sure that her husband was well fed.

In those same years Professor Schaer of the University of Neuchâtel asked me to help him plan and then administer a course of invited lectures on mountain ranges around the world, for the Francophone Swiss universities. Among many others we invited Professor Martin, and he told us about the geology of the Damara mountain belt in Namibia/SW Africa.

In 1989 I began to hear that Professor and Frau Martin were both seriously ill. In 1990 I came back to Göttingen for a geological meeting; I was unable to see Professor Martin, but I did have the chance to give him my greetings over the phone.

Douglas Saxon Coombs

NEW ZEALAND CONSISTS OF TWO ISLANDS; its four universities are equally divided between them — from north to south: Auckland, Wellington, Christchurch, and Otago (in Dunedin, the capital city of Otago). With its spectacular, active, geology — volcanoes and earthquakes — New Zealand has produced a number of outstanding geologists, some of whom spent much of their lives elsewhere; e.g., Francis Turner. I met Frank Turner and his charming wife Esmé when he came to New Haven in 1948 to work with Mrs. Knopf on her specialties; later he was called to the University of California at Berkeley, where he had an illustrious career.

Professor Douglas Coombs, on the other hand, stayed in New Zealand all his life at the University of Otago, though he was often a welcome visitor elsewhere. He was a Visiting Professor in the Yale Department of Geology during the second term of 1967-68; later we tried to appoint him to a chair in the Department but failed. I met him again in Moscow in 1973 at the Ophiolite Conference where he gave an outstanding paper (by himself and colleagues), which I then persuaded him to publish in the *American Journal of Science* (v. 276, p. 561-603, 1976); later he became an Associate Editor of the *Journal*. Then I saw him again and again during his visits to the United States; he was named a Foreign Associate of the U.S. National Academy of Sciences in 1977 and an Honorary Fellow of the Geological Society of America in 1984.

Metamorphism is the process by which rocks of all kinds are altered in the solid state, when subjected to heat and pressure within the Earth. If they melt, they become igneous rocks — lava if they are then erupted at the Earth's surface, magma if they remain beneath it to solidify there — and transitions from metamorphic to magmatic are known. If the metamorphic heat has been high and long-lasting, the materials of the rock form large crystals and the rocks can be quite handsome, spangled with crystals of garnet, staurolite, and kyanite. But Professor Coombs made his reputation by studying the minerals formed in the early stages of the metamorphic process, minute and difficultly recognizable crystals visible only through the microscope; he was recognized as the world authority on those early stages.

During my Australian year, I visited New Zealand twice, each time for nearly a month; both times I began at Dunedin. The first time I divided my visit between the Universities of Otago and Christchurch; the second time I visited all four universities. Actually I spent more time on field trips seeing the geology than at the universities or in their cities. Professor Coombs was very cordial and helpful to me during my visits, and I went on field trips with him and with Drs. Graham Bishop and Charles Landis to see the rocks of the Southern Alps, rocks that their work had made well known to geologists everywhere.

From Christchurch, on the first trip, Dr. Douglas Lewis took me to see the geology along the Alpine fault on the northwest side of the South Island, whence it crosses Cook Strait to the southeast side of the North Island near Wellington; that fault is very much like the San Andreas fault of California, and as active. On the second trip I went with Drs. Roger Cooper and George Grindley to see the geology of the Nelson Mountains at the north end of the South Island, and it turned out to be strikingly like that of the Gordon belt in eastern Tasmania, showing that at a geologically earlier time New Zealand, with a part of Antarctica, was attached to Tasmania and adjacent Australia and has since drifted away.

In Wellington my host was Dr. Ian Speden, who received his doctor's degree from Yale in 1965 but who in 1974 was well up in the ranks of the New Zealand Geological Survey. During my visit to Wellington I didn't have the opportunity to meet Professor Harold Wellman, which, as I noted in my diary, was rather like seeing *Hamlet* with Hamlet's part left out. In Auckland my host was Professor Arnold Lillie; I suppose I shouldn't admit that my chief memory of Professor Lillie is that he tried to inveigle me into joining a game of cricket, about the playing of which I then knew, and still know, nothing.

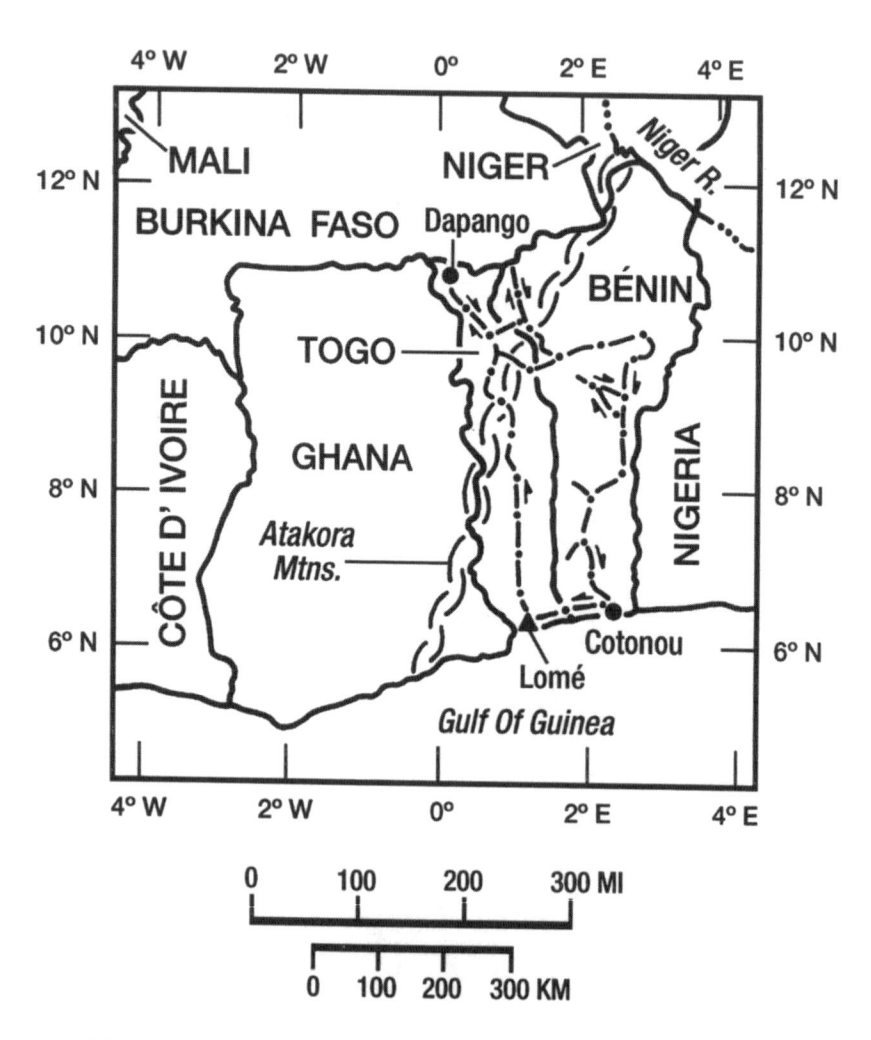

Map 16–11. *Togo, Bénin, and Adjacent Countries*

16 — In Africa and China

Pascal Affaton

I FIRST MET PASCAL AFFATON in 1983, in Professor Sougy's laboratory in Marseille; he was a black student from Bénin, the former French colony of Dahomey in West Africa. Some time before that, as I learned later on, the Bénin government had sent him to the United States to study hydrogeology at the University of Arizona but, while he was there, a change of government occurred in Bénin, and he decided not to go back. He and his wife, a Frenchwoman who had gone to Bénin to teach science in secondary schools, went instead to France, where he became a French citizen and began working for his *doctorat* at Marseille. I met him there again in 1984, and late one afternoon he "suddenly invited me to come to supper. As I like him a lot and respect his work, I accepted. It was a very delightful occasion. They have two charming children, and the love and spontaneity in the whole family was wonderful to behold. But I keep wondering what future he (or they) have. I expect he has cut himself off from hope of promotion at home, and wonder how he could get a post in France. The human waste seems so terrible, and so unnecessary." (quotation from my diary.)

Affaton had been working on a fairly old, fairly worn down mountain range in West Africa, commonly called the Dahomeyide or Atakora range, which diagonals north-northeastward from the southeast corner of Ghana (the old British Gold Coast) across Togo and Bénin to the "W" Bends of the Niger River in Niger (those countries had been French colonies). That range was to be the subject of his doctoral thesis; indeed in 1980 the *American Journal of Science* published an article by Affaton, Sougy, and Trompette describing the range. In 1987, Professor Sougy asked me to come to Marseille as a member of *le jury* for Affaton's *défense de thèse*, and I was happy to accept, the defense was timed to follow my wonderful trip across Turkey with Professor Ketin of Istanbul. Not only was the written thesis a fine and thorough job, the oral defense too "was magnificent — my respect and admiration for him increased steadily through the whole thing. His presentation was clear, methodical, and beautifully arranged; then he handled the questions clearly, forcibly, and indeed occasionally rather aggressively — no panic, no undue deference, quite extraordinary." We, le *jury*, were very pleased to award him his doctor's degree. At that time also I learned that he had a position at the University at Lomé in Togo; it was a six-year contract, a *mission co-opérative* with France.

The history of Togo is complicated. To the east was "the empire that the French called Dahomey and that held them up for a couple of decades, as the Ashanti did the British in the Gold Coast, now Ghana. The Germans sneaked in between the two empires, and Togo is in good part populated by groups that fled there from the imperial armies, well before the white man came to take over the country." After the First World War, the German colony was split between the French and the British; the British zone is still part of Ghana, but after *décolonisation* the former French zone declared its independence from Dahomey-Bénin. As a result Togo is a long skinny country, 600 kilometers from north to south but only about 100 kilometers wide.

In 1989 I got a letter from Affaton in Togo, "inviting me to come there, see some geology, and give a lecture or two. Affaton is practically the only person who could lure me to undeveloped black Africa, but he can, so I wrote a letter accepting." We set up my trip for January 1991, but unfortunately I had to have my second prostate operation in December 1990, so the visit to Togo had to be put off till January 1992; that year I was able to go.

I was in West Africa for two weeks. The first days, in Lomé, I did my duty by giving lectures, in French of course: four hour-long lectures on the Appalachians on one day, with pauses between the hours, and a *Conférence Grand-Publique* on the next, in which I compared the recent plate-tectonic revolution in geology to the Copernican revolution in astronomy four and a half centuries ago, for both replaced "fixist" by "mobilist" ideas. I was pleased that as many of the good and pertinent questions afterwards came from the students as from the faculty; so often in foreign countries only the professors ask questions of the lecturer.

Affaton then took me for a week's field trip during which we crisscrossed his range, first south to north in Togo, then north to south in Bénin. We even got beyond the range in northwesternmost Togo where, at Dapaong in the corner against Ghana and Burkina Faso (the old Haute Volta), we were on the very old rocks of the West African craton, the western component of the "Saharan" block, though still some distance south of the real Sahara Desert. Then on the way back, when we were close to the Nigerian border, we came into a region with much granite, commonly making rounded, bare-rock hills or mountains; Stone Mountain in Georgia would be a close analogue. "In artificial depressions" in the rock of one such hill, "the ladies of the village (nude from the waist up) were grinding flour. As we left, I remarked that it was a fine granite for making flour, which amused Jack (our chauffeur) as well as Pascal."

Near Dapaong, "trying to go down a steep slope" to see the outcrop, "I slipped on loose rounded gravel and fell forward on my nose, my right wrist, and my right knee; the nose bled, and the wrist was badly scratched, so Affaton at once covered them with bright red mercurochrome or something like it. The nose must have been pretty spectacular; I think he got a picture!" This was the first of the bad falls I've been having in recent years as my leg muscles gradually deteriorated, incapacitating me for the geological field excursions and field work that I have always loved so much.

At the end of the trip we came to Cotonou on the coast, the largest city in Bénin though not the capital; there Affaton found a real M. D., the French wife of an African geophysicist whom he knew, who could dress up properly the wounds from my fall at Dapaong.

On this trip we took our lunches in whatever village we were near at midday. As we went along, they became more and more informal, and "African," and I began "to wonder if my dear friend Pascal Affaton is trying to find out just how native I'll consent to go, like Ted Díaz and the others on that great trip from Monterrey to Ciudad México on 2-3 September 1956."

During these traverses across "his" range, I was struck again and again by parallels with the structure of "my" Appalachians, especially the southern Appalachians, though "my" mountains are younger than "his."

We actually crossed the Togo-Bénin border six times, three times each way, on this trip, yet we checked in at the pairs of border posts only three and a half times; the other times either they were closed up tight or there weren't any. This led to a certain difficulty the third time we came into Bénin, but he was able to talk our way out of it.

We came to Cotonou because of a meeting on mineral deposit in West Africa that Affaton wanted at attend, a small meeting (no more than a dozen, it turned out) of geologists from the countries from Bénin west to la Côte d'Ivoire; I met them all, but "I got the strong impression that Affaton stands head and shoulders above the others in his comprehension of the regional geology and its implications in modern theoretical terms, even for the mineral deposits." Afterwards we drove back along the coast to Lomé. There I got them "to figure out the distance we'd driven on this trip — 2,294 kilometers in eight days. Two days later I flew back to the United States via Amsterdam.

On his 1993 New Year's card, Affaton wrote me that he'd been elected President, the first I think, of the Geological Society of Africa, for a three-year term ending in 1995 at a meeting at Nairobi in Kenya, to which he invited me. Naturally I wanted to go and began to make plans, but later a fall that injured one of my vertebrae made that impossible. In the meantime, he had "had to leave Togo for political reasons" and return to France; later he was sent to Niamey, the capital of Niger, on a similar *mission coopérative*.

Yang Zunyi (Tsun-yi Yang) — and my Trips to China

WHEN I CAME TO YALE as a graduate student in 1937, there were two Chinese graduate students in Geology, Chen Shu and Yang Zunyi. I have almost no memory of Mr. Chen, who left in June 1938, but Tsun-yi Yang, as we called him, was a delightful person to know, friendly and full of life but also a very serious student; he was studying paleontology with Professor Dunbar. He went with us on field trips and to parties; in particular he sometimes went to the Chinese restaurant downtown and arranged with the proprietor for a Chinese banquet for our whole group of graduate students, with many fine Chinese dishes yet still within our none-too-plentiful means. In 1939 he completed his doctoral dissertation on Middle Devonian fossil brachiopods from north-central Michigan; he then returned to China.

At first we heard good things about his career there — that he had been named Director of the Geological Survey of not one but two provinces in southern China, whence he came — but in 1949 the Communists took over, and we heard nothing. We knew his having spent several years studying in the United States would now be a black mark against him, and we dared not write for fear of increasing his difficulties. Only once in the next thirty years did I learn anything about him. As mentioned above, when I was Secretary of the International Commission on Stratigraphy, our Subcommission on the Stratigraphic Lexicon was headed by M. Jean Roger of the French BRGM, *mon frère jumeau*; we had been warned in 1952 that he was a Communist, but actually that meant that he obtained lexicons from both the Soviet Union and mainland China and republished them in French. In the Chinese lexicon I discovered references to several articles that Zunyi had published in those years, showing that for at least part of that time he had been actively doing geology. He did suffer very considerably during the "Cultural Revolution," but later he was rehabilitated and became again a highly respected professor of paleontology.

In February 1979, at the start of another trip around the world, I spent three weeks on Taiwan, having invited myself there to visit John Suppe of Princeton, a former Yale graduate student, in the area where he was doing his geological field research. During that trip I had naturally met and come to know many Chinese geologists who had left the mainland when the Communists took over; I asked several of them if they knew Yang Zunyi, and they happily answered: "Why, he taught us paleontology!" Later in that trip I took a field excursion on the island of Cyprus

Fig. 16-25. Taken during trip to see the "Pan-Xi rift" in Sichuan, China, September 1985.

to see the well known Troödos ophiolite complex, and there I encountered a group of Chinese geologists from the mainland; when I asked them the same question, I got the same happy answer. Moreover they took pictures of me to give, with my address, to Professor Yang, so soon we were writing back and forth. A few years later, my friend Preston Cloud, who had been our fellow graduate student at Yale, got to China and saw him, and in 1984 I saw him myself at the International Geological Congress in Moscow, where he was a member of the official Chinese delegation.

My trip to Taiwan was very successful, and indeed I found that I related very warmly to the Chinese people I met, even though at that time I had only a bare idea of the Chinese language. But during the 1920s the Chinese game Mah Jongg had been very popular in the United States, and our family had a fine set of the tiles; from them I learned the Chinese characters for the numbers from 1 to 9 and for the four winds, at least an introduction to the character system. Moreover, because of the missionary aunts and uncles in our family, we had always been brought up with a great respect for China and her civilization — very different from ours but equally great on its own terms. My experience on Taiwan was so rewarding that I said to myself: "It was wonderful to see the side-show, but now I want to see the main tent." In the preceding years President Nixon had made the diplomatic breakthrough with the government of Communist China — Nixon of all people, but he was the one to do it precisely

Fig. 16–26:
*Turkey, 19 September 1987
Left to right: Dogan Perincek, John Rodgers, Prof. Ihsan Ketin. Lake in background is that behind the Keban Dam on the upper Firat (Euphrates) River in eastern Turkey.*

because his anti-Communist credentials were so impeccable — and exchange visits with China had become possible.

In the spring of 1985, Professor Yang came to the United States, and of course we welcomed him in New Haven; he visited us twice in April, giving us a lecture the second time, but actually he spent much of his visit with an old friend from graduate-student days, Mr. Jerry Stein, who lives near Torrington, Connecticut. I saw Zunyi there several times, then and in later years.

In Moscow in 1984, Yang Zunyi had introduced me to Dr. Ma Xingyüan, whom I had in fact met on a field excursion in the Pyrenees after the International Congress in Paris in 1980, and Dr. Ma invited me to a meeting in Chengdu in western China the next September; naturally I happily accepted. Thus in 1985 I made my first trip to mainland China. I went in and came out by Beijing, and both times Professor Yang welcomed me, showed me around, and introduced me to many Chinese geologists, among whom was Dr. Sun Shu, Director of the Geological Institute of the Academia Sinica (the political relations between the main groups of geologists in China are much like, and probably patterned after, those in the Soviet Union, described above). I was already working from our end to arrange an exchange visit for several months in 1986, and Dr. Sun was the person to pass on exchanges for China; he assured me that he would request me for the exchange, thus making my visit virtually certain.

The meeting in Chengdu, in Sichuan province, was about rift valleys; e.g., East Africa, Lake Baykal, but especially those in China. There were two field trips after that meeting; I chose to take the one to the so-called Pan-Xi rift southwest of Chengdu rather than the one to the Fen-Wei rift in northern China. When I talked later to those who'd taken the other trip I found I'd made the right choice. Our trip took us as far as the city of Dukou (Ferry City) where the Jinsha Jiang (Golden Sands River) comes out of the eastern edge of the high Tibetan Plateau and becomes the Chang Jiang (Long River, commonly called the Yangzi, a name coined for it by the British). The city, of half a million people, had grown up in the last twenty years near a big iron mine and around a major steel mill. The geology was interesting, but for me the Pan-Xi belt is not properly a "rift;" I cited it, in an article I published a few years later, as an example of a quite different kind of structure, though I never converted many others to my point of view.

My exchange visit was first planned for three months in the fall of 1986, but then the Chinese cut it down to six weeks; later we got it back up to two months. I was supposed to go over in early September, but then Kenneth Hsü (or Xü Jinghua) got me invited to join the trip he was taking with Chinese geologists from Dr. Sun's Institute, which was to gather in Beijing on 31 August. So I left New York on 29 August and flew over Alaska to Tokyo and then Beijing; it was a long, long afternoon, thirteen and a half hours of it, even if divided between the 29th and the 30th as we crossed the date line, yet we fell only three hours behind the sun. The trip we took with Hsü, which lasted two and a half weeks, is described in my sketch for him. Dr. Sun Shu was with us for part of that field trip; also present was Dr. Celal Sengör from Turkey (Turkish c is pronounced like English j). I met Celal first in the late 1970s when he was a student of Prof. John Dewey at the State University of New York in Albany, then again at the International Geological Congresses in Paris in 1980 and in Moscow in 1984; after the latter, we were roommates on the field trip in the Caucasus. In the meantime he had been appointed to the faculty of the Istanbul Technical University; I visited him there in 1985 on the occasion of a very fine conference on the Alpine-Himalayan mountain belt he organized in honor of Professor Ihsan Ketin, the grand old man of Turkish geology. In 1987 moreover he arranged for Professor Ketin to guide me on a ten-day trip right across Turkey, a wonderful experience.

Toward the end of our field excursion with Ken Hsü we crossed the Chang Jiang and spent two days in the Dabieshan, a very interesting

FIG. 16–27. *Hills north of Beijing, China, 9 October 1986. Photo taken by Song Tiennu; others are Yang Zunyi (in blue blouse), John Rodgers, and Qiao Xianfu.*

range at the east end of the Qinling, the great mountain range that separates the basin of the Chang Jiang (Yangzi River) from that of the Huang He (Yellow River), middle China from north China. After that Hsü left us, but Sengör and I had the opportunity to spend nearly another week in the Dabieshan, which contains some remarkable rocks, though how remarkable they are wasn't known when we were there. They show clear evidence of having been under extreme pressure deep in the Earth, and they actually contain minute diamonds formed at that depth and pressure. Then we went to Hefei, the capital of Anhui, where Sengör and I each gave a lecture at the Institute of Geology of the Anhui Bureau of Geology and Mineral Resources, I on the Appalachians, he on Turkey. We were then put on a train that brought us through the hills of western Shandong to Beijing.

In Beijing Professor Yang made arrangements, first for my stay there, including four days of field trips nearby plus the Great Wall and the tombs of the Ming emperors, then for visits to Colleges of Geology in Chengdu (Sichuan) and Wuhan (Hubei), at both of which I gave lectures. From Chengdu I was able to take field excursions for ten days into the mountains to the west, excursions quite different from the field trip I took the year before and including one to the Longmenshan (Dragon Gate Mountains). These mountains are on the south side of the Qinling Range, whose eastern end I had just seen in the Dabieshan, enabling me to make some interesting comparisons. At Wuhan, in between, I saw the very southern outliers of the Qinling Range facing the very northern outliers of the Yangzi fold-belt. I felt very lucky to get to see all these different parts of these two major mountain ranges.

I came back to Beijing then at the end of my two months, but there I was offered the chance to join a field excursion the Chinese were planning to collect specimens for geochemical work in the province of Fujian in southeast China, facing Taiwan. Naturally I jumped at the chance but, because it involved a third month not covered by the exchange agreement, I was asked to pay for my share of it; I was glad to do so. The arrangements for my paying got quite confused, but ultimately things seemed to straighten out; anyway, I paid and went on the excursion.

We flew down to Fuzhou and made a sort of rectangular tour through the province; on the tour there were some delightful incidents. Early in the trip we came into a fair-sized village or town where the local Chairman, of the Party Committee I presume, particularly asked me to sign his guest book because, he said, I was the first Westerner (*dàbízi* – big nose; the final i is like a mute e) ever to get there. He would certainly have known of any after 1949 and, if any got there before that, they would have had to come on muleback, for the roads we drove are certainly more recent. Later in the trip we drove to the dam of a fairly new reservoir, hired a boat with its owner and his son for guides, crossed the reservoir, and walked up a valley through a village (I think it was their village) to see some rocks. Because of the reservoir, there was no way to drive to that village, and it was the only one I saw without electric lights, for rural electrification seemed to be almost universal; like the reservoirs and the roads, that all happened after 1949. Climbing the nearby hill, I looked all around at the peaceful valley where the farmers were going about their work, paying no attention whatever to us intruders; I was forcibly reminded of Brueghel's painting *The Fall of Icaros*, which shows just such farmers paying just such attention to Icaros' two bare legs sticking up out of the sea. Yet a new electric powerline was being built there, a tractor (brought by boat?) was pushing power poles around, and I expect that village too was electrified before long.

In Fujian, as elsewhere, we were given very pleasant banquets in quite a few places, and toward the end of our tour I asked for the privilege of giving a banquet of my own for all my companions on the trip. It took a bit of arranging, but we finally had it in the Agate Gardens Restaurant attached to the Oceanographic Institute of Xiamen University — all seafood and all very good.

In Fuzhou, at both the start and the end of our trip, I had an afternoon free of any obligations, so I put on field pants, field shoes, and a sweater, and walked around the city for four hours or so. I visited a couple of parks, those built around the famous Black and White Pagodas, and in one I discovered, each time, a concert of real Chinese music, most of it strictly five-tone with a bare octave range, played on the local instruments (one time it was an "opera," so there was singing as well). I listened, fascinated, and I also noticed that the listeners, and indeed the musicians, were all old men. One asked me, in English, how old I was, and he was quite pleased to discover that he was four years older — 76 instead of 72. The younger Chinese whom I observed, like the drivers and their buddies when they got canned music for their long drives, chose Western rock-and-roll or Chinese imitations. On those two walks, I never saw another Westerner — another *dàbízi*.

For some reason, stone lions kept turning up on this trip. I had already memorized a tongue-twister: *sì-shí-sì-zhi shí-shì-zi*, meaning 44 stone lions (the i's are almost mute and those after -h- are better expressed by weak r's), for I was working quite hard on my Chinese during the whole three months, and by the end I was making up sentences to say from time to time, to everyone's amusement. I think one can say that, for a command of English, one needs a minimum of 5,000 words; I succeeded in memorizing and mastering the use of perhaps 1,600 Chinese words and characters, which shows how far I'd got. Then we came to the town of Shí-shì, Stone Lion, which is close to the coast between Xiamen (Amoy) and Fuzhou, opposite Taiwan. That coast has many small headlands and bays and is therefore ideal for smuggling; goods come in not only from Taiwan but also from Hongkong (Xianggang) and perhaps even Singapore. The point of visiting Shí-shì was exactly that it had the largest "free market" in mainland China, with all sorts of colorful goods for sale, clearly smuggled in from those places. I should say, by the way, that during my three months in mainland China I was struck again and again by how well, though certainly not luxuriously, the people were clothed, especially the children, who were frequently dressed in bright colors. People who visited China a decade or so earlier reported a depressing dullness in dress and a depressing monotony in people's actions, but I certainly saw nothing of the sort.

Later I saw the "Marco Polo" Bridge outside Beijing, which was decorated with stone lions of many different designs — some with, some without cubs, though many had lost their heads. And I was given a set of ten tiny stone lions carved out of pyrophyllite, a material something like talc.

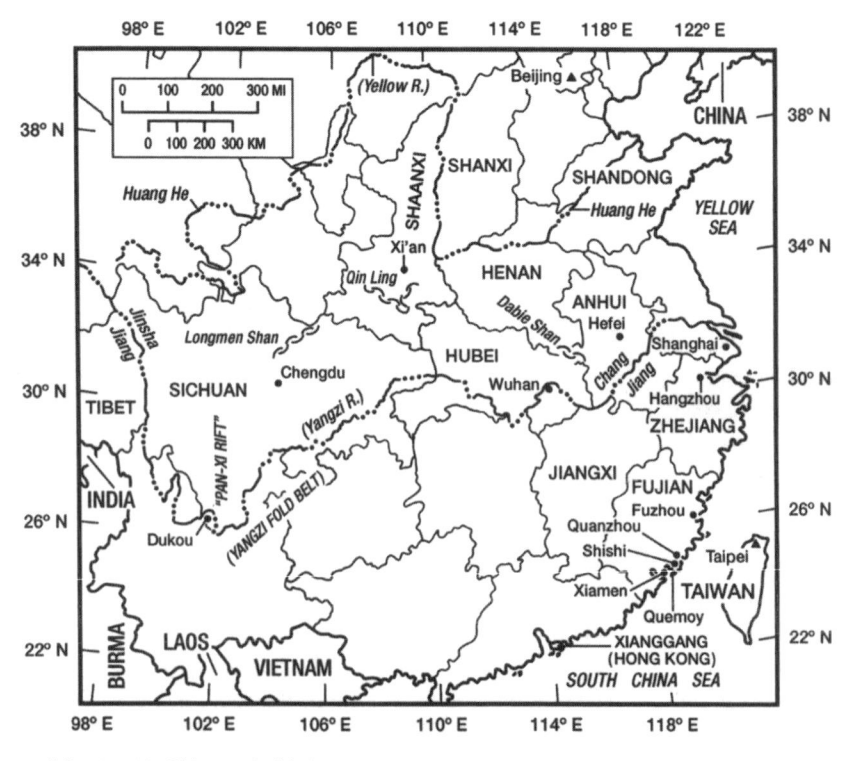

Map 16–12. *China and vicinity*

The final side of the rectangle was along the coast from Xiamen (Amoy) back to Fuzhou. Visiting the peninsulas and islands around Xiamen and Jimei, we saw not too far away islands belonging to Quemoy and still in the hands of the Taiwan government. In Qüanzhou, partway up the coast, and in Fuzhou, I was even asked to give lectures. Like all the others I gave in China, these were of course in English with translation, generally quite good as far as I could determine, but by this time I was able to salt them with Chinese words and even phrases, amusing everybody.

So finally I got back to Beijing, where Professor Yang again took me in hand; I even gave a couple of lectures there. Then I flew back to the United States during two rather short, successive, 30ths of November, for I was going east and the day went west around the world to meet me again.

Late in 1991 Dr. Sun Shu, knowing that I wanted to see even more of China's geology, advised me to make contact with Professor Zhang Guowei of Northwest University in Xi'an in Shaanxi province. I did so, and we began to plan a cooperative project between Northwest and Yale. We both worked hard on it, trying to bring in our younger colleagues, but in the long run our proposals were turned down by the U.S. National Science Foundation. Nevertheless Professor Zhang encouraged me to come to Xi'an in September 1992 following the International Geological Congress in Japan, which he knew I would be attending. Professor Zhang didn't get to that Congress, but Professor Yang and Dr. Sun did; when I flew to Beijing, they both met me again and put me on the proper plane for Xi'an. There Professor Zhang and his English-speaking assistant, Dr.

FIG. 16–28. Lecture at Anhui Bureau of Geology and Mineral Resources, Hefei, Anhui, China, 22 September 1986.

Meng Qingren, met me and showed me around that famous city; it was the capital of the Chinese empire rather longer than Beijing has been and is the site of the great terra-cotta armies dating from the third century BC. They then took me on a two-week excursion right across the Qinling mountain range within Shaanxi; we got to the southern margin of the range between the places where I'd seen it in 1986, west of the Dabieshan in Anhui and of Wuhan in Hubei but east of the Longmenshan in Sichuan. Needless to say, I was asked to give several talks, some of them more discussion sessions than formal lectures, both about "my" Appalachians and about mountain ranges more generally, also but only at the end of course, comparisons of the Qinling with others. My Chinese had slipped pretty badly between 1986 and 1992, but I had my dictionaries with me, as I always did while I was in China. At one point I had five on the dashboard in front of me, one Chinese-Chinese (a very useful pocket dictionary), two for Chinese-English but with different romanizations of Chinese, one for English-Chinese, and one for geological terms.

All through these trips to China, Taiwan included, I felt warmly related to Chinese people. Like us, like the Russians, the Canadians, and the Australians, they possess a very big continental country, and many of their reactions, notably their sense of humor, are much like ours. That I find those reactions more familiar and more easily understandable than those of island peoples, like the British, the Japanese, and the New Zealanders, says more about me of course than about those other peoples.

I did what I could to pay my share of the costs of the trips that Professor Zhang arranged for me in China, but in fact he covered most of them for me. It was therefore understood that I would invite Professor Zhang and colleagues to come to the United States for similar trips; we chose September and October 1994. Both Professor Zhang and Dr. Meng were able to come; I met them at Kennedy Airport on 19 September and brought them to New Haven. There I took one day to explain the geology of central Connecticut and one day to go see it. After that we took a day to drive up to Millinocket, Maine, to the fall field meeting of the New England Intercollegiate Geological Conference (NEIGC) in the vicinity of Mt. Katahdin; we took the same field trip on the first day of the meeting, different trips on the second.

After we came back to New Haven I took them for two days on my standard excursion to the lower Hudson Valley, including a trip up into the Catskill Mountains. A few days later we flew to Knoxville, Tennessee, where I had arranged with a long-time friend in the Geology Department of the University of Tennessee at Knoxville, Dr. Robert Hatcher, to help me show them a full cross-section of the southern Appalachians from Augusta, Georgia, to Cumberland Gap, Virginia. After we got back from that, we made a short trip to Albany, New York, where indeed Professor Zhang and Dr. Meng gave a joint lecture, Zhang giving it in Chinese and Meng in English (later we heard the same lecture in New Haven), then on to look at rocks in Vermont.

After all this tripping in the East, it was time to fly them out to Seattle for the annual meeting of the Geological Society of America, where of course they had the opportunity to meet many more American geologists. Before the meeting we took a trip into northern Washington State together; after the meeting I didn't see them again, for they took a trip into British Columbia while I took one in Washington. They were then to fly back to Denver to visit a former student of Professor Zhang's working there as an oil geologist, who would see that they caught their plane home from San Francisco.

Earlier that same year, Professor Yang came back to the United States to receive a Wilbur Cross Medal from the Graduate School of Yale University, a medal specifically for distinguished scholars who received their PhDs from Yale. As before he stayed mainly with his friends the Steins in Torrington, but of course I visited him there and also saw him in New Haven. It happened that Professor Yang had a daughter working in Los Angeles; when her daughter, his granddaughter, was going to Hotchkiss School in Connecticut, the Steins had welcomed her into their home. In 1995 I had the privilege of seeing Professor Yang there again, but in 1996 I felt I shouldn't go to the International Geological Congress in China on account of my age and failing health, so I was unable to see him that year. In May 1998, however, I saw him once more in New Haven, 60 years after we first met, this time when his granddaughter graduated from the Yale School of Organization and Management.

Epilogue

It has long seemed to me that, basically, life is an immense lottery. In that lottery I was dealt an extremely good, indeed an unfairly good hand; the extraordinary luck I've had throughout my career must be obvious to anyone who reads this account, and I've not hesitated to exploit it to the best of my ability. It began already with my being born into a loving and reasonably well-to-do family, in which intellectual achievements were considered rather more important than either athletic prowess or wealth. Added to that was the luck of my finding the right vocation by the time I was halfway through high school; so many of my contemporaries only discovered a vocation toward the end of their college years, if then. Despite the Great Depression of the 1930s, I never had to worry about where my next meal was coming from; by the time I was into my Master's year, I could count on geological employment, as with the U. S. Geological Survey, and my various geological jobs led me from one valuable experience to another. They also permitted the Survey to ask for my deferment from the wartime draft; thus I was soon deep into "war-work," yet I never stopped doing, and learning, geology.

As I've mentioned above, I deliberately requested the Survey to assign me to field work in the eastern United States, in the Appalachian Mountains, and I have made that range the core of my scientific research. At the end of the War and just after, on the other hand, my Survey work took me abroad, and since then I have seized every chance that came my way to see new countries and new geology, going for example to twelve successive International Geological Congresses; by now I have seen and studied geology on every continent. For all this my early start in foreign languages was a very great help; in particular my opportunities to see geology in so many parts of the Soviet Union would have been unusable or indeed impossible without a reasonable command of the Russian language.

Finally I had the luck that my most active years as a geologist coincided with a geological revolution, the theory of plate tectonics, and that by training and geological perspective I was preadapted, as the paleontologists say, to accept that theory with fervor and delight and to see its implications for all the geology I was doing. All this extraordinary luck has been the basis for whatever I have been able to achieve as a geologist — and as a person.

Publications

Abbreviations:
AAPGB: American Association of Petroleum Geologists Bulletin, AJS: American Journal of Science, CtGNHSB: Connecticut Geological and Natural History Survey Bulletin, EcG: Economic Geology, GSAB: Geological Society of America Bulletin, GACP: Geological Association of Canada Proceedings, TnDGB: Tennessee Division of Geology Bulletin, USGS: United States Geological Survey

1937
Tilting of proglacial lakes: AJS, 5th series, v. 34.
Stratigraphy and structure in the Upper Champlain Valley: GSAB, v. 48.
1940
Distinction between calcite and dolomite on polished surfaces: AJS, v. 238.
1944
P. B. King, H. W. Ferguson, L. C. Craig, and JR, Geology and manganese deposits of
 northeastern Tennessee: TnDGB 52.
1945
Manganese content of the Shady dolomite in Bumpass Cove, Tennessee: EcG, v. 40.
1948
Geology & mineral resources of Bumpass Cove, Unicoi and Washington Counties, Tennessee:
 TnDGB 54.
Phosphate deposits of the former Japanese islands in the Pacific: EcG, v. 43.
JR and D. F. Kent, Stratigraphic section at Lee Valley, Hawkins County, Tennessee:
 TnDGB 55.
1949
Evolution of thought on structure of middle and southern Appalachians: AAPGB, v. 33.
1950
Mechanics of Appalachian folding illustrated by Sequatchie anticline, Tennessee & Alabama:
 AAPGB, v. 34
The nomenclature and classification of sedimentary rocks: AJS, v. 248.
1952
Absolute ages of radioactive minerals from the Appalachian region: AJS, v. 250.
M. P. Billings, JR, and J. B. Thompson, Jr., Geology of the Appalachian highlands of east-central
 New York, southern Vermont, and southern New Hampshire: GSA Annual Meeting,
 1952, Guidebook.
1953
The folds & faults of the Appalachian Valley and Ridge province: Kentucky Geological Survey,
 Special Pub. 1.
1952
Geology of the Niota quadrangle, Tennessee: USGS Geological Quadrangle Map [18]
Geology of the Athens quadrangle, Tennessee: USGS Geological Quadrangle Map [19]
Geologic map of East Tennessee with explanatory text: TnDGB 58, pt. 2.
1954
Nature, usage, and nomenclature of stratigraphic units: a minority report: AAPGB, v. 38.
Terminology of limestone and related rocks: an interim report: Journal of Sedimentary Petrology,
 v. 24.
1956
JR, R. M. Gates, E. N. Cameron, and R. J. Ross, Jr., Preliminary geological map of Connecticut:
 Ct GNHSB.

The known Cambrian deposits of the southern and central Appalachian Mountains: Cambrian symposium, International Geological Congress, 20th, Mexico City 1956, v. 2.
The clastic sequence basal to the Cambrian system in the central and southern Appalachians: ibid.
1957
The distribution of carbonate sediments, a review (with record of panel discussion): Society of Economic Paleontologists and Mineralogists Special Publication 5.
C. O. Dunbar & JR, Principles of Stratigraphy: New York , John Wiley ; also in Russian, Spanish, Arabic, Chinese.
1959
JR, R. M. Gates, and J. L. Rosenfeld, compilers, Explanatory text for preliminary geological map of Connecticut, 1956: CtGNHSB 84.
JR and R. B. McConnell, Need for rock-stratigraphic units larger than group: AAPGB, v. 43.
The meaning of correlation: AJS, v. 257.
1960
JR and Peter Bearth, Sur la "nappe" de Lebendun: Académie des Sciences (Paris) Comptes Rendus, v. 250.
JR and Peter Bearth, Zum Problem der Lebendundecke: Eclogae geologicae Helvetiae, v. 53.
1962
L'emploi pratique de la schistosité dans la tectonique locale: Société géologique de France, Mémoire hors série [1] (Livre à la mémoire du Professeur Paul Fallot), v. 1.
1963
Mechanics of Appalachian foreland folding in Pennsylvania and West Virginia: AAPGB, v. 47.
JR and E. R. W. Neale, Possible "Taconic" kllippen in western Newfoundland: AJS, v. 261.
1964
Basement and no-basement hypotheses in the Jura and the Appalachian Valley and Ridge: Virginia Polytechnic Institute Department of Geological Sciences Memoir 1.
1965
Long Point and Clam Bank Formations, western Newfoundland: GACP, v. 16, p. 83-94
1967
Chronology of tectonic movements in the Appalachian region of eastern N. America: AJS, v. 265.
1968
Nekotoriye voprosy tektoniki Appalachey: Geotektonika, no. 3 (English translation: Some aspects of the tectonics of the Appalachians: Geotectonics)
The eastern edge of the North American continent during the Cambrian and Early Ordovician: Studies of Appalachian Geology, northern and maritime (Billings volume).
1969
Gnathostomulida: is there a fossil record? Science, v. 164.
1970
The Pulaski fault, and the extent of Cambrian evaporites in the central and southern Appalachians: Studies of Appalachian Geology, central and southern (Cloos volume).
The tectonics of the Appalachians: Wiley-Interscience, New York (John Wiley & Sons), 271 p., 2 maps
1971
The Taconic orogeny: GSA Bulletin, v. 82.
1972
Evolution of thought on structure of middle and southern Appalachians: second paper: *In*: Kanes, W. H., Seminar Director, Appalachian structures -origin, evolution, and possible potential for new exploration frontiers - a seminar: West Virginia University and West Virginia Geological Survey.
Latest Precambrian (post-Grenville) rocks in the Appalachian region: AJS, v. 272.
W. M. Poole and JR, with 25 collaborators, Appalachian geotectonic elements of the Atlantic Provinces and southern Quebec: International Geological Congress, 24th, Montreal

1972, Guidebook to Field Excursion A63-C63, 200 p. (French translation by Jacques Béland, 209 p., 1973).

1974 [1972]

L'orogenèse avalonienne (fini-précambrienne) dans les montagnes des Appalaches: Service géologique du Maroc Notes et Mémoires, n. 230 (Centre nationale des recherches scientifiques (Paris) Colloques internationaux n. 192).

1975

Rogers, Henry Darwin, and Rogers, William Barton: Dictionary of Scientific Biography, v. 11.

The geological history of Connecticut: Discovery (New Haven, Yale U. Peabody Museum), v. 15, no. 1.

The Merrimack synclinorium in northeastern Connecticut: AJS, v. 281.

1982

Stratigraphic relationships and detrital composition of the medial Ordovician flysch of western New England: implications for the tectonic evolution of the Taconic orogeny: a discussion: Journal of Geology, v. 90.

(Peter Robinson and Robert D. Tucker) Discussion (of) The Merrimack synclinorium in northeastern Connecticut; (JR) Not a reply but a further discussion: AJS, v. 282

1983

The life history of a mountain range - the Appalachians: Mountain Building Processes (K. J. Hsü, ed.), Academic Press, London.

1984

A geologic reconnaissance of the Cycladic blueschist belt, Greece: Discussion: GSAB, v. 95.

1985

Witnessing revolutions in the Earth Sciences: Annual Reviews of Earth and Planetary Sciences, v. 13.

JR, compiler, Bedrock geological map of Connecticut: Connecticut Geological and Natural History Survey.

1987

West-running Brook: the enigma of Schoharie Creek: Northeastern Geology, v. 9.

Differences between mountain ranges: The Anatomy of Mountain Ranges (J.-P. Schaer and John Rodgers, editors), Princeton University Press.

The Appalachian geosyncline: ibid.

Chains of basement uplifts within cratons marginal to orogenic belts: AJS, v. 287.

1988

The Appalachian-Ouachita orogenic belt: Episodes (International Union of Geological Sciences) v. 10.

Fourth time-slice: mid-Devonian to Permian synthesis: In Harris, A. J., and Fettes, D. J., eds., The Caledonian-Appalachian orogen: Geological Society [London] Special Publication 18.

Allen J. Krill, JR, and Bjorn Sundvoll), Alternative to the Finnmarkian-Scandian interpretation on Mageroya, northern Norway: Norsk geologisk Tidskrift, v. 68.

1989

William M. Jordan, ed., Thomas X. Grasso, JR, Edward S. Belt, Markes E. Johnson, and Richard E. Naylor, Boston to Buffalo, in the footsteps of Amos Eaton and Edward Hitchcock: International Geological Congress, 28th, Washington 1989, Field TripGuidebook T-169.

1990

Fold-and-thrust belts in sedimentary rocks. Part 1: Typical examples: AJS, v. 290.

1991

Fold-and-thrust belts in sedimentary rocks. Part 2: Other examples, especially variants: AJS, v. 291.

Evolution of ideas about The Ocoee Conglomerates and Slates: In Kish, S. A., ed., Studies of Precambrian and Paleozoic stratigraphy in the Western Blue Ridge: Carolina Geological Society.
1992
Trzcienski, Walter E., Jr., JR, and Guidotti, Charles V., Alternate hypotheses for the Chain Lakes "massif", Maine and Quebec: AJS, v. 292.
1993
Les Appalaches dans le cadre péri-atlantique: Service géologique du Maroc Notes et Mémoires, n. 366.
1994
Is the West Karmöy complex igneous or metasedimentary?: Tectonophysics, v. 231.
1995
Lines of basement uplifts within the external parts of orogenic belts: AJS, v. 295.
1997
Exotic nappes in external parts of orogenic belts: AJS, v. 297.
James Dwight Dana and the Taconic controversy: AJS, v. 297.

Non-geological articles
1957
Historic house comes to University for College of Architecture Use: Cornell Alumni News, October 15, 1957
1968
The seventh American revolution: Yale Review, v. 57 (Japanese trans: Japan-America Forum, v. 15, no. 5)
1979
JR and Willie Ruff. Kepler's Harmony of the World: a realization for the ear: American Scientist, v. 67.
1983
Four Preludes ascribed to Yulian Skriabin: 19th Century Music, v. 6.
1988
A contribution to philosophy: New Haven [North Haven], 90 p.
1997
The ironies of evolution: The Centennial Review, v. 41, no. 1 (Winter 1997).

Biographical memoirs
1974
Rudolf Ruedemann, 1864-1956: National Academy of Sciences Biographical Memoirs, v. 44.
1977
Memorial to Eleanora Bliss Knopf, 1883-1974: Geological Society of America Memorials, v. 6.
1982
Chester Ray Longwell, 1887-1975: National Academy of Sciences Biographical Memoirs, v. 53.
1985
Carl Owen Dunbar, 1891-1979: National Academy of Sciences Biographical Memoirs, v. 55.
1990
Memorial to Philip B. King, 1903-1987: Geological Society of America Memorials, v. 20.
1992
[Biographical Memoir] Preston Cloud, 1912-1991: American Philosophical Society Proc., v. 136.
Richard Lee Armstrong, 1937-1991, American Journal of Science, v. 292.

Index of Names

A
Ackerman, Louise Allen 18
Ackerman, William 23
Affaton, Pascal 203
Allen, Thomas 17
Andrews, David 62
Andrusov, Dmitri 184
Armstrong, Richard Lee 120
Arnold, Gary 192

B
Badoux, Héli 133
Bambach, Richard 144
Banks, Maxwell 195
Bascom, Florence 51
Bateman, Alan 87
Beach, Hugh 59, 61
Bearth, Peter 133
Behre, Charles H., Jr. 66
Belousov, V. V. 157
Belov, Aleksandr 163, 183
Bick, Kenneth 120
Billings, Marland Pratt 56, 83
Bird, John M. 118, 142, 184
Bishop, Graham 201
Bloom, Arthur 166
Boatwright, Howard 91
Bogdanov, Aleksey 155, 162
Bogdanov, Nikita 167
Boucot, Arthur 144
Bragg, William Lawrence 35
Branford Quartet 89, 91
Brewster, Kingman 116
Bridge, Josiah 65
Buck, Norman S. 87
Burchfiel, B. Clark 124
Burfoot, J. Dabney 34
Burtman, Valentin S. 164

C
Cadisch, Joos 132
Carey, S. Warren 125, 194
Caster, Kenneth 32
Choubert, Georges 102
Churkin, Michael 159
Clar, Eberhard 137, 138, 184
Clarke, John M. 26

Cloos, Ernst 83
Cloos, Hans 199
Cloud, Preston 58, 136
Club, The 85
Colom, Guilliermo 113
Conklin Family 94
Conklin, George and Anne 95, 178
Coombs, Douglas Saxon 200
Cooper, Byron Nelson 82, 144
Cooper, Gustav Arthur 100
Cooper, John 196
Cooper, Roger 201
Corbett, Keith 195
Craig, Lawrence C. 66
Crook, Keith 191, 192
Crowley, William 157
Currier, Donald 91

D
Daley, Brian 193
de Cserna, Zoltán 122
de Sitter, Ulbo 102
Debelmas, Jacques 131
Dewey, John 143, 209
Díaz, Teodoro 122
Diegel, Fred 84
Dunbar, Carl Owen 40, 156

E
Elter, Piero 139
Evans, David 100
Exner, Christof 137

F
Fallot, Paul 110
Felton, Anne 191
Ferguson, Herman W. 65
Flint, Richard Foster 120
Ford, William E. 58
Frakes, Lawrence 193

G
Gagnebin, Elie 102
Gardner, Julia 52
Gardner, Louis 63
Garrels, Robert M. 70
Gèze, Bernard 106, 122

Gilluly, James 51
Goldring, Winifred 26
Goold, Charles 151
Granath, James 192
Grindley, George 201

H
Hansen, Edward 128
Harrington, Larry 193
Harris, Gilbert D. 32
Hartnagel, Chris Andrew 24
Hedberg, Hollis 127
Heller, Howard H. 36
Hendricks, Tom 79
Hendrickson, George Lincoln 88
Hess, Harry 64
Hill, Dorothy 198
Hindemith, Paul 174
Hobbs, Bruce 192
Hobbs, Warren 59
Holtedahl, Olaf 126
Hsü, Kenneth 147, 209
Hutchinson, G. Evelyn 84, 175

J
Jenkins, Iredell 92
Jennings, Ian 195
Jonas, Anna 52
Jones, Owen T. 100
Julivert, Manuel 170

K
Kamaletdinov, M. A. 163
Keller, Boris M. 163
Ketin, Ihsan 209
King, Helen Carter 65
King, Philip Burke 64
Knopf, Adolph 40
Knopf, Eleanora Bliss 51
Knox, Bernard 93
Knox, Betty 85, 93
Korzhinskiy, D. S. 169
Krill, Alison and Allan 128
Kröner, Alfred 199
Krumbein, William 70

L
Ladd, Harry 77
Lamont, Archie 100
Landis, Charles 201
Leitch, Evan 198
Lekkas, Spyros 151
Lemoine, Marcel 131, 136
Lewis, Douglas 201
Lillie, Arnold 202
Longwell, Chester 48, 125
Longyear, John 38
Loughlin, Gerald 62
Lowman, Shepard 142
Lull, Richard Swan 49

M
Ma Xingyüan 208
Mansfield, George Rogers 63
Martin, Henno 198
Mattauer, Maurice 109
Mattice, Paul 38
Maxwell, John 92, 139, 152
Mazarovich, Oleg A. 160
McAlester, Lee 144
McConnell, Richard 99, 103
McKerrow, Stuart 144
Mendell, Clare 89
Meng Qingren 214
Menner, V. V. 155, 162, 169
Merla, Giovanni 139
Michot, Paul 168
Mitchell, Dwike 173, 178
Miyashiro, Akiho 143
Moores, Eldridge 153

N
Nabholz, Walter 132
Nalivkin, Dmitri V. 155, 168
Nesbitt, Robert 194
Nevin, Charles Merrick 28
Newcomb, Ethel 38
Nielsen, Elizabeth 22
Niggli, Ernst 132
Nolan, Thomas B. 120

O
Oliver, Jack 143
Osborne, F. Fitz 118

P
Peyve, Aleksandr 155, 169, 183
Platt, John 196

Platt, Lucian 157
Pond, Walter F. 65
Poole, William 136, 157
Porter, Lois and Quincy 90
Pugh, William J. 100
Purvis, Lillian 36

Q
Quarrier, Sidney 118

R
Raaben, Maria 158
Raymond, Percy 47
Ries, Heinrich 32
Roberts, Ralph 59
Rodgers, Henry Allen 18
Rodgers, Henry Darling 16
Rodgers, James 15
Rodgers, John 15
Rodgers, Jonathan 97, 177
Rodgers, Prentice 18, 96
Roger, Jean 127
Rogers, William B. 68
Rosenberg, Mark 175
Rosenfeld, John 102
Rubenach, Michael 192
Rubey, William Walden 62, 63
Ruedemann, Rudolf 26
Ruff, Willie 86, 173, 178
Runnegar, Bruce 193
Rutland, Roye 193, 196

S
Sander, Bruno 52
Schaer, Jean-Paul 190, 200
Scheibner, Erwin 185, 187
Schenck, Hugh 75, 124
Schreiner, Olive 21
Schuchert, Charles 27
Sculthorpe, Peter 92, 194
Sengör, Celal 209
Shaw, Russell 192
Shenon, Philip 71
Singleton, Owen 196
Skinner, Brian 165, 194
Skinner, Catherine 197
Sougy, Jean 188, 203
Speden, Ian 201
Stein, Jerry 208
Stewart, Alastair 192
Stille, Hans 157
Sullivan, Walter 169
Sun Shu 208, 213
Suppe, John 147, 149

T
Tatge, Eleanor 70
Tercier, Jean 133
Thomas, William A. 83
Thompson, James 57
Tollman, Alexander 137
Trevisan, Livio 139
Trinkaus, John 116, 173
Trümpy, Rudolf 135, 187
Tsagareli, Archin 166
Tucker, Robert 183
Turekian, Karl 121
Turner, Francis 200

U
Ulrich, E. O. 46

V
von Engeln, O. D. 32

W
Warren, Charles 73
Webby, Barry 193
Whittington, Harry 145
Williams, Emyr 195
Williams, Neil 60
Wilson, Keith and Rachel 90, 116, 194

X
Xü Jinghua. *See* Hsü, Ken

Y
Yang Zunyi 182, 206

Z
Zambetakes-Lekkas, Alexandra 151
Zen, E-an 57, 117, 143, 184
Zhang Guowei 213
Zimmerman, Jay 152, 179

Transactions

The constitution of the Connecticut Academy of Arts and Sciences declared in 1799 that "the object of this Academy is to cultivate every art and science which may tend to advance the interest of a free and virtuous people." The goal of the Academy is to represent the arts, humanities, and sciences in Connecticut through its meetings and publications. Members and guests gather at educational institutions around the State at least eight times a year. From 1810 to 1816, the Academy published 25 papers in the first volume of the Memoirs. In 1818, the Academy abandoned publication of *Memoirs* when Benjamin Silliman the elder inaugurated the *American Journal of Science*, which still continues to publish. However, considerable publishable material in a variety of fields led to a new series. *Transactions*, with a volume completed every two or three years, has a 6" x 9" format. Josiah Willard Gibbs's *On the Equilibrium of Heterogeneous Substances* was published in the third volume of the *Transactions* (1877). *Memoirs* reappeared in 1910, in quarto format for major illustrated works. A third series of publications, *The Manual of the Writings in Middle English 1000-1500*, began in 1967 with Volume 11 due in 2002. In celebration of 200 years as a learned society, the Academy instituted a series of *Facsimiles* of earlier, presently out of print, materials.

RECENT PUBLICATIONS

ROBERT GORDON AND MICHAEL RABER
Industrial Heritage in Northwest Connecticut
2000   ME 25   220 pages $39.00

HUGH CLARK, JULIUS ELIAS, AND PETER BERGMANN
The Antecedents Of Nazism: Weimar
2000   TR 56: 181-372 $18.95

MARY ELLEN ELLSWORTH
A History of the Connecticut Academy of Arts and Sciences
1999   TR 55   254 pages $35.00/paper $17.50

LEOPOLD POPISIL
Obernberg: A Quantitative Analysis of a Tirolean Peasant Economy
1995   ME 24   427 pages $59.50

For further information call 203-432-3113
e-mail: CAAS@YALE.EDU or visit us at: WWW.YALE.EDU/CAAS